W9-BVF-237

Mountain of Storms

MOUNTAIN OF STORMS

The American Expeditions to Dhaulagiri, 1969 & 1973

by
Andrew Harvard
and Todd Thompson

Chelsea House
New York University Press
1974

Library of Congress Catalogue Card Number 74-13925
ISBN 0-8147-3366-2

Acknowledgment is made for permission to quote from the following published sources: *Annapurna* by Maurice Herzog, 1952, E. P. Dutton & Co., Inc., publishers; "Dhaulagiri, Mind Odyssey" by James Janney, published in *Ascent* magazine, the Sierra Club mountaineering journal, 1970, Sierra Club, Inc., publishers.

Photo credits: 1969 ADE, pages 12, 20, 21, 22, 42; Craig Anderson, pages 9, 11, 60, 97, 110, 142 (top), 144; Terrence Bech, page 183; Barbara Duenwald, page 35; Jeffrey Duenwald, page 58; Ronald E. Fear, pages 36 (b.r.), 38 (t.l.), 39 (t.l.), 40 (t.r.); 70, 100, 120, 141, 142 (bottom), 169, color plate 10; Andrew Harvard, pages 37 (t.l.), 38 (t.l.), 69 (top), 87, 129, 131, 189 (bottom), color plates 2, 5, 8, 16; Del Langbauer, pages 170, 174, color plate 9; Karen Langbauer, page 36 (t.l.); Peter Lev, page 41 (b.l.), color plate 12; Thomas Lyman, pages 39 (bottom), 67, 99; James D.Morrissey, pages 36 (t.r.), 37 (t.r.), 38 (b.r.), 41 (top), 59 (top), 59 (b.l.), 69 (bottom); Kathy Reichardt, page 40 (t.l.); Louis Reichardt, pages 38 (b.l.), 68, 156, color plate 13; Drummond Rennie, pages 39 (t.r.), 41 (b.r.), 117, 158, 182; John Roskelley, page 88, color plate 4; John Skow, pages 89, 119, 157; Lowell Smith, pages 36 (b.l.), 37 (bottom), 90, 109, 117; Todd Thompson, pages 40 (bottom), 57, 118, 132, 189 (top), color plates 1, 3, 7, 11, 14, 15. Maps by Stephen E. Harvard.

Authors' Note

The authors' aim has been to produce a journalistic account of an adventure from a perspective which considers what the adventure meant to a number of people. We hope to show that while a large expedition team does operate as an entity, it is in fact a loose affiliation of individuals, not a tightly structured campaign as is often supposed. Combining the observations, impressions, and recollections of others with our own, we have chosen a middle ground between the two traditions of expedition writing: first person reports which have immediacy but little perspective, and broad official accounts which have a generalized perspective but no immediacy. Along the way, we tried to show that climbers on a mountain do not spend all of their time bravely surmounting insurmountable obstacles, and, at times life in the mountains differs from life everywhere else only in that it is life in the most beautiful of surroundings. We have directed this book toward those who do not know everything there is to know about mountaineering in general and expeditions to the Himalaya in particular: there are a few asides to the close world of climbers, but not many, because a great deal has already been written by climbers for themselves alone.

The expeditions, in 1969 and 1973, owed their existence and eventual success to a long list of friends, supporters, and contributors. Some are acknowledged in the text, some in an appendix, but many more are not mentioned simply because there is not space to do so. We could not have done without them; we thank them all.

All the members of the expeditions helped in the preparation of this book; the diaries and letters of Louis Reichardt, Ron Fear, and Jeffrey Duenwald, as well as the recollections of John Roskelley, Del Langbauer and Jim Janney, were particularly important: the cooperation, encouragement, and assistance of Drummond Rennie were essential.

The authors would further like to thank Bruce McEllresh and Andrew Brown of *National Geographic* for their cooperation, and Professor Chauncey Loomis of Dartmouth College for his editorial advice.

The geographical information contained in the maps and the text follows data in Dr. Harka Gurung's *Annapurna Dhaulagiri: A Decade of Mountaineering in the Nepal Himalaya 1950–1960,* published in 1968 by His Majesty's Government of Nepal. The English spelling of Sherpa names follows the usage of Terry Bech.

Special appreciation is due Jim Morrissey, a man of strength and humanity; a man of violent contrasts, hence deep resources. Emerging as the leader in 1969, he led the 1973 expedition as perhaps no other man could have.

A.H., T.T.

Galpin House
Hardwick, Massachusetts
Summer, 1973

Contents

List of Illustrations

COLOR PLATES, FOLLOWING PAGE 148

MAPS

Mountain of Storms

Dhaulagiri

In the Dolpo region of central Nepal, on the west side of the Kali Gandaki River valley, high above the old road to the holy city of Muktinath and the kingdom of Mustang, is the Dhaulagiri massif. Dhaulagiri I, the White Mountain, stands aloof from the four other peaks in the group, separated from them by the gorge of the Myagdi Khola river. Almost three miles above the valley floor, the east side of Dhaulagiri forms the west wall of one of the deepest canyons in the world. At 26,795 feet, the summit of Dhaulagiri I is one of the world's highest, and it was among the last to be climbed.

In 1809, the Survey of India sent Captain William Webb to map the Ganges River and to find the place at which it crosses the Himalaya. Webb did not learn the secrets of the Ganges, but he did become the first European to observe Dhaulagiri I. From four survey stations in the plains of northern India he estimated its height at 26,862 feet, a figure that was mocked because surveyors at the time believed the Andes of South America to be the highest mountains in the world.

After 1949, when the government of Nepal ended a long-standing policy of political isolation, opening the country to foreigners, mountaineering expedition activity in the Nepalese Himalaya was concentrated on finding, reconnoitering and climbing the peaks over eight thousand meters, the fourteen highest mountains in the world.

The first seven expeditions to Dhaulagiri failed to reach the summit. The Fédération Française de la Montagne expedition led by Maurice Herzog made the first thorough reconnaissance of Dhaulagiri in 1950. The team left France with a broad assignment: find and climb either Annapurna I (26,493) or Dhaulagiri I, climb the first eight-thousand-meter peak. Dhaulagiri seemed inaccessible, so the expedition turned its attention to Annapurna, making an epic first ascent late in the season. Gaston Rebuffat and Jean Couzy went up a subsidiary section of the southeast ridge to have a look at the south face and the southeast ridge of Dhaulagiri. In his account of the expedition, Herzog recalls the conversation on their return:

"What about the southeast ridge? The other day when we saw it from the east glacier, you were most hopeful, you said . . ."

"I was absolutely wrong. To begin with, it's incredibly long, it's all very high up, and above all it's technically very difficult: great walls and towers of ice, some rock, broken ground, gendarmes—there's no end to it."

"Any possible camp sites?"

"None."

"Well," I said, "all that's not exactly encouraging."

"Oh," he replied, "there's absolutely no possibility of going that way."

Meanwhile, Jacques Oudot and Lionel Terray explored the route to the north side of Dhaulagiri. From a 17,500-foot saddle below Tukche Peak, known now as French Pass, they studied the glaciers and ridges before them. Neither the long approach, which porters would refuse to make, nor the routes on the north side interested the French. Terray called it "the foulest looking place."

In spite of the discouraging reports from the French, Dhaulagiri was still a choice mountaineering prize, so other expeditions followed in rapid succession. The first attempt came in 1953, when a Swiss team pioneered an approach route up the Myagdi Khola River valley. The team had to cut trails through dense vegetation and build bridges across glacial streams, but the route was lower than the French approach had been, and was free of snow. From a camp at 13,000 feet on the Myagdi Khola Glacier, they reconnoitered the north side of the mountain, choosing the northwest ridge as a route to the summit. Above a broken bottom section and an intermediate glacial terrace, they identified snow fingers protruding into the formidable upper rock wall. The snow fingers suggested the shape of a pear, an ordinarily pedestrian image rendered meaningful by weeks above the snow line, so the route became known as the Pear route. They reached 25,400 feet, but were unable to find a suitable campsite for a summit attempt. An Argentine expedition in the following year attempted the Pear route, placing a high camp at 25,000 feet. From there, a summit party crossed the last difficult rock section and bivouacked at 26,250 feet on the easy summit ridge. Heavy snows turned them back the next day.

A Swiss-German team on a special vegetarian diet designed by a commercial sponsor took the field in 1955, reaching about 24,300 feet. The Argentinians returned in 1956 to reach only 25,000 feet. The team's sponsor, President Juan Peron, fell from power while they were on the mountain, so they had to scratch his name from their equipment before returning home. A Swiss team in 1958 made the final attempt on the Pear, faring little better. In 1959, a team of Austrians, seeking a better route, made the dangerous approach up the Myagdi icefall to the northeast col at 19,300 feet. The approach brought them under a spectacular rock face about three thousand feet high, which they christened the Eiger, after the infamous Eigerwand in the Bernese Oberland. They made their highest camp at 24,300 feet on the northeast spur. From there a summit team reached 25,600 feet, but was beaten back by high winds on three successive attempts.

The summit was finally reached by the International Swiss Expedition in 1960. The team, led by Max Eiselin, a veteran of the 1958 attempt, followed the Austrian route up the northeast spur. In very good weather, eight men reached the summit. Dhaulagiri became the highest mountain climbed without oxygen.

The first Nepalese eight-thousand-meter peak to be reconnoitered, and the last to be climbed, Dhaulagiri developed a sinister reputation as it taxed the endurance and ingenuity of team after team of climbers. The high winds and unpredictable snowstorms became legendary; it was first called "Mountain of Storms" by the Swiss. The price of the summit was high: Francisco Ibañez, the leader of the 1954 Argentine Expedition, died of frostbite injuries incurred during his bivouac at the high point on the Pear route. Bal Bahadur, a porter, died in an avalanche at 17,400 feet in 1956. Heini Roiss, a member of the Austrian team in 1958, died in a crevasse on the northeast col. Climbing methods stretched the resources of technology; the Argentines in 1954 used dynamite to blast campsites in the rock slopes of the Pear; the Swiss in 1958 used bedframes to build tent platforms, a noisy, windy, and unstable solution to the same problem of sloping campsites. In 1960, a Swiss Pilatus airplane dubbed "Yeti" ferried men and equipment to the northeast col, making successful landings at 19,300 feet, before crashing in Hidden Valley, northeast of French Pass.

In the nineteen-sixties internal politics of Nepal, reflecting cold war pressure on the tiny state sandwiched between India and the Chinese in Tibet, forced the government to close the country to foreign mountaineers for most of the decade. In 1969, an American reconnaissance expedition, led by Boyd Everett, explored the approach to the southeast ridge from Lete before an avalanche stopped them on the southeast glacier. A Japanese expedition in 1970 made the second ascent of Dhaulagiri by the northeast spur in extremely bad weather. Using oxygen, they put one Japanese and one Sherpa on the summit; the Sherpa refused oxygen because the mountain had been climbed once without it.

Organized by Boyd N. Everett, Jr., the 1969 American expedition was hastily formed after a surprise announcement from Nepal that the high mountains in Nepal were again open to foreigners. The goal was to explore and try to climb the southeast ridge, Rebuffat's impossible ridge. In March of 1969, Everett, an experienced mountaineer in the unlikely person of a Wall Street securities analyst, wrote: "In three weeks personnel will have to be organized, equipment and food bought and shipped, and funds raised. It has never been done on such short notice, but I think it can be done." Everett was the man to do it. He had long kept a foot in two small close-knit worlds, each jealous of its own and suspicious of outsiders: climbing and Wall Street. He was able to combine the skills of a businessman with the wisdom of a mountaineer to pick the finest route up a mountain, assess its difficulty and then assemble a team with the necessary strengths to climb it. He was a competent expedition climber, a resourceful leader, and above all a good manager.

Everett's route choice was typical of his expeditions. There are two well-defined styles of climbing a big mountain. The first, "expedition style," is the assault on a mountain by a large team using a logistic pyramid of camps. Progression toward the summit is methodical; a new camp is not established until existing ones are consolidated and supplied. Fixed ropes guarantee safety and the ability to retreat, and speed is sacrificed for security. Because of their incredible scale, uncertain weather, and debilitating altitude, virtually all of the highest mountains are climbed in this way. In the second style, "alpine style," two or four climbers make a continuous unsupported push from a base camp to the summit using bivouacs rather than stocked camps. No fixed ropes are used. This second style is an accepted method for attempts on difficult routes on peaks of moderate altitude; climbers rely on skill and grace-under-pressure, rather than heavy support, to overcome climbing problems. A general but by no means universal characterization of objectives in climbing follows the stylistic differences. The goal in early mountaineering was the summit, and first ascents are normally done by the easiest route and in the safest style. But by the late sixties, most of the big mountains of the world had been climbed at least once, and attention turned to routes which offered greater technical difficulty, a straighter line, or a more beautiful approach. The route became as important a goal as the summit: the technical difficulty of a new route became an attraction, not an unwanted obstacle.

In American climbing in 1969, the advocates of the two styles tended toward confrontation. Everett favored synthesis, taking wherever possible an alpine-style approach to expedition-style problems. In 1967 his large expedition to Mount McKinley in Alaska ascended the mountain by three routes, including a four-man ascent of a hard new route on the south face. In 1969, he organized a small, lightly equipped party to attempt the southeast ridge of Dhaulagiri, a route considerably more difficult than anything done in the Himalaya up to that time. Everett realistically considered the hastily formed expedition a reconnaissance to explore the southeast ridge for the larger effort that would probably be necessary, but he did not rule out the possibility of completing the route.

Foray into the Icefall

The team that assembled in Kathmandu in April of 1969 was small by Himalayan standards, but it included some of the most active American expedition mountaineers. With Everett were Al Read, a professional guide from the Tetons; Vin Hoeman, a guide from Alaska; David Seidman, a photographer who had climbed the direct south face route on McKinley and had made the first ascent on the north ridge of Mount Kennedy in the Yukon; Jeffrey Duenwald, a veterinarian from the wheat country of eastern Washington, and Jim Janney, a medical student, both veterans of several South American and Alaskan climbs; Lou Reichardt, a biochemist, and Paul Gerhard, a computer scientist, both with Alaskan and Yukon experience; and two physicians, Bill Ross, who had climbed in the Andes, and Jim Morrissey, whose climbing had been in Canada and East Africa. They were joined by Terry Bech, an American musicologist in Nepal with an undisclosed number of first ascents of minor Himalayan peaks and thousands of miles of mountain trails to his credit.

In Kathmandu, they struggled with final arrangements for the expedition. Morrissey pirated oxygen cylinders from a wrecked plane. Bech bought food in the bazaar. Reichardt conducted tripartite negotiations with the Indian Army and the U.S. Department of State to get oxygen cylinders from India. Al Read courted an American volunteer teacher working for the Dooley Foundation. Everett scrambled to hire Sherpas for the expedition. The others explored the joys of Kathmandu's streets and alleys.

There are not always enough trained climbing Sherpas for all the expeditions in a season, so expeditions must compete for those who are available. The number of working Sherpas increases only slowly, and experienced Sherpas choose their expeditions carefully, because, as devout Buddhists, many work only during specific seasons when the stars are right. By the time Everett reached the Himalayan Society, the Sherpa guild hall, most of the Sherpas had jobs for that season. After a search, he was able to hire an experienced sirdar, Phu Dorje II, four high altitude porters, two cooks, and a mailrunner.

On April 15, the team flew to the town of Pokhara, northwest of Kathmandu, where the trail leading to the Dhaulagiri and Annapurna massifs begins. There, Phu Dorje hired sixty Tibetan and thirty Nepali porters to carry the expedition's five thousand pounds of baggage up the Kali Gandaki trail to the hamlet of Lete, six days' march away. At Lete, Everett planned to climb directly up the west side of the Kali Gandaki Valley to Dhaulagiri's southeast glacier and from there to the southeast ridge. Bech, Hoeman, Sherpa Panboche Tenzing, and Read formed an advance party, leaving Pokhara shortly after the plane landed. Their objective was to walk to Lete as quickly as possible, climb up the grassy slopes above the town to the snowline and establish an expedition base camp at fifteen thousand feet on the southeast glacier. They made the trip to Lete in four days while the main group, slowed by the porters, left Pokhara on April 16 and reached Lete on the twenty-first.

The towns along the trek—Lumle, Tirke, Chitre, Tatopani and Ghasa—are only distinct in memory by association with specific disagreements with porters, refreshing swimming holes, or painful gastro-intestinal infirmities. Everett played tape-recorded symphonies, and constant repetition taught everyone the customary Nepali greeting, *namaste*. The Sherpas knew the trail well, and its campsites, lunch stops, and resting places were a matter of tradition centuries old. Quickly, unobtrusively, they took command of the party from the time they woke the climbers with a morning cup of tea until they dropped their loads and asked "Camp here, sahib?" with every intention of doing just that. Everett, not one to let others take charge or to sit back and sample the particular character of local custom, was annoyed with the Sherpas' *de facto* leadership, writing "Sherpas cooking and doing it their way, which isn't bad, . . . but who is in control?"

The advance party established base camp at fifteen thousand feet on April 20. Snow and poor visibility kept them in tents most of the twenty-first. Communication between the sections of the expedition was through radio contact twice a day. On the evening of the twenty-first, Hoeman reported to the main party that all at base camp was well. Al Read had been suffering the minor symptoms of mountain sickness—poor appetite, fitful sleep, headache and cough—but those symptoms are not uncommon and not necessarily threatening. Read took a Darvon pain suppressant and tried to sleep. During the night he lost consciousness and remained unconscious, near death, for the next thirty-two hours.

The physiological problems of high altitude constitute one of the chief hazards of climbing in the Himalaya. To function properly at high altitude, the human body must physically adjust to compensate for the decrease in available oxygen in the air. This adjustment, called acclimatization, occurs naturally with gradual increases in altitude. A safe rate of ascent above ten thousand feet would be a combination of climbing days and rest days that averaged a thousand feet of altitude gain per day. Climbing quickly without proper acclimatization often causes dizziness, shortness of breath, and general malaise. This set of symptoms is called acute mountain sickness: it is often a trivial problem but it can have dangerous complications leading to pulmonary and cerebral edema if the climber remains at altitude. The only effective treatments are rapid descent to low altitude and application of oxygen to regularize breathing: both must be done quickly if the victim is to survive.

Loud groaning from Read woke Hoeman at 3:00 A.M. on the twenty-second. Read could not be roused, and Hoeman and Bech suspected pulmonary edema so they wrapped him in a tent in preparation for an evacuation to lower altitude. At the morning radio contact Hoeman was instructed to begin the evacuation while Morrissey, the expedition doctor, started up to meet the rescue party. Despite well-known, recognizable symptoms and a classical pattern of deterioration, pulmonary edema almost always comes as a surprise to healthy climbers. It is something that happens often to tourists, and occasionally to good mountaineers, but never to oneself. In their impatience to push the new route, all three had overlooked Read's developing symptoms.

This critical situation precipitated a search for the expedition medical supplies in the pile of over a hundred unmarked boxes of equipment. Ross, who had the only list of the boxes' contents, was off hiking down the valley. The oxygen system was a shambles. The oxygen bottles from the wrecked plane were found first, and Mingma Norbu, one of the porters, was sent up the mountain with a bottle but no mask, and written instructions from Morrissey to use a plastic bag and rubber bands for a makeshift regulator. The Indian Army regulators did not fit the aircraft bottles, and adapters were still being fabricated back in Kathmandu. A complete Indian system was eventually found and sent up the mountain, with Reichardt and Morrissey breathlessly following the Sherpa who carried the load. Reichardt wrote: "While we ascended at a pace that revealed that we had not yet been this high, Terry, Tenzing, and Vin dragged Al down two thousand feet in Paul's tent. It was a heroic task; the terrain was very hairy and they had to lower him down steep ice slopes and gulleys with only sixteen feet of sling rope. I left Jim about one thousand feet below Al and continued ahead alone to find him. When I finally did, he had been on oxygen for an hour at thirteen thousand feet and the 3,600-liter bottle was blown. He was still unconscious and unresponsive."

Morrissey arrived quickly with the announcement that he had fainted on the way up and had awakened to find himself face down in the glacial mud. They dragged Read down another four hundred feet over relatively easy snow. Then Morrissey gave him some adrenalin and a diuretic, a bladder catheter, and intravenous fluid. It was snowing and cold. They continued to drag him down across very rocky terrain to a camp the others were establishing at 12,400 feet.

Two hours of oxygen inside a tent left Read marginally better, but the doctors were still pessimistic about his survival. They decided to evacuate him as low as possible before nightfall.

Reichardt continued, "As always, it had been snowing since midmorning and the descent was agonizing and hazardous. It was just as well Al did not know what was happening. The trail was only a collection of ice-covered rocks and these were often just above steep cliffs. Eleven people proved none too many to manage the stretcher over such terrain. It left me beyond exhaustion."

Read was at 10,400 feet before dark and was left there with Morrissey and the oxygen in a tent. The drop in altitude reversed his symptomatic momentum toward death. He had become steadily more responsive as the party descended; they left confident that he would live.

Morrissey attended Read through the night of the twenty-second, and by morning of the twenty-third Read could repeat his name, answer simple questions, swallow water and recognize the beast grazing nearby as a yak. At noon they began the 2,500-foot descent to the valley. On the walk to the valley, Read's recovery was quicker than expected. That night, as Read lay fitfully asleep and Morrissey law awake trying to sleep, Read's breathing suddenly stopped. Morrissey sat bolt upright and lunged for Read to resuscitate him. Read's laughter broke the tension and he gasped "Had you going, didn't I?" Morrissey, relieved, muttered "Bastard!" under his breath and went back to bed.

On April 25, Reichardt and Hoeman continued the search for a route up the southeast glacier to the long southeast ridge, making a reconnaissance from the fifteen-thousand-foot base camp to seventeen thousand feet. In the meantime, a confrontation with the Sherpas below was threatening the progress of the expedition. Confrontation is a familiar part of the step from valley to mountain, as much a stalling ritual as anything, but in this case, the Sherpas had a legitimate grievance. Normally, high altitude Sherpas are given the same equipment that expedition members receive. The 1969 expedition had been organized on such short notice that Everett was unable to purchase leather boots for the Sherpas, and had given them ungainly, army surplus rubber boots instead: the Sherpas wanted leather boots. Also, Phu Dorje did not like his power diluted by the presence of Terry Bech, whose considerable knowledge of Nepal, its languages and peoples threatened Phu Dorje's role as

Dhaulagiri from the south.

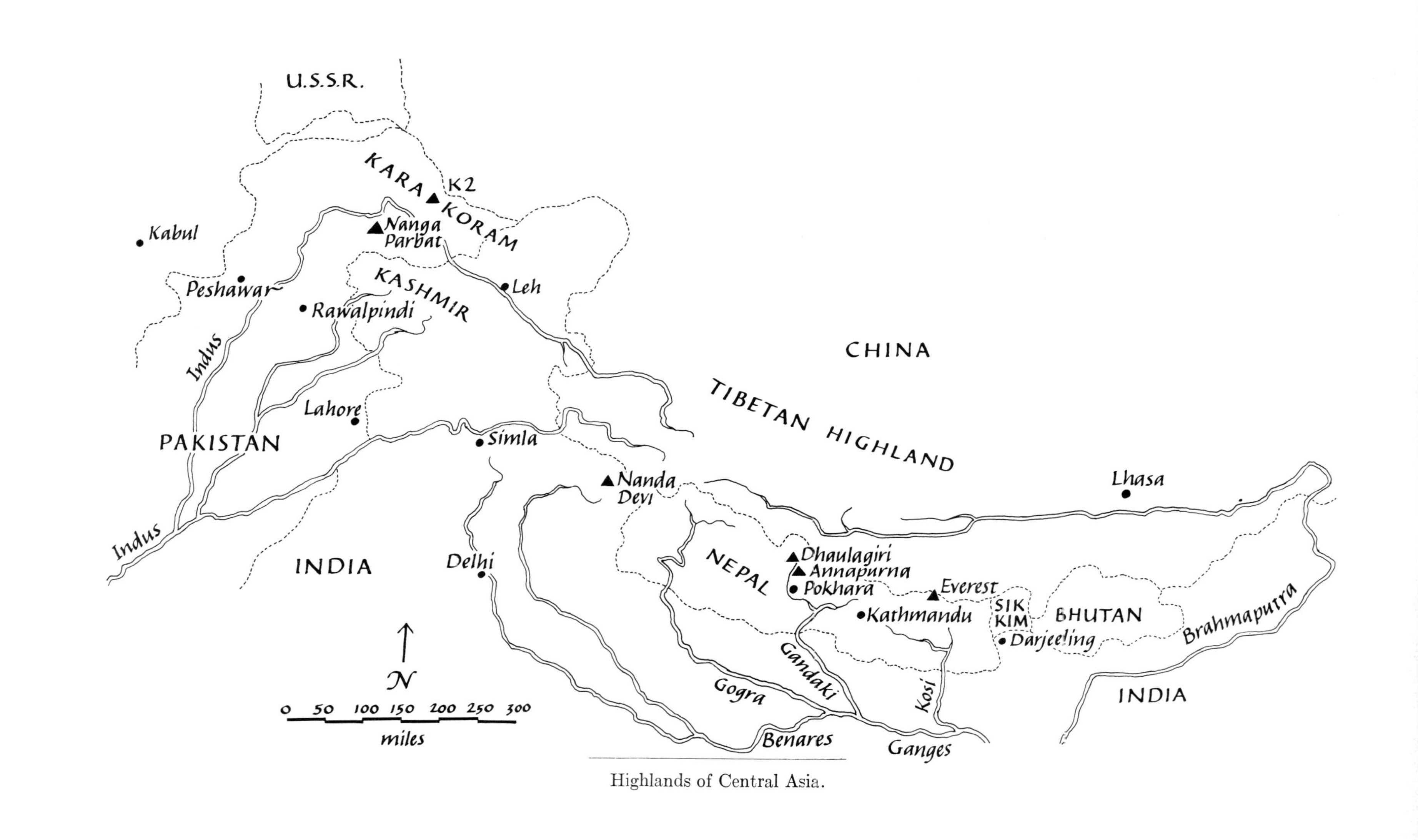

Highlands of Central Asia.

oracle on local custom. Reacting to Phu Dorje's hostility, Bech nearly left the mountain in disgust. All of the Sherpas were vaguely apprehensive about Dhaulagiri's reputation for bad weather, and specifically did not like the location of the fifteen-thousand-foot base camp, which they considered dangerously exposed to avalanches.

Hoeman and Reichardt were joined by Paul Gerhard on April 26, and the three pushed their reconnaissance to 17,500 feet, the level at which they intended to leave the glacier and climb onto the southeast ridge. There, on the edge of a wide basin leading to the southeast ridge, a large crevasse cut across the route. Above the basin was the upper icefall of the southeast glacier. The route through the icefall was straightforward, easily climbable and without unusual danger. At the evening radio contact, Reichardt asked Everett, who was at 12,500 feet, to get logs from the forest in the valley and send them up for a bridge over the crevasse.

Pemba Phutar and Panboche Tenzing joined Reichardt, Hoeman, and Gerhard at fifteen thousand feet on the twenty-seventh for a carry of food and equipment to a camp at 17,500 feet, just below the crevasse. Everett, Ross, and Seidman moved up to base camp with the news that the logs could not be brought up until the following day. That evening they argued about the best route to the ridge. There were two choices: go onto the ridge close to base camp and make a longer, more technically difficult traverse along the lowest section of ridge crest toward the summit, or gain altitude on the glacier above them and begin dealing with the technical problems of the ridge higher up. Either choice could be argued, and both were. Everett worried about avalanches falling on the glacier route from a large hanging glacier on the ridge and so favored the first alternative. They agreed to cross the crevasse at 17,500 feet and see what developed.

On the morning of April 28, Seidman, Everett, Hoeman, Pemba Phutar, and Panboche Tenzing began the carry to 17,500 feet while Reichardt and Ross waited for Mingma Norbu to bring logs up from below. Men moved upward at different speeds, most still acclimatizing—all with the idea that the effort was a reconnaissance, the route unsettled. The morning was sunny; the talk was light and friendly.

Reichardt and Ross reached the crevasse with the logs and began to rig ropes for a bridge. The regular Dhaulagiri fog settled in. Seidman arrived next leading the second rope. He kidded Hoeman about setting him up to lead an impossible section: he was excited about the route, and wanted to head straight for the ridge. With easy confidence he said "crossing avalanche chutes like this is standard, but it would be Russian roulette with that hanging glacier

Dhaulagiri from the Kali Gandaki.

Evacuation of Al Read.

up there." The snow chute that led to the ridge was just ahead, across the basin on the other side of the crevasse. The hanging glacier was out of sight in the fog. The others arrived at the crevasse. Hoeman organized the bridge-making while Gerhard and Reichardt took pictures.

Eight men stood in the afternoon fog, concentrating on the log bridge which was the key to the route above, engaged with each other and with the mountain. After the avalanche passed over them, only Louis Reichardt remained. Seven men, numberless dreams, and incidentally another expedition, died in the afternoon fog.

After the avalanche, when the pace of living resumed as abruptly for the survivors as it had just been halted for the others, Reichardt wrote:

"It began with the noise of an avalanche, not rare that day, then a mutual realization that it might hit us. A moment to duck, but only a change of slope angle for shelter. A roar. A pelting on my back and head of ice. A struggle to remain in a fetal position with an air pocket, then a slackening in intensity of the avalanche. Curiosity compelled me to raise my head. I got sharply whacked on the skull as a reward for my effort.

"Then there was silence. No screams, just silence. First came the realization that I was not hurt. It couldn't have been that bad! Then there was a search for the familiar; friends, tents, cache, and gear; then the discovery that nothing was there—no tents, no cache, no ice axe, and no friends. A moment of hope. It was just a snow avalanche. Why just to dig them out would do. Yells of reassurance: Hey, Boyd! Hey, Paul! Hey, Dave! Hey, Bill! Hey, Vin! I'm alive and OK; here to dig you out. Just let me know where you are. No answers.

"A glance at my watch. I must plan. Then three pickets, the first remains. Profound discouragement. The terrain was unrecognizable. How little to be left. The tents were sheltered; dug into the hill, but the platform had been scoured away. A systematic search, criss-crossing the hill. Yelling and probing; listening and hoping. Alternately moving and stopping. No luck.

"But then a pack. Hope again. It is Paul's and virtually undamaged. Only the top bar is crushed. Like me it is a fugitive. The only other human thing on the mountain. I put it on; I need it.

"On down the slope, but then an ominous discovery and fear: I was treading on ice, not the snow that was there before. The angle increased; the slope became quite steep and my position without an ice axe quite precarious. Cliffs I had never realized were there appeared in the mists below. That way went the avalanche, that way my friends.

"A mixture of emotions—what I wanted to avoid at this time. They boded ill for my rationality and future self-esteem. Fear, completely absent when the avalanche struck, now raised its ugly head. What if I were to fall? With my lousy dark glasses in the mist, I cannot see a thing. My God! How I feared fear, because it should be completely absent when I make my decision of life and death. A recklessness. The normal rules of caution do not apply when friends are in need. Over the cliffs, through the crevasses: find them or die with them. If I am reckless and am injured or killed, who will save them—who will ever know their tale. Both responsibility and history beckon me away.

"How long to stay? To descend and leave the scene—to bring help—shovels, medical aid, clothing, and assistance for them: guidance and reassurance for me. How I hate this decision. Yet time is important. A swift departure and those below may be intercepted at fifteen thousand feet; the same descent may condemn a friend to death, one in need of immediate succor. A late departure: same type of argument, but reversed: no help, no digging, no large rescue party until morning.

"A rationally agreed-to compromise: one hour of searching, then descent. More beating and yelling. When hope ran low, at ten minutes before 1:00, the upper slopes seemed futile for further searching and I made a descent. However, first my duty to history: photos of the scene with the same roll of film on which I had been so happily recording our work before. Through the lens the scene was so different. All snow scoured off the slope; absolutely no cover over the hard glacier ice; a full two feet of surface gone. In its place, large ice blocks up to six feet in diameter scattered over the slope. Such a feeling of barrenness, like the mountains of the moon where erosion and lichens never reduce the corners on the boulders to sand. Then the crevasse: paradoxically filled to the brim in the precise spot where we had been lowering the logs, and only there, as if the entire mass of ice and snow had been funneled through an hourglass. No sign of the logs themselves, large as they were. What cruel fate to have held everyone within yards of that spot to witness the lowering of the boom across the crevasse, then in the same act which destroyed them to fill the barrier which had been the magnet which lured and trapped us.

"The descent: only fifty feet to the left, the wands stand undamaged. The glacier three hundred feet down: new cracks in the familiar basin at seventeen thousand feet, and some debris. What force, what weight to open crevasses.

"Why me? To fear, to be responsible? Is this right? If only some friend were looking for me, then confidence would not be misplaced.

"Yelling and listening. The fog is clearing to the left, revealing debris, but crevasses are in between. To risk it or not? This is five hundred feet vertically down; it seems impossible for a man to have survived this fall in the midst of those ice blocks, but I must see. The way is hazardous; the others must be informed. I remove my pack as a sign and find the map inside. I must write a message to leave so the story may be told. My pen won't write. Frantically, I scribble, trying to force the words into the paper so that even without ink they will be visible: 'Survived avalanche. Looking for survivors.' No luck. Only white indentations on the paper—invisible to the unknowing eye. Why was it so important for someone to know? I yell again and listen; no response.

"Down to base camp: speed is impossible in the soft deep snow. I was always slow going down anyway since my cartilage was removed, leaving me an awkward clod with bad knees. No one is there. On down to twelve thousand feet, shedding first crampons, then overboots, and finally disbelief on the way. Down snow and rock; faster and faster; time the more critical the closer the others are. There are the Sherpas—I pass them on the fly, yelling the news, and receiving stupefied disbelief. Into camp: 'Avalanche. I think seven are dead. I am the only one left. Come. We must dig and search.' Janney visibly folds, thinking of Dave and his own past close escape. Morrissey seizes command, a self-appointed leader, and a very good thing. Duenwald offers me tranquilizers, but this is a time when I need my adrenalin. It is for them to bring what is needed. I must return to continue the search and show the way. They approve my leaving and make plans on what to carry, mostly medical gear. I yell what is needed and what is available at base camp.

"Up the hill. Can I make it? Somehow I must. This day I must be a god. Other lives may depend on it; knowing that, I know that my own does as well. To base camp is no sweat, but we have to melt water. I stop for fifteen minutes with Terry for this chore. Jeff comes in tired, his second trip up today, and assumes our watermaking task. The Sherpas are slow. Only Phu has arrived when we leave; the others are mysteriously absent. We leave without him; just Terry and me on a quarter-inch rope, Terry without jumars.

"(In retrospect, I failed completely to gauge the reaction of the others to this search, to appreciate that in their minds the glacier was a mortally dangerous place on which to tread and had great danger of new avalanches. While I *felt* my place was at seventeen thousand feet and still felt curiously at home there; they knew what had happened, accepted my rational judgment, and felt it an alien place, one waiting greedily to finish what fate had begun.)

"Terry and I go the 16,400 feet alone, then cross on now solid snow bridges over many crevasses to the avalanche debris. The hour is late. My impressions from the morning are confirmed; there is no hope.

"We play the role of scavengers and pick up what we can. Much was frozen, solidly imbedded in the ice. My hat for example, the relic of so many other climbs, half appears, but is solidly claimed by the glacier and has to be abandoned. After the initial flurry of activity, we try to be systematic. We cover the whole slope. Our rope is quite a handicap; it is continually being entangled in the ice blocks. Terry goes up; I follow at a distance; I go down;

he holds my rope. I cross large crevasses, mostly filled, but still large enough for me. A look down a hundred feet, still more debris. No bodies showing. Relief. No time to recover them.

"Darkness and mist come together. It is time to depart. A bivouac is mentioned and then rejected. A storm seems to be coming and it would comfort us but not our lost friends. We collect our belongings and leave. My desires are ambiguous; my mind lures me to seventeen thousand feet to spend weeks and weeks; my stomach and feet lure me downward to rejoin the living. Living comrades prevail over dead ones. Down it is to camp and a nervous meal, followed by a strangely solid sleep."

An ice cliff just above the basin collapsed, starting an avalanche which swept across the crevasse. Glaciers move, and a steep Himalayan icefall is in fact animated and noisy, seeming to be still only because it is so vast. The ominous hanging glacier which had been discussed the evening before the avalanche had done nothing. The avalanche was a chance occurrence, accidental, without meaning. The conversation it interrupted was not profound or important; the interruption was as unexpected, as abrupt and as complete as only uncontemplated annihilation can be. Meaning lay in the lives of those men who had chosen to be in Nepal on the southeast glacier of Dhaulagiri on the afternoon of April 28, 1969, and had died there. Meaning lay in the effect that those deaths had on the survivors of the 1969 American Dhaulagiri Expedition, and in the tension that those deaths caused between the survivors. Meaning lay in the effect that the dead and the living of the expedition would have on their friends, and on those who would later go to Dhaulagiri and to other mountains.

Later Janney wrote: "Only Lou survived to tell those of us below. The clouds sense the tragedy and send snow. They pay their respects, as does the full moon which now peeks sheepishly through the clouds, kindly assisting the forlorn search for any sign of life. We ascend. The procession, the wake, is good for us. Submerged in the pain of our upward paths, we forget some of the shock, some of the inexplicable ugliness of what has happened. For a time we forget the questions which may never be answered.

"Dead. I cannot see, hear or touch them. Understanding the reality of their death is like seeing a vacuum, like listening for an echo which is never returned. Somethingness disappearing into nothingness; the final period of a sentence which was never completed. The full moon will wane. It speaks of the paradox that life also wanes. Life even at its height cannot escape the fact of death. Lived at a mountaineer's rhythm, life tends towards death. Pushing hard against life, the seven have been pulled away by death." Still later, considering the jarring events that took place in that beautiful setting, and the dissonance in trying to truly record those events in beautiful prose, he wrote, "Keats was not a climber."

The avalanche area was carefully searched. There was no question of going on. The immediate concern of the expedition was to withdraw from the mountain in a respectable manner. The behavior of the living in cleaning up the expedition's debris would reflect on the lives of the dead. There was disagreement among the survivors on how to make the withdrawal. Morrissey, whose introduction to the expedition had been as a footnote on Everett's recruiting list, emerged as the natural leader, and took command.

"I have respect for Morrissey," Reichardt wrote in his journal. "He had the best reasons for not going up to the avalanche site. He was up from eight thousand feet for the first time, and this after having fainted on his previous trip on the way to thirteen thousand feet, the day Al nearly died. Yet he came and not only that, he had the strength to exert badly needed leadership. He was the only one to prevent a rout from the mountain. Terry is quiet and dependable. He is another essential member of our team, doing all the work with the least reason to do so. A demand for self-respect will keep me here until all the work is done. We led ourselves into this and must ensure that the mess is cleaned. Our behavior now reflects on the character and image of those we must leave behind. Those with a right to flee are the dead. We, the living, have suffered only what we rendered ourselves liable for and must stand before the emotional hurricane. We are conquered physically, but must not let ourselves be beaten mentally as well. Otherwise we too lose our lives here on these slopes, and in losing ours, deny theirs."

Late that night the survivors took shelter in the small tents below the glacier. Compelled to talk, they spoke awkwardly at first just to break the silence, then to try to fathom what had happened, and then to shore themselves against the desolation they suddenly felt. The headlong rush of events had left their accustomed circle of conversation incomplete: they brought in Everett's tape recorder, and found they could talk more easily. Reichardt, who had suppressed his response to the avalanche for so long, sat down at last to rest. When he finally untied his swami belt, emotion overwhelmed him, and he found that he could cry. Duenwald spoke of his sons, and of the children his friends would never have. Would it be better, or worse, to die without children? He could not decide. But he did know, as they all knew, that it was a time to cry. Janney searched the past weeks for the things which were lasting and good, finding comfort in the joy that had characterized the expedition. Though he could call their enthusiasm childlike, he saw that it was indestructible, and saw it as inseparable now from the lives of those who had died, and those who had survived that day.

About a week was spent in dismantling camps and ferrying loads down to

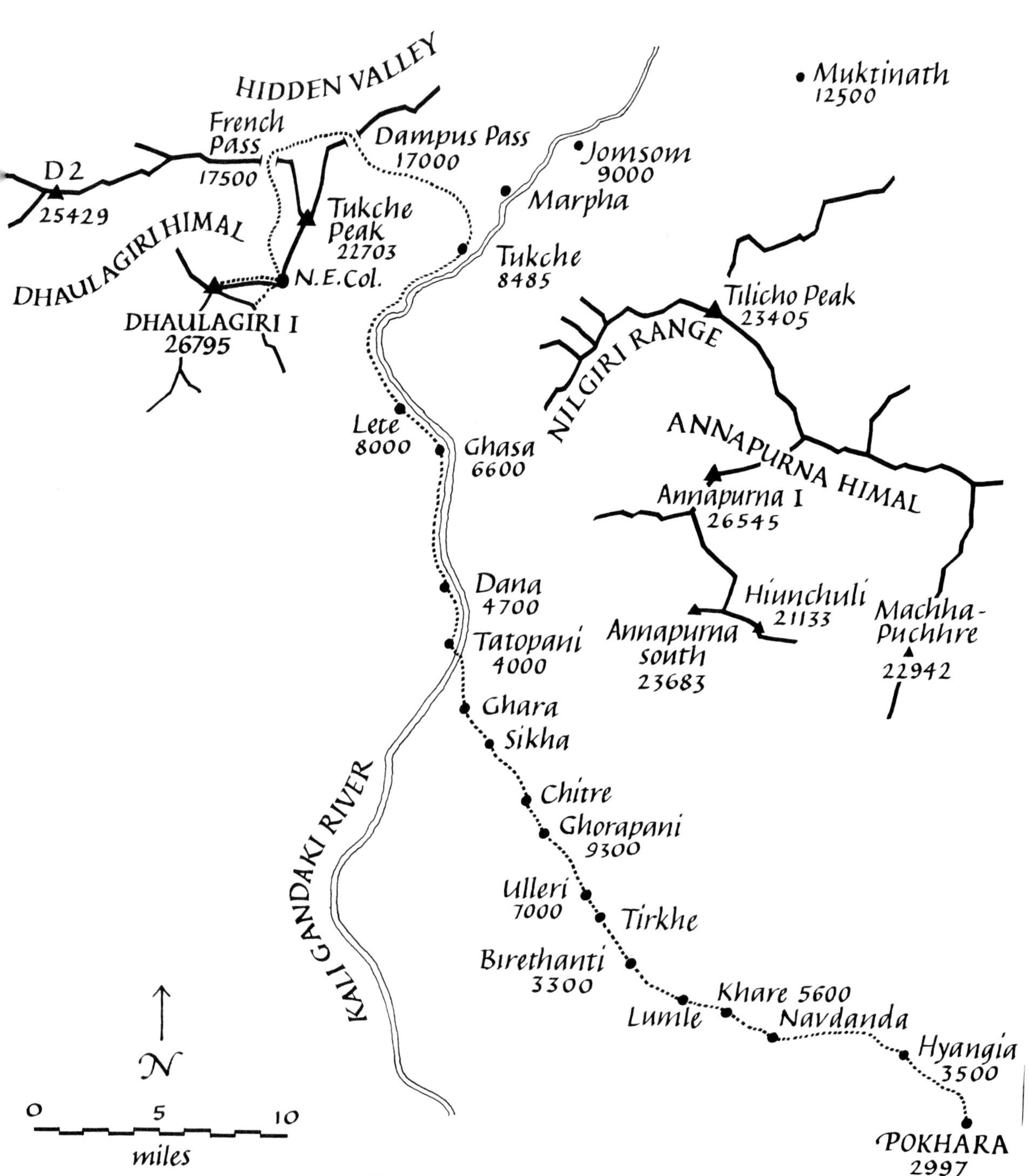

Pokhara to the Dhaulagiri region.

Boyd Everett.

David Seidman.

Vin Hoeman.

Bill Ross.

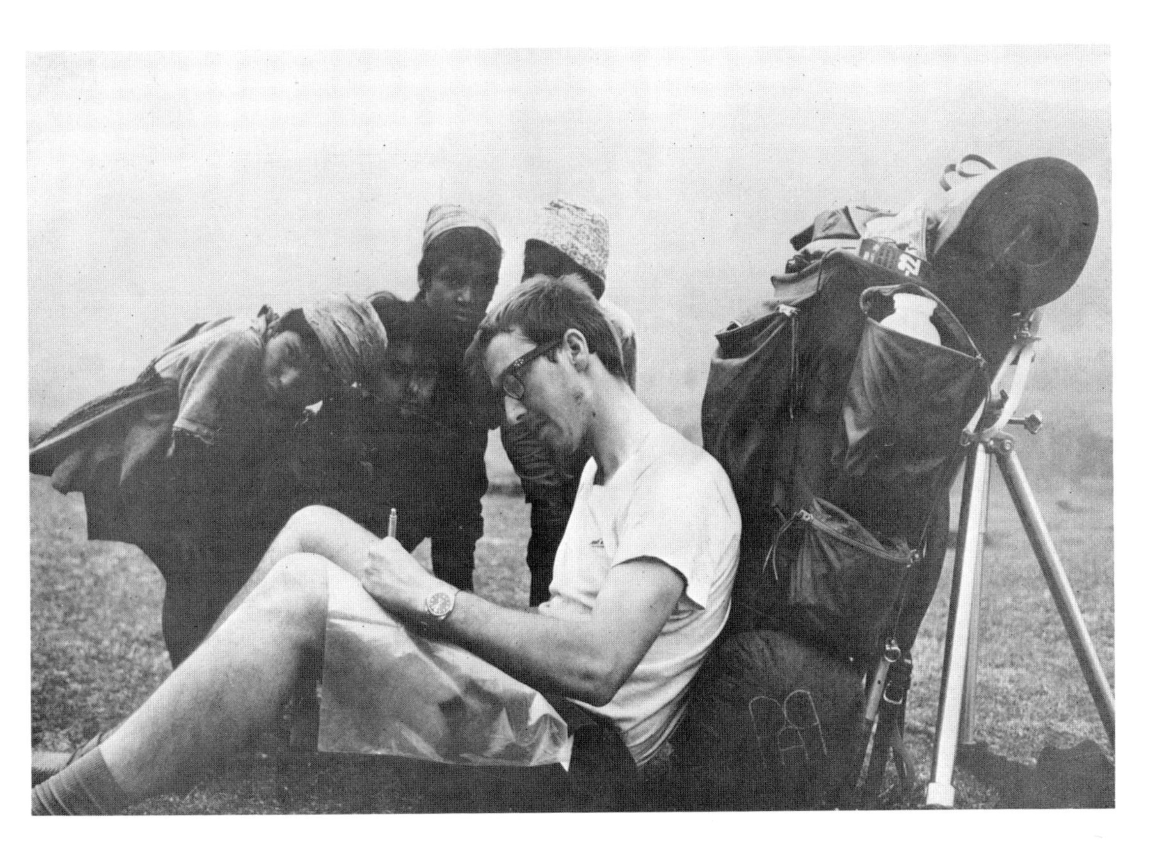

Paul Gerhard.

the valley. News of the accident was released to the world on May 1. Phu Dorje lit seven candles in the expedition's cookshed in Lete to help direct the dead men's souls to their next incarnation, and chanted Buddhist prayers as the last man came down from the glacier on May 5.

The tragedy was not over. On the trek to Pokhara, Phu Dorje showed increasing signs of emotional strain. He became irascible, launching into tirades and petulantly challenging the expedition members. One night he camped on the wrong side of the river, four miles from the appointed destination. He spent the night laughing hysterically over the Radio Peking political broadcast, trying to bait the American expedition members. He left the expedition in Pokhara, and the team saw little of him after that. They learned in Kathmandu that he had tried to throw two Sherpa women from a third-story balcony, and that four men had had to subdue him forcibly. Janney last saw him wandering through the Kathmandu bazaar wearing a necklace of flowers and a blank expression, followed by a handful of jeering Nepalis. They had just stopped him from drowning himself, they said, as he grabbed Janney around the neck in a confusion of grappling and embrace. Finally, Phu Dorje's wife went to Kathmandu and took him home to Namche Bazaar.

The team left Nepal one by one, shaken, but also strengthened by the events they had lived. Janney wrote: "They could never have realized how much they took from us when they died, nor could they have realized how much they gave us. We take the energy and vitality of their souls and of their dreams. Taking a little bit of each individual which truly inspired us, we incorporate it into our lives, along with a knowledge of their faults, and descend. And continue living."

A small stone on the trail in the valley where the runoff from the southeast glacier joins the Kali Gandaki River reads, in Nepali and in English:

THE LIVES OF BOYD N. EVERETT, JR., WILLIAM B. ROSS, PAUL ALEXANDER GERHARD, DAVID SEIDMAN, JOHN VINCENT HOEMAN, TENZING SHERPA AND PEMBA PHUTAR SHERPA WERE LOST IN AN ICE AVALANCHE ON THE S.E. GLACIER OF DHAULAGIRI, APRIL 28, 1969. THEIR ENERGY SHALL BE CARRIED ON.

Hoeman lowers a log across the crevasse at 17,000 feet.

The Making of an Expedition

Before they left Nepal the six survivors, Morrissey, Read, Reichardt, Duenwald, Bech, and Janney, agreed to return to Dhaulagiri to try again the southeast ridge. The initial impulse was emotional. In June of 1969, Morrissey wrote:

> The ancient hemlocks saw our passing.
> How could we know that some of us
> Would rest forever in the snow . . .
> We searched for them by moonlight.
> We listened, standing in the tangled ice . . .
> White Mountain, grey shrouded mountain,
> You came to us like thunder in the night . . .
> White mountain, shining siren,
> You whore. We shall return to have you.
> A thousand pins will pierce your shoulders.
> We shall not rest 'till then.

As time passed, this sense of mission diminished. The real motivation to climb Dhaulagiri, as simple and enigmatic as the reason for all climbing, had endured. If there had been a reason to climb Dhaulagiri in the first place, then that reason still existed and that enduring reason, itself indefinable, would define the new expedition.

They decided to return with a team large enough to handle comfortably the foreseeable mountaineering obstacles, and to ensure that the 1969 survivors were a minority. As a nucleus, their cohesion was as tenuous as their common bond was accidental; as the impact of the accident was eroded by time, its importance in molding the character of the team diminished. The survivors submerged themselves as individuals in a new group, a group whose goals would not be tied to the events of 1969.

In 1970 and early 1971 the expedition's total assets were a large pile of newly printed stationery, a slim file of prospective climbers and the enthusiasm of six members. Building on the leadership he had won in 1969, Jim

Morrissey charged the project with his tremendous, if not wholly organized, energy. Morrissey is all that is good in the stereotype of a black Irishman. In bright sunlight, but never in a social situation, his face becomes exceedingly red; he sweepingly commits himself to more projects than he can reasonably handle, eventually completing the undertakings only after they have far outgrown their original dimensions. He has a healthy disregard for details, and the conviction that all obstacles can be finessed, coerced or, if need be, physically overwhelmed. He is a natural politician. He was an All-American lacrosse player and as a college wrestling star claims to have beaten Jim Brown, the well-known football player. After earning a degree at the New York State School of Forestry, he studied medicine at Syracuse, spent three years in Tanzania as a Peace Corps doctor, then finally finished a residency in cardiothoracic surgery, which he now enthusiastically practices. He is straightforward, guileless, energetic, and sentimental. He will try anything, and he wanted to go to Dhaulagiri.

Morrissey's style of leadership defined the organization and set the tone for the expedition. His technique was simple, informal, and effective: he allowed the members enough initiative in decision-making to give them a feeling of personal responsibility for the results. No one could tell if the technique was calculated or accidental, but design or the lack of it wasn't important. The inclination to delegate responsibility and the willingness of the members of the team to accept it kept the organization decentralized. Duenwald summed up Morrissey's technique as leader: "There's a fine line between the king and the court jester. Jim stands on both sides of the line."

Late in 1970 Morrissey applied to the Nepalese government for official permission to climb Dhaulagiri in 1973. The rhetoric of the application was formal and the petition was accompanied by a U.S. State Department endorsement. Both quickly disappeared into the dark recesses of Singha Durbar, a maze of a thousand anterooms and offices housing, among other things, the bureaucracies of His Majesty Mahendra's Foreign Ministry and Mountaineering Division. Once inside the building, our application did not emerge for almost two years.* Singha Durbar was built as a palace for the Rana family, Nepal's hereditary prime ministers from 1846 to 1951; a favorite story in Kathmandu tells of a USAID official who spent his entire tour of duty trying, unsuccessfully, to chart a floor plan of the ministerial offices it now houses.

The process of expanding the expedition and adding new members began, a process which was to continue up to the month of our departure. The six

* Singha Durbar, guarding its mysteries to the end, burned to the ground in July, 1973. Speculation has it that the cause of the fire was spontaneous combustion in the piles of forms and records heaped in a courtyard. In any case, the bureaucracy is said to function more efficiently now.

named on the letterhead formed the initial core which set the rules for recruiting the twelve to fourteen additional climbers needed. Since it was to be, as far as possible, a national expedition, an announcement and an invitation to apply were sent to most American climbing organizations, circulated in climbing areas, and mailed to a hastily compiled list of active American expedition mountaineers. Applicants were expected to have, in addition to sufficient mountaineering skill and demonstrated competence, a willingness to work for a team goal even at the cost of personal ambitions. High altitude experience was considered particularly important because it entails exposure to the paced, often monotonous climbing that a big mountain demands: most American climbers are accustomed to the faster alpine climbing that does not require much patience.

New members were selected by consensus, and, obviously, in the inbred world of expedition climbers, personal contacts were important. We decided that the expedition should have a full complement of members by early 1972, a year in advance of the climb. The early selection of the team would ensure some stability in the party and provide a bulwark against disorganization in hectic last-minute preparations. Applications began to come in, increasing in number as interest in the expedition grew, and correspondingly, as the number of remaining places decreased.

The first two additions to the team were Roman Laba, a Fordham graduate working as a steeplejack in New York City, and Del Langbauer, an assistant professor of philosophy at the University of Puget Sound in Tacoma—both in their late twenties with years of expedition experience. They had been with Everett on the 1967 McKinley South Face Expedition, and both had been on the list for the 1969 Dhaulagiri expedition. Rather than go to Dhaulagiri in 1969, Laba had chosen to climb in Patagonia, and Langbauer's attention had turned that year to a new wife and an old Ph.D. thesis. Langbauer took on the job of organizing the equipment for the expedition, a task which grew continually until it threatened to turn him into a businessman. In December, 1972, after reassessing his personal commitment to the expedition, and evaluating the team's chance of success, Laba resigned, to travel in Central America. In its infancy the expedition organization was loose and contact among members was sporadic. The process of action by consensus was slow: sometimes an application would inspire an obvious yes or no, but more often applications from prospective members sat, like the expedition's application to Singha Durbar, immobilized by administrative procrastination.

Don Anderson, Lowell Smith, Andrew Harvard, Todd Thompson, Dave Dornan, and Drummond Rennie joined during the spring and summer of 1971. Dornan, a public health educator, and Anderson, a veterinarian, later dropped out of the expedition, Dornan because of its conflict with his job, and Anderson because of its conflict with his current lack of one. Smith, thirty-five, who delicately balances his career as a space radiation physicist for a defense contractor with a role as a prominent Sierra Club agitator, took no part in the preparations for the expedition, but later made strong contributions on the mountain. Rennie, a renal physiologist with a secret life as a *literatus;* Thompson, a conscientious objector assigned to a road-building section of the California Ecology Corps; and Harvard, who had a timber stand management contract with the U.S. Forest Service in Vermont, took on most of the pre-expedition administrative and fund-raising chores. Thompson had climbed throughout North and South America and made a climb of high standard in the Yukon; Harvard had completed difficult new alpine routes at high altitude in the Bolivian Andes and had climbed in Peru, Canada, and around the United States. Both were in their early twenties and had climbed with several members of the team on previous expeditions. Smith was not well known but he was strongly recommended by Reichardt, whose opinion was respected. Rennie, at thirty-six, had a colorful background in high altitude physiological research, a pursuit which had taken him from his native Scottish hills to the high mountains of Peru, the Yukon, and central Nepal. His flair for histrionics had once put off several of the team members during a chance meeting in the Andes in 1970, where American climbers were involved in earthquake relief work, but Morrissey, who knew him better, fortunately overrode mutterings about "arrogant Englishmen."

With a number of applications unanswered and with details of the preparation to be settled, Morrissey decided to bring the expedition together at the 1971 American Alpine Club annual meeting, held that year in Portland, Oregon. A summons was sent out and those members who could went to the northwest by plane, car, or thumb. The meeting was held in an odd place to begin a mountain venture, but climbers have long been attuned to ironically unlikely beginnings. We arrived in Portland, known to most of us only as a city one passes on the way from the Canadian Rockies to Yosemite, to find that the meeting would be held in the Thunderbird Motel, a shiny new complex of multi-colored buildings right off the interstate highway. Shades of purple dominated the design. Such a scene deserves a backdrop of either a brilliant sunset, or rain. As we converged on the motel it started to rain.

The AAC meeting offered most who attended a sleepy atmosphere for socializing and low-key politicking. The quiet conversation and predominance of grey business suits belied the fact that many of America's best climbers were present. Cocktails in hand, the climbers were far from the bright dawns, stormy nights, cold bivouacs, and narrow escapes which dominated the lazy conversations. The gathering gave us a forum to publicize the expedition and a chance to plumb past Himalayan climbers for information.

We rented a room in a remote wing of the motel, turning a quiet double into a bedlam for twelve. For a room with seven hundred occupants a year, it looked completely unlived-in, a guarantee of the anonymity of its past and future occupants. Like all its other transients, we briefly gave life to the room, the mass of our presence temporarily desterilizing its subdued plastic and masonite surfaces.

During that cold December weekend the 1973 expedition began to make the transition from an idea which could be ignored to a promise which would be kept. We picked up momentum with individual enthusiasms snowballing into a group *élan* that carried us through some difficult decisions and awkward confrontations. We tried to synthesize individual ideas and preconceptions and fought over the details of our goals and priorities. Adrenalin and emotion ran high; we expressed our differences quickly and openly, settling some and tabling others.

Six climbers were added to the expedition in what was intended to be the final selection. The number, now twenty in all, was a compromise between two points of view. Most of the younger members favored a small, streamlined expedition at the expense of extra reserves of manpower, which could be either a margin of safety or a source of redundancy in individual effort. Others cited discouraging health statistics from past expeditions and the difficulty of our objectives as reasons for needing a large group. If the southeast ridge proved as difficult as it looked, we could not expect Sherpas to carry loads on that route. The question was never more than temporarily settled, but in compromising we agreed to accept twenty, expecting some to drop out, but to make replacements only when the group dropped below sixteen.

The additions were: David Peterson, an intern at Harborview Hospital in Seattle, who had been an expedition doctor on the ill-fated 1971 International Himalayan (Everest) Expedition; Ron Fear, a manufacturer's representative, or "racer chaser" for the Raichle ski boot company, who had been to the summit of Dhaulagiri II with an Austro-American team in 1971; Del Young, a graduate student, logger, and Mount Rainier guide who had climbed many of the hardest alpine and rock routes in the country; Tom Lyman, then the manager of a guide service in New England; Jack Miller, a well-known mountaineer and cartographer with expedition experience from Alaska to southern Chile and Argentina, then working as a guide in Yosemite, California; and Lute Jerstad, a mountaineering entrepreneur from Portland, Oregon, who had been to the summit of Mount Everest with the American Everest Expedition in 1963 and has since been involved in a number of mountain-oriented business ventures. Peterson and Fear were in Portland to look at the expedition while it looked at them, and they were able to pitch in quickly and add to the chaos. Young and Miller had both climbed with several members of the team;

their reputations were good and their interest seemed high, but Miller, like most of us wary of the large size of the team, dropped out at the last minute to climb instead in Patagonia. Lyman had had extensive high altitude experience on Mount Logan in the Yukon with Arctic Institute of North America research projects. As preparations progressed, Jerstad's business interests began to conflict with his role as an expedition member; in the flare-up and confusion that resulted, good will was lost on both sides and he resigned.

The experience, background, education, and careers of members varied widely. We were from all parts of the country and some of us seemed to be from several parts at once. In a way, mountaineering itself was the thing which brought out our differences. Beyond a shared love of the mountains and a common fascination with the hardships, pressures, rewards, and challenges of climbing, our styles of climbing, our motivations to climb, and our approaches to climbing problems varied greatly, sometimes bringing us into conflict. Alpine experience was unequal, and was understandably a sensitive issue in a venture purporting to be capable of a most difficult Himalayan ridge. Some expedition members had made obscure or clandestine climbs in remote corners of the world but had not reported them in the customary high-profile way. Others had been responsible for important, well-publicized first ascents in Alaska, the Andes, the Canadian Rockies, or Yosemite Valley that required high competence and advanced techniques. Some had helped define the limitations of alpine climbing, others were only vaguely aware of those limitations. Eight members had been to the Himalaya before; a few knew appallingly little about mountaineering. Some regarded themselves as professional climbers, others clung to non-professional status. (The difference between "professionals" and "non-professionals" often reflects not a difference in degrees of skill, experience, or even amount of time devoted to mountaineering, but simply a difference in how non-climbing time is spent.) Yet these inequalities were not unwelcome. A large expedition needs a certain latitude in the personalities and qualifications of its members: tolerance would have to be the common quality.

A desire to climb Dhaulagiri brought us together and ultimately held us together, but that desire meant something different to each of us and could only be defined in very broad terms. We were able to reach a workable compromise on how to climb Dhaulagiri; it would have been pointless to attempt agreement on why to climb it.

The mountaineering goal of the expedition was to reach the summit by the southeast ridge, the object of Everett's reconnaissance in 1969, the "impossible ridge" of the French attempt in 1950. Improvement in techniques and equipment, growing familiarity with high altitude, and the search for new climbing problems constantly brings more difficult routes into the realm of possibility.

Unattractive in 1950, the northeast spur presented no insurmountable problems for the Swiss in 1960; unthinkable in 1950, the southeast ridge began to look possible in the early seventies.

The plan for a dual ascent, with a small party climbing the northeast spur while the expedition concentrated on the southeast ridge, grew from the knowledge that if a successful ascent of the ridge were made, a safe descent back along the ridge would be difficult. A route which follows a straight line up a steep face can be descended easily by a series of rappels on fixed ropes. The southeast ridge crest, however, has long sections where rappels would be impossible, and the descent would require climbing along, rather than sliding down, fixed ropes. We wanted to stock camps along the northeast spur's gentle slope, so that a summit party from the southeast ridge could walk safely down. With the uncertainty of the southeast ridge—nobody calls anything "impossible" in the mountains any more, but the southeast ridge was not a sure thing—interest in the spur as an alternative route to the summit, as an expedition goal in itself, began to grow.

Both routes are difficult, both throw the obstacles of high altitude, merciless wind, and unpredictable weather across a climber's path. The southeast ridge stretches the most advanced techniques for ice climbing, and requires an innovative approach to logistics. The sharp, steep profile of the ridge clearly defines its problems in a confrontation between a series of specific physical obstacles and the collective skill, strength, imagination and will that an expedition team can bring to bear.

Just as the southeast ridge requires breaking new ground in mountaineering practice, the spur route demands familiarity with the cumulative experience of a hundred years of mountaineering lessons. In the gentle, wandering topography of a low angle snow climb which appears to offer no technical difficulties, the problems: routefinding, crevasses at twenty-three thousand feet, and avalanches above twenty-five thousand feet, are more subtle than those of the southeast ridge, but no less serious.

It was clear at the meeting in Portland that a definite split existed in the group between those whose attention and commitment centered on the new route, the southeast ridge, and those who respected the challenge of the ridge but were primarily interested in reaching the summit, regardless of the route of ascent. This basic difference in approach, a fundamental difference in climbing motivation, was reflected in almost all the decisions we had to make, including the size of the group, the qualifications of its members, logistic needs and priorities, and even the style of our fund-raising efforts. Some members, among them Young, Langbauer, Duenwald, Harvard, and Thompson, were clearly oriented by temperament and experience to the southeast ridge. Others, including Bech, Rennie, Smith, Fear, and Peterson, clearly saw the summit, not the new route, as the overriding goal. Everyone agreed that the expedition's primary objective was to try to climb Dhaulagiri by the southeast ridge, but just how much effort would be devoted to climbing the northeast spur as well was left for circumstance on the mountain to define. We effectively postponed a confrontation over the relative importance of each route until one might really be necessary, but the resulting ambiguity caused some tension in our discussions. Morrissey, as leader, arbitrated between the two groups; he was emotionally drawn to the southeast ridge, but his mountaineering experience threw him in with the northeast spur group.

As we started to work together, to size each other up, and to speculate on our future together, it seemed that accident more than design had ruled the selection of the group. Random events and chance associations had brought us together and had kept others off the team. Late the first night in Portland Rennie soliloquized in the darkness about the excitement of meeting people whom one did not yet know but on whom one's life might soon depend. Sleepy responses followed. We would be dependent upon each other not only in extreme climbing situations, but also in the mundane rounds of our daily routine, in sickness and in health. We fell asleep in the face of a growing awareness of the scope of our contract.

The preparations for a large Himalayan expedition are extensive, involving laborious and intricate planning of food, equipment, transportation, and financing in the months before departure. Irregular or unforeseen local circumstances and transportation problems then usually make it necessary to repeat the process in Nepal. We had an unusually long lead time in our preparations because a sense of continuity with the 1969 expedition kept at least some interest and organizational activity going for almost four years. The growth of the project was slow, but over four years, even slow growth is measurable. By 1972, the plan for the small, inexpensive, streamlined expedition that most of us had originally envisioned was no longer relevant. We were clearly going to Dhaulagiri with the ponderous logistic strength and depth of manpower that Himalayan peaks traditionally required.

An expedition as big as ours was getting to be would need a well-coordinated logistic operation beyond the means of the individual climbers. We would need national publicity and credibility outside the close world of climbers to organize sponsorship and raise the necessary funds. Some climbers genuinely dislike publicizing their climbs and adventures; some pretend to dislike it; some welcome personal publicity, and some openly seek it. At first we had to scramble for attention in an undignified manner regardless of our individual ideas about the place of publicity in mountaineering.

As the original expedition letterhead, a line drawing vaguely similar in shape to Dhaulagiri's profile, was used up, the new stationery reflected a subtle but important shift in the expedition's tone. Black Letter gave way to monotype Bembo, and the scratchy mountain was replaced by an impish face peering out of an initial letter "D," copied in woodcut from a manuscript of obscene thirteenth century songs.

Many large expeditions are the creation of a single leader who devotes all of his time to organization and promotion while drawing a salary from the funds he raises. Some expeditions incorporate, and the American Mount Everest Expedition in 1963 even created an independent foundation to facilitate pre-expedition administration. Such a leader-dominated system was ill-suited to both the individual and collective tastes of our group. While a one-man organization may be efficient, it tends to de-emphasize the responsibility of each member to the expedition and to isolate the leader. A loose, easy relationship of general participation and accountability was evolving under Morrissey's leadership, and we wanted to keep it that way. Consequently, our organization relied on shared responsibility and therefore came dangerously close to leadership by committee. Like the proverbial committee whose design for a horse resulted in a camel, we roughly divided the work with the hope that the pieces would fit together in the end.

The National Geographic Society had supported the 1969 expedition and had followed its progress, but chose to drop the story after the accident. They were aware of our preparations, and were about due for a mountain adventure story.

In 1971 Morrissey asked for renewed support, invoking generations of explorers from Columbus to the astronauts in a moving appeal to the society to "continue its leading role in Man's challenge of his physical boundaries." The society, presumably with tears in its official eyes, contracted for a picture story for its magazine. The contract gave us enough money to open a bank account, and of much greater importance, associated us with the most universally recognized name in travel, expeditions, and exploration. People who had never heard of Dhaulagiri, of the American Alpine Club, or certainly of us might well have subscribed to the *National Geographic Magazine* for twenty years and be quite willing to take the society's word for our credentials. Their support so early in our preparation was extremely important; we were grateful, because the magic of their name helped to make each of us aware of what it would mean to be involved in the ADE (American Dhaulagiri Expedition): climbing expeditions have emotional roots in the sandbox, but the *Geographic* was something to be taken seriously. We hoped we could still have fun. Our agreement with the magazine gave them exclusive rights to our story and required their approval of any subsequent projects which involved us in films, books, or news releases. Since climbing, not promoting, was our real interest, we were glad to sign. But as we grew from the quiet little expedition that the

Geographic had adopted and we had perceived ourselves to be, to a large organization with a fiscal deficit and momentum for expansion, that contract became frustrating, particularly when fund-raising expedience tempted us to sell the same story to all of the bidders at once. With the patience of a father who had heard it all before, our editor at *Geographic* ruled out some schemes and approved others; with the exuberance of adolescents new to the business we tried his patience as often as we could. Our relationship with the society was marked by a cordial but slightly aloof formality which never failed to cow us. In 1969 Everett and Seidman had argued over Seidman's wearing levis to meet an editor. In the winter of 1972 Morrissey carefully shined his shoes and Harvard combed his hair before a meeting at the society's Washington headquarters.

Dr. Rennie's "Protocol of Scientific Work to Be Carried Out During the American Expedition to Dhaulagiri," and, in fact, Rennie himself, like the *National Geographic Magazine,* gave us a feeling of solid legitimacy, a source of strength, when talking with potential sponsors. Rennie, in a continuation of previous research, wanted to investigate the relationship between exertion and altitude with particular reference to the effect of these on the blood vessels of the retina of the eye. He had worked with unacclimatized volunteer subjects up to 17,600 feet on Mount Logan and he wanted to observe the response of well-acclimatized subjects actively exercising at higher altitude. His tools were a portable retinal camera, a gasoline generator, and a ubiquitous ophthalmoscope. As a control, he took pictures of everyone's eyes before leaving the United States; the photos would be compared with those made at the 19,300-foot Base Camp on Dhaulagiri. The expedition was perfect for his purpose because only climbers are silly enough to perform the kind of work at the kind of altitudes that Rennie needed for his results.

Building on our *Geographic* contract, our enthusiasm for the expedition, we could turn our attention to that powerful yet delightfully vulnerable big brother in American society, The Business World. We had to equip and feed ourselves as cheaply as possible, so we set out to trade product-testing, endorsements, photographs, and potential publicity for goods and services. To this end we appealed to over two hundred suppliers for specific things we would need, offering everything from serious field evaluations of products to a tax write-off for donations. We were engaged in an age-old mountaineering activity called "counter-marketing" by some and begging by others.

Climbing can be a pure form of exploration, free of the trappings of a reason for being, but on a large expedition, one seems to venture forth for mercantile interests as did the explorers and voyagers of old. In a consumer-oriented

Food planners Harvard and Duenwald at the warehouse in Seattle.

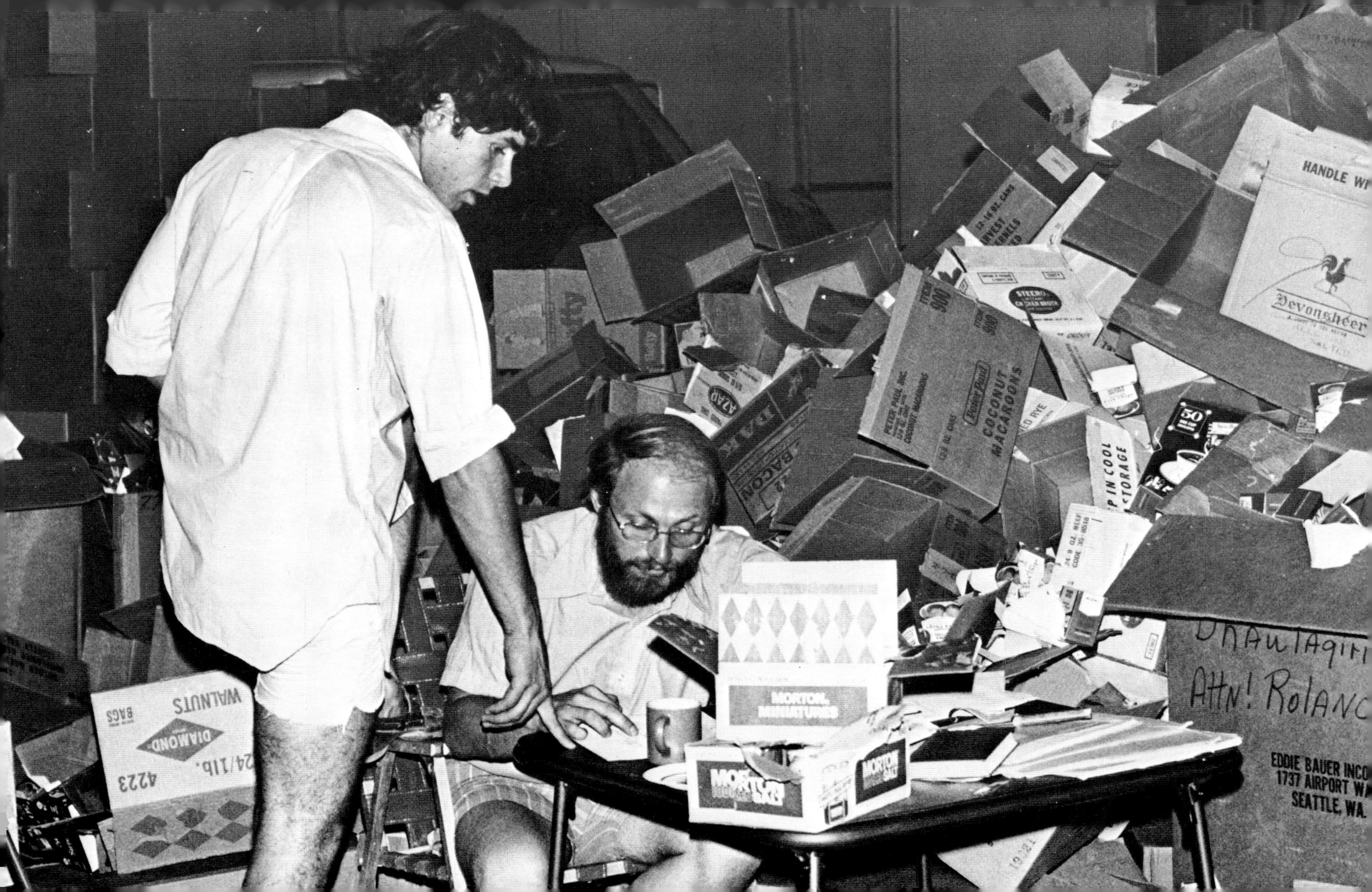
HANDLE WI
Devonsheer
COCONUT MACAROONS
PETER PAUL INC.
BACON
P IN COOL
STORAGE
MORTON MINIATURES
MORTON
WALNUTS
DIAMOND
24/1lb.
4223
BAGS
Attn! Roland
EDDIE BAUER INCO
1737 AIRPORT WA
SEATTLE, WA.

Del Langbauer.

Jeffrey Duenwald.

Del Young.

Ngawang Samden.

Terry Bech.

Andy Harvard.

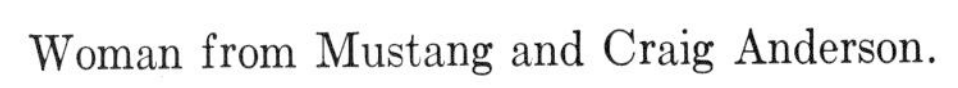

Woman from Mustang and Craig Anderson.

Peter Lev.

Sonam Girmi.

Lowell Smith.

Todd Thompson.

Jim Morrissey.

John Roskelley.

Ang Mingyur.

Lou Reichardt.

Pasang Tenzing.

David Peterson.

Drummond Rennie.

Ron Fear.

Tom Lyman.

society, where attractive marketing is important to commercial success, a high-profile expedition can offer an ideal vehicle for capturing consumer attention. The system is simple: a manufacturer makes a product that is either useful or necessary in the high mountains, a climber uses it in severe conditions, the manufacturer advertises that the toughest nail-eating mountaineer ever to walk down the pike used it, and the consumer, both wanting an adequate piece of goods and wishing to identify with nail-eating, buys. Suffering in the mountains for consumer marketing may not sound as romantic as freezing to death in the fur trade for the Hudson's Bay Company, but it is essentially the same activity.

The response to our dunning was slow at first. As a few prominent suppliers took an interest in the project, others noticed that interest, and as more companies involved themselves, others were more easily attracted. In the end, the campaign was so successful that we overshot the mark. By the time we left for Nepal, we were in the agonizing position of having to turn down offers of things we wanted but did not really need. Active climbers, perennially short of cash, rarely see shiny new equipment, so we had to fight a strong temptation to stockpile.

It took most of 1972 to amass the needed food and equipment, and our project turned out to be a genuinely nationwide operation. Morrissey, Rennie, and Fear shook hands and hefted packs at a Chicago sports show; Langbauer and Peterson argued our case in the board room of Eddie Bauer, Inc., the Seattle expedition outfitter whose down-insulated clothing and high altitude tents we selected. Morrissey petitioned patients with good business connections for support as he wheeled them into the operating room. Members who worked as mountain guides or climbing equipment salesmen turned around and nailed their bosses for contributions. Long-ignored relatives and friends were resurrected and tapped for contacts. A steady stream of letters descended on manufacturers and suppliers around the country until some begged for mercy. (After an exchange of polite letters, a gracious offer of a donation from a food manufacturer starts, "I do not wish to engage in further correspondence; just tell me what you need . . .") Harvard typed so many letters that he increased his typing speed from ten to fifteen words per minute. Langbauer hired one of his students as a secretary. We developed a great debt for office supplies and secretarial services to such seemingly impersonal institutions as the California Division of Forestry and Barnes Hospital in St. Louis.

Dealing with our suppliers was often frustrating but almost always fun. Our relationship with them was positive because each of us was getting from the other something which could not be bought. We, who could not afford to

Porter, 1969 expedition.

buy supplies, were able to offer promotion at little expense to ourselves while the suppliers, who could easily budget our needs, got publicity and a chance to join the expedition vicariously at a very low price. Lunches from New York City to San Francisco began with a glass of gin and "It's a fantastic ridge . . . they say it's impossible, but we think . . ." then ran to "Why do you do it, anyway?", answered by "How can you ask?". and ended with a cup of coffee and "Well, good luck . . . I think you're crazy, but I'm glad we can help."

Our equipment requirements were clear. We needed essential technical climbing hardware, strong tents designed for the devastating winds of a high mountain, five miles of the highest quality synthetic rope to anchor along the routes, dependable stoves, and fuel. We needed clothing and boots to give to the Sherpas we would hire. In addition, we had a long list of things which the members would have to supply for themselves if the expedition could not provide them: packs, boots, down-insulated clothing, windsuits, sleeping bags, and protective eyeglasses. The list was endless and would have amounted to a large, possibly prohibitive, outlay for each member, had not a large number of firms and individuals joined the ranks.

A small amount of oxygen was needed for medical use, but we would use no climbing oxygen. A route as difficult as the southeast ridge narrowly defines the way in which it can be climbed. The ridge's length and steepness, dictating the logistics of expedition progress, would allow little margin for wasted time in the ascent. We would have to set up and supply five or six camps, a day's climbing apart, along the ridge's one-and-a-half to two-mile length. A conventional climbing oxygen system, with its cylinders, regulators, and masks, is heavy. The coordinated movement of an expedition's people, food, fuel, and equipment—its logistics—is determined by the flow of loads, the roughly forty-pound units that one man can carry from point to point in one day. The use of oxygen for daily climbing and sleeping doubles by weight the minimum number of loads necessary to support a route at high altitude because it adds more loads: more loads mean more carrying days, in turn increasing food and fuel requirements to further slow progress. The added burden of climbing oxygen on our logistics, its health and safety advantages notwithstanding, would cancel the potential benefits.

The decision was controversial. The Swiss planned to use oxygen on Dhaulagiri in 1960, but made their ascent without it when their oxygen bottles proved defective. The Japanese used oxygen in 1970. Form dictated that we repeat the spur without oxygen, but the southeast ridge was different. No one had attempted a route of such difficulty without oxygen before. It is physically possible to climb at above twenty-five thousand feet without oxygen, but debate continues as to whether it is advisable to do so. The British used oxygen in 1970 on the south face of Annapurna, a difficult route, but agreed later that oxygen probably wasn't worth the trouble. Our decision was discussed and second-guessed at length. Conflicting advice came from all corners of the mountaineering world.

Our food needs were less clear. We had to feed the expedition team for the time it would be in Nepal and on the mountain, so we used the liberal estimate of thirty men (sahibs and Sherpas) for four months, our outside estimate of the expedition's duration. That meant that we needed 3,600 man-days or 10,800 meals' worth of food. The packaged weight of food for a large expedition normally runs to about four pounds per man-day, which meant we could expect a gross weight of around 14,400 pounds, or over seven tons of food. A liberal estimate, of course. For a climb on an eight-thousand-meter peak, the overall bulk of supplies is so great that concern for the weight of individual food items is important only high on the mountain; most of the supplies go no farther than base camp.

From experience we knew that although eating well is essential on a long climb, a monotonous diet sometimes makes doing so a chore, so we wanted an attractive diet with a normal variety of foods. Most of us were accustomed to climbing on budget rations of rice and tuna fish, so the prospect of an unlimited menu was too good to pass up. Since weight was not a severe limitation we chose to use whole foods of familiar brands rather than the customary lighter, but often less palatable, dried foods. This decision took us out of the protected realm of the specialized outdoor market in our search for sponsors, and we suddenly found ourselves vying with UNICEF, the Salvation Army, and the NFL training table for the attention of manufacturers' public relations men. Our initial address list came from a supermarket in the San Juan Islands where the tolerant store manager watched Thompson and Harvard copy down manufacturers' home office addresses from the backs of almost every can or box on the shelves. From that list grew others, until we eventually accumulated enough, then more than enough, food.

We decided to reduce the potential for complaints about the food by letting each member of the expedition list his menu preferences and veto foods which he knew from experience he wouldn't be able to stand in a small tent. By initially catering to a few idiosyncrasies, we reasoned, we could avoid problems later on. Unfortunately, when we polled the members about tastes, their responses were virtually irreconcilable. Almost everything that was someone's favorite food couldn't be stomached by someone else—eight men couldn't live without granola, for example, while six couldn't stand it and two had never heard of it. Even chocolate was rated at both ends of the scale. It was clear that we couldn't fool all of the people all of the time. In desperation the food committee—Duenwald, Harvard, and Thompson—chose the foods that they themselves liked best, assuming that they could at least eat well on the mountain while listening to complaints. This basic principle varied only with the exigencies of the donation market.

As had happened with equipment, the absolute essentials seemed to be the last to come, and it was not until Hickory Farms of Ohio provided large amounts of cheese, soup, and canned goods late in 1972 that our basic nutritional requirements were assured.

When we assembled in Seattle on Labor Day of 1972 to sort and pack our supplies, the scale of what we were undertaking was suddenly and shockingly apparent. Some of us knew, in theory, what was in our warehouse: we had calculated the numbers, allocated weights and amounts, and followed invoices by mail. We had even seen some of the shipments here and there, and we were aware of the murmurings of amazement that came from the Raichle-Molitor warehouseman who was receiving the contributions of equipment and food. Langbauer could have estimated the tonnage of equipment; Duenwald and Harvard had even calculated the net weight of food in ounces, but no one was prepared for the sight of our hoard massed together in one place. There are famous rock-climbing problems which are not as high as was our pile of cartons! Young wandered among the boxes, a dazed expression on his face, murmuring about multi-day climbs done on a can of sardines and a handful of raisins.

We ran out of space in the suburban Raichle-Molitor warehouse, so we rented a truck and moved to the garage and storeroom adjoining Eddie Bauer's retail store on a busy corner in downtown Seattle. There, for four days, we performed our packing chores for a small but loyal gallery of regular passers-by. Our intent was to pack the supplies for efficient daily use in camps on the trail and on the mountain, so our tasks in Seattle were primarily mechanical: we took things out of big boxes, put them in small packages, made piles of assorted small packages, and then put everything back in big boxes. The incoming boxes were of every shape, size, and color and boldly advertised their contents. The boxes to be shipped out were of uniform size and shape, and the only hint of their contents was a stenciled code number. As the pile of boxes grew, the code book became very, very important.

The story of the packing boxes, at first a seemingly minor detail, gives a good idea of how our organization worked. We knew we would need something in which to pack and carry our goods, so a large Northwestern timber and paper products firm was approached. The dialogue ran somewhat as follows:

Expedition: "We are a team of American mountaineers, supported by the . . ."
Large Timber Firm: "We know, we know . . . We gave boxes to the Everest

expedition. You know, that guy from the Seattle Co-op and Sherpa what's-his-name . . ."

Expedition: "We know, we know . . . your boxes are doubtless the only ones that can save us . . ."

Large Timber Firm: "OK, what kind of boxes do you need?"

Expedition: "Nothing special, just a good strong box the size of a couple of beer cases."

Large Timber Firm: "Look, we make boxes that can do anything. Give us your specifications."

Expedition: "OK. Each box has to be exactly 12 x 10 x 28 inches to fit our packs, and strong enough to be dropped from a plane doing ninety miles per hour at four hundred feet over ice, but cannot weigh more than ten ounces. It's got to be flexible at sub-zero temperatures, completely waterproof, brightly colored, reusable, combustible, and if possible, edible."

Large Timber Firm: (Pause) "Well, thanks for calling. One of our subsidiaries will send you some good strong boxes about the size of a couple of beer cases."

The boxes alone, as sheets of unstapled cardboard, weighed over a ton. We needed an industrial stapler to put them together, but everything in Seattle was closed for Labor Day. The owners of the Northwest Staple Company jokingly offered to let us use a machine in their back yard. To their amusement and their neighbors' amazement, we set up an assembly line and shuttled hundreds of finished boxes from there to the warehouse in cars, vans, and a rented truck. The boxes turned out to be entirely satisfactory, some surviving the expedition from start to finish.

The packing session was our first chance to work together, under pressure, on a single project. Everyone seemed to be conscious of the testing of the group inherent in that situation. During four long days tempers flared and cooled as energy peaked, drained, and finally began to disappear. Good will fluctuated between the spontaneous and genuine and the rationalized and calculated. Members who had not involved themselves in planning expressed surprise at some of the decisions that had been made. The nagging questions of the size of the party and of route priorities surfaced again, and were again only temporarily settled. But, overall, we could be optimistic. Eight members and about as many wives and friends had done a staggering amount of work in a short time, and when we parted, tempers were cool and good will was real. We knew each other better, and if that meant greater awareness of weaknesses, it also, on reflection, meant greater appreciation of strengths. The project became viable through a growing synthesis of its participants. Pleased and a little surprised at how well things had gone, Harvard noted that Morrissey had done a good job of putting the pieces together. Morrissey's uncomplicated response summed up the hopes and precarious strength of the expedition: "I didn't put anything together . . . things fit by themselves."

Our baggage was shipped by sea, a risky business when the expedition depended on the cargo arriving safely and on time. By steamer from Seattle to Calcutta and then across India to Pokhara by truck, the route is far from secure: all along it our shipment was at the mercy of striking longshoremen, careless sailors, confused shipping agents, predatory truck drivers, and grasping customs officials. Weather, coincidence, accident, and the bakshish system could all threaten delay, disruption, and taxation. Because so many expeditions to the Himalaya have had trouble in getting supplies to Nepal, it is almost axiomatic that when transport problems can occur, they will occur. We could only pack carefully, ship early, and hope for the best.

The final months of preparation meant something different to each of us. Everyone in his own way examined his motivation for going to Dhaulagiri. The strong impulse to go was tested against the hard question "Why?" Some found no need for an answer deeper than "I want to." Others simply never questioned a commitment once made. Men changed with time, and some questioned, found no satisfactory answer, and dropped out. Janney found his interest to be too strongly rooted in the past, so he withdrew. Duenwald looked to Dhaulagiri as the last in a series of big mountains; Young saw it as the first, to Rennie it was the only, big mountain. Some saw the project as a once in a lifetime event; to others, it was just another year, another expedition.

We had no formal program of training; no one considered it his business how anyone else got in shape, and everyone was accustomed to regular exercise anyway. Morrissey ran and did pull-ups; Fear skied and consumed large amounts of energy pills and health foods; Young guided in the Cascades; Don Anderson chased women, and Rennie thought about chasing women. The most popular theory was "Duenwald's Scientific Fat Factor" which called for climbers to arrive in Nepal strong but a bit overweight. The hike-in would take care of muscle tone, and the extra weight would be useful as a buttress against the debilitation of high altitude living. Langbauer, possibly because his wife is a superb cook, was the most dedicated student of the Fat Factor theory.

Most of the members climb regularly, and the expedition as an entity developed a colorful reputation in the ranger's lodge on Mount Rainier. Janney, Langbauer, and Don Anderson were rescued by helicopter after being hit by an avalanche on Fuhrer's Finger; Thompson and Harvard sat out a storm in a snow hole near the top of Liberty Ridge, barely escaping a rescue by descending quickly when the weather cleared; then Duenwald and Morrissey were chased off Fuhrer's Finger by rockfall. Smith, unwilling to risk Mount Rainier, went to climb in Wyoming where he promptly broke his leg.

While the large and increasingly noisy organizational effort was going on in the United States, Bech was running an important parallel operation in Nepal. It was fortunate that Bech was one of the most resourceful men on the expedition, because his tasks in Nepal were a challenge to imagination and initiative. Bech was responsible for our relations with Nepal's government, for our financial arrangements in Nepal, and for the efficient transfer of funds to and from the United States. He had to find dozens of things we would need and to arrange to receive and store equipment when it arrived.

Bech knew many of the working Sherpas, and he wanted to hire the best for the trip. Circumventing the Himalayan Society and working a year in advance, he retained as sirdar Sonam Girmi, a man who has commanded the respect of both Sherpas and sahibs on eighteen expeditions. Ngawang Samden, an experienced sirdar who had once been a Buddhist monk, agreed to become the assistant sirdar. Both devout Buddhists, Sonam Girmi and Ngawang Samden epitomize the Sherpas' attitude toward their religion: Sonam consulted lamas in Tibet and in Kathmandu to see if climbing Dhaulagiri by the southeast ridge with the Americans in 1973 would be safe before he agreed to go. Ngawang, who had been a monk for several years, deemed it inauspicious to go to any mountain during his forty-third year, but sat down with Bech and a Tibetan calendar to discover that the proscribed period ended just days before our scheduled arrival in Kathmandu. Sonam Girmi and Ngawang Samden chose the rest of our Sherpa contingent.

Sonam Girmi and Ngawang Samden are typical of the best of the working Sherpas. They come from Namche Bazaar (12,800 feet), near Mount Everest, the largest town in the Solu-Pharak-Khumbu region, the home of the Sherpa clans. They had worked their way up through the ranks of the expedition system, from low altitude porter to cook or mailrunner, to icefall porter, to high altitude porter, the "Sherpa" job familiar to westerners, and ultimately to positions of responsibility and leadership as expedition sirdars, or chief sherpas. They spoke rudimentary English and French, with a smattering of Spanish and German, and were, of course, fluent in Sherpa, Tibetan and Nepali. They had learned the confusing ways of sahibs and the intricacies of mountaineering on numerous expeditions. Sonam Girmi, related by marriage to Tenzing Norgay, had lived and studied at the Institute of Mountaineering in Darjeeling.

Bech carefully explored all the possible logistic schemes for getting us to the mountain. His detailed cost analysis of various combinations of mules, porters, and airdrops over the two possible approach routes is perhaps the only document in the expedition archive hinting at the use of modern business practices.

In loose coordination with the growing operation in the United States,

Bech made a reconnaissance of Dhaulagiri in the spring of 1971. Under the umbrella of the expedition's permission for 1973, Bech was permitted to climb to twenty thousand feet in an exploration of the approaches to Dhaulagiri. He and his wife, Cherie, and a handful of porters trekked to the mountain along the Myagdi Khola approach, establishing camps at 15,000 feet, 17,000 feet, and on the northeast col at 19,300 feet. From the northeast col at the base of the northeast spur they could see and photograph the southeast ridge clearly. Instead of attempting a reconnaissance to the crest of the ridge, they chose to try for the summit by way of the northeast spur. Tolerable weather held, and they started carrying loads up the spur. Careful logistics and long, hard days of carrying brought them to 24,600 feet. There the high winds characteristic of Dhaulagiri's weather stopped them, and they had to retreat. They were agonizingly close to success, but their failure to reach the summit does not detract from the remarkable feat of getting as far as they did without the customary heavy support. They demonstrated once again that a small party can reasonably attempt a non-technical route on an eight-thousand-meter peak with little support. The climb was rewarding for the Bechs, who met the dangers of a big mountain with the slimmest possible margin of safety. They pirated oxygen and food supplies from camps left by the Japanese a year before, and left a little blood and sweat in crevasses on the Myagdi Glacier. A few months later Cherie, a native Australian who is a trained nurse and a skilled climber, gave birth to a daughter. They named her Annapurna.

Most of the crucial decisions for the expedition's movements to the mountain were based on Bech's research. His isolation gave him freedom, but also kept him guessing as to what the rest of us were up to. Communication with him was spotty at best, but when Morrissey's secretary in Stockton started sending letters to Nepal by sea mail, it all but ceased.

As the tempo of activity increased toward the end of 1972, the scope of our involvement grew. We explored several options for making a commercial film but never received an offer which guaranteed a return great enough to compensate for the demands on our logistics, and the potential distraction, that a film crew would entail. The fact that we were looking for a guarantee, not grabbing a speculative offer, is a fair indication of how stable we considered ourselves by then. We had grown up considerably in a year: even the circulating rumors reflected it. A year before we had spent hours in raucous speculation on the possible results of Rennie's secret negotiations with an editor of *Playboy Magazine*—Dhaulagiri as a centerfold? Hefner's jet? In December of 1972 when Morrissey closeted himself with representatives from the Columbia Pictures' overseas marketing operation, the possibilities associated with a magical Hollywood name caused little excitement.

The climb, not the organization, was our object, and clearly our attention had run beyond the preparation, focusing on the mountain. In the last months, the pace increased but the presentation became more polished and mechanical. Lyman, Fear, Morrissey, and Harvard attended the American Alpine Club annual meeting in Boston and quietly raised a few thousand dollars in contributions while the rest of the club membership bickered about such heady issues as the average age of the AAC Board members. A serious meeting in the boardroom of Fuji Photo Film USA in New York, at which thousands of dollars worth of film, cameras, and equipment were being discussed, was interrupted by a long distance call for Dr. Morrissey. The call, which brought a respectful silence in the room, was from Morrissey's mother on Long Island, who wanted her car back.

We began to think of our commercial sponsors as truly a part of the expedition. Some of them, as individuals or corporate beings, became part of its folklore. Of course, we could not have made the trip without their help, but more than that, personal friendships grew out of formal business contracts. We watched the operation of large corporations from the privileged vantage point of a mendicant stranger at a feast who finds himself magically elevated to the head table.

In January of 1973, Craig Anderson, Peter Lev, and John Roskelley were added to bring the team up to sixteen climbers. Roskelley, the proprietor of a climbing shop in Spokane, had never climbed above fourteen thousand feet but had performed well on difficult climbs in Yosemite and on alpine climbs of his own design in the American Northwest and the Canadian Rockies.

Lev is an ageless greybeard of the mountains who acts with the slow deliberation of one who knows how to get where he is going. He has an uncounted number of mountain exploits in his long and murky history. He works during the summer guiding in the Tetons of Wyoming and in winter as a snow ranger at the Alta Ski Area in Utah. He had broad knowledge of snow conditions and avalanches, so he devised a research project to carry out for the U.S. Forest Service while on Dhaulagiri. Anderson spoke Nepali, learned during years in Nepal as a Peace Corps volunteer. He had made the first ascent of Huinchuli (21,133 feet), an outrider of Annapurna, and had earlier thrown his good-natured enthusiasm into the packing effort in Seattle, so he joined us as an old friend.

We gathered in New York on February 16, 1973, a few days before our departure, to turn the quiet club house of the American Alpine Club into a busy office, warehouse, workshop, laboratory, and campsite. We had countless last-minute details to attend to, many of which actually did get attention. Rennie set up his retinal camera and photographed our eyes. There was still more packing to do and an air freight deadline to meet. Thompson and Harvard still had a list of companies to approach for contributions and had to be dragged from the phone for the trip to the airport. Members had to sign insurance agreements, commercial and editorial contracts, and financial statements. Some still had to get tickets and visas; many still needed vaccinations.

Two or three reporters wandered around the building during those days, cornering climbers for comments and explanations. No one paid much attention to the press, an oversight reflected in the results: one story gave the expedition a few lines, then rambled on about how the AAC building was a firehouse in the nineteenth century. Thompson was quoted as saying that climbing is safer than living in New York City, while Langbauer, who wasn't sure he liked reporters at all, somehow got the headline "Black Humorist Dr. Del Langbauer Predicts That 1.6 of the 16 Climbers Leaving for the Himalaya Today Will Die on the Mountain."

We had negotiated with Air India for months to arrange an exchange of publicity for dollars with which we would then buy transportation to Nepal on Air India; IATA rules demand such circuitousness. The discussions continued up to the last minute. In a gallery at Kennedy Airport the night we left, we briefly stopped quibbling over excess baggage charges to pose with forced smiles, holding a banner which advertised Air India and a New York ticket agency. As climbers have done for years, we trooped onto the plane wearing our heavy double boots to save the cost of their weight as baggage.

We settled into our seats strangely quiet, almost subdued. Many of the other passengers were Indians returning to their land. As the plane roared off toward Nepal, toward the mountains, toward our mountain, we too seemed to be going home.

Approach to Dhaulagiri

The thirty hours that measured half a world were punctuated by brief stops in London, Paris, Rome, Kuwait, and New Delhi; as airport citizens and transit lounge inhabitants, we were thrust through time and space. Suspended in the neutral zone between departure and arrival, we had little to distinguish the places in which we paused: there were the *Times,* Italian butter at dinner, women in purdah, and oil fires in a dark, flat desert. At proper times we expressed either actual or strategically pretended outrage when our excess baggage was questioned or our air freight delayed. Months of intensive planning were over. As we flew east from New Delhi on Sunday, February 18, and saw the Himalaya, hazy white peaks in a dark blue sky, we longed to cut through peripheral nonsense and get on with the climbing.

Terry Bech and Al Read met us at Tribhuvan Airport in Kathmandu with the exasperating but not entirely surprising news that our sea shipment had not arrived in Pokhara as planned. The shipping agent in Kathmandu informed us that the ship containing all of our food and equipment had been unable to find a berth in Calcutta, so had gone on to Rangoon. The rumor was that the ship would be back in Calcutta and ready to off-load within a few days. After that, more time would be required to truck the seventeen shipping containers across India and through Nepali customs, and the expedition could not really get under way until the trucks arrived. Careful plans were aborted by circumstances, and we faced an open-ended period of waiting when we most needed action.

Kathmandu was a fruitful place for us to wait: it is a culturally eclectic city that shows the history of religions in south Asia and the influence, particularly western, of other cultures on the once-isolated kingdom. The seal of Nepal reflects these East-West, Buddhist-Hindu mixes: the Hindu deity Shiva with a trident, which is his symbol, is shown in a European heraldic escutcheon against a background of the Himalaya; below the escutcheon are Latin and Sanskrit mottoes; above are the footprints of the Buddha. As students of the history of religions, we wandered about the temple viewing, and listening to clear explanations of unfamiliar things given to us by Professor Langbauer, whose academic field includes Hindu and Buddhist phenomena, and Kathy Peterson, David's wife, who is a Tibetan scholar. Pilgrims travel great distances to the Hindu and Buddhist shrines of the Kathmandu Valley; our pilgrimage was to the mountains, but we savored a privileged view of the Tibetan Buddhist Mahakala ritual at the hill-with-monkeys temple of Swayambhu, and cremations at the Hindu shrine of Pashupatinath on the sacred Bagmati River.

We moved into the basement of the Kathmandu Guest House, an inexpensive hotel known to a clientele of itinerant young foreigners by its cable address, KATHOUSE, where we were joined by some of our Sherpas. We set up our own kitchen in the hotel and quarantined ourselves from local food, hoping to avoid tourists' intestinal shock during the wait. We should have enjoyed the luxury of ample free time as events beyond our control unfolded, but we soon realized that we were incapable of relaxing on such ill-defined terms. Information about the status of our shipment was very soft; the shipping agents told us what they thought we wanted to hear, and it was doubtful that anyone we dealt with really did know where the ship was. The members of the expedition responded to the real but insubstantial problem of waiting in a variety of ways. Some became tourists, some retired to peaceful contemplation, and others frantically sought activity. Some who had little interest in Kathmandu or who felt the need of physical conditioning suggested that the expedition borrow or buy enough equipment to make an acclimatization camp somewhere near Dhaulagiri, returning to Pokhara for the repacking when the boxes arrived. The idea was heartily debated, but finally canned as busy work. Most took the waiting as a windfall for personal indulgence as the fascination of the Kathmandu Valley became apparent.

The bazaar, which fills the winding streets through the center of town, drew us in and held us for hours each day. Stall after stall of goods—ancient goods, modern goods, modern renderings of ancient goods, aging modern goods—piled upon each other. In and around the stalls a steady stream of humanity flowed: Gurkhas, Newaris, Indians, Tibetans, saddhus, beggars, Brahmans, wide-eyed tourists, foreigners stoned on drugs, hustlers, soldiers, priests, small children, and old men and women filled the streets.

Some necessary discussions and many superfluous ones were born of a definite impulse to do anything, however ineffectual or inefficient. We decided to stay in Kathmandu, learning as we could the fabled patience and the pace of the East while working on final negotiations and preparations. As though the mere anticipation of four months walking and climbing were not enough to sate the drive for physical activity, some of the hardier members spent the time hiking up jungle-covered mountains around Kathmandu "for the exercise."

Much to everyone's relief, Sonam Girmi made it plain from the start that he as sirdar would take responsibility for the smooth operation of our supply train, and for the organization and discipline of our porters. A good sirdar functions as a co-equal administrator with the expedition leader; each is at the top of his own organizational pyramid. Morrissey was grateful for Sonam Girmi's professionalism; he could put the 1969 nightmare of Phu Dorje II behind him. The rest of us saw him as a good counterweight to Morrissey, balancing by contrast or complement the things which distinguished Morrissey's style. Sonam Girmi is soft spoken, almost invisible at times; he is organized almost to the point of being methodical, and he is extremely efficient. Neither is particularly intimidated by human or natural obstacles; in solving problems, Sonam Girmi compared to his American counterparts as a rapier compares to a broadsword.

Important and not so important details made equal demands on our time and attention. Boots for the low altitude Sherpas, extra crampons for the climbers, and fuel containers for the airdrops had to be found. The Sherpas' preferred food—rice and lentils—had to be bought in staggering quantities in the Kathmandu bazaar. Carol Laise, the U.S. Ambassador to Nepal, generously held a reception for us at the Residence, where we stretched good manners and taxed the resources of her staff by making a meal out of the hors d'oeuvres. She showed a film of the British Annapurna Expedition. Some of the soundtrack was a recording of slow, heavy breathing at high altitude: too many cocktails, the warm, dark room, and that breathing made most of the climbers tax her hospitality further by falling asleep.

Lev received a telegram from our New York ticket agent informing him that the check for his airline tickets had bounced. He claimed indignantly that it was a bank error, as we gleefully pictured the agent's frustration. Morrissey held press conferences. He arranged for Elizabeth Hawley, the Reuters correspondent in Kathmandu and a long-time friend of expeditions, to handle our mail. We met with Samrajya Bahadur Pande, a subinspector of police attached to us by the Nepali government as our liaison officer. Pande, a portly man in his thirties, is a member of the Hindu ruling class in Nepal who preferred the cosmopolitan life of Kathmandu to the austerity of the mountains. He had little relish for his assignment with the expedition, but regarded it as a necessary step in his career.

Bech handled delicate negotiations with the Royal Nepalese Air Corporation for airdrops to French Pass and the northeast col. We wanted to use airdrops rather than a long porter train, but we were not certain that the government would give permission to RNAC and the expedition to make the drops, even though an extremely large Italian expedition was using two cargo helicopters on Mount Everest at the time. The government prefers to have expeditions employ Nepali porters, but in 1973 the Italians had hired just about every available porter. In addition, though RNAC owned two Pilatus Porters and was anxious to make the drops, they were not certain that they could maintain an operation from Pokhara, our planned staging area, to which fuel would have to be trucked from a depot near the Indian border. Emil Wick, who was working as a charter pilot for RNAC in 1973, was very eager to do the flying, so we relied on him to make the operation work once a base was established at the dirt airstrip in Pokhara.

Airdrops were logistically important to us. We wanted to avoid using the southeast glacier, where the avalanche had occurred in 1969, as an approach to the northeast col, so we would have to go from Pokhara to Tukche and then over Dampus and French Passes to the Myagdi Glacier, under the Eiger and up to the col, following the approach route of the Swiss in 1960. It was a lengthy approach, possibly the longest in Nepal, and, including time for acclimatization, would require three weeks between Pokhara and the northeast col. It would have been dangerous and impractical to use untrained porters over the proposed route, which traversed two seventeen-thousand-foot passes and a glacier. Without airdrops, we would need more than seven hundred porters: to take them from the local labor force at harvest time would have been impossible, and to bring that many in from another region would have severely taxed the resources of the valley, so delicate is the food balance along the Kali Gandaki.

Therefore, carefully planned airdrops to French Pass and the northeast col allowed the expedition to travel relatively light, carrying only what it would need for the three-week walk, and the breakable scientific instruments and medical supplies we were afraid to airdrop. Without porter support we would remain flexible and independent; would expose no untrained porters to unnecessary risks in the Myagdi icefall, and would have a cheaper operation. In gaining these advantages, of course, we became very dependent on timely and successful airdrops, and no one had made airdrops as high as 19,300 feet before. We counted on near-perfect drop conditions, low breakage, and high recovery rate for our system to work well.

After much haggling, the government granted permission for the drops. John Skow, an old Peace Corps friend of Craig Anderson's, volunteered for the job of airdrop "kicker." When his Peace Corps tour was over, Skow had remained in Nepal to climb and to explore the possibilities of setting up a search-and-rescue service as an adjunct to the growing expedition trade. For us, he would be responsible not only for sorting and stacking the boxes in the plane, and for making the actual drops with Wick, but also for regulating

Bagmati River at the Hindu temple Pashupatinath, Kathmandu.

Girl, Kathmandu.

the flow of our baggage to us and acting as our agent in clearing snags in our official dealings with RNAC.

In the evenings we met at the Kathouse to fine-tune our logistic scheme and to jockey pet projects into expedition policy. Langbauer expanded the equipment committee to include Young, and together they performed the drudgery of dividing the equipment between the two airdrop sites and the trek in. Mismanagement would mean snow shovels on the walk and no climbing hardware when it came time to climb. The food committee guessed how many man-days would be spent on each section of the trip and allocated food resources accordingly. The tasks were dull, and the size of the group turned simple ideas into unwieldy abstractions. The mountain seemed remote. Reichardt turned Bech's 1971 reconnaissance diary into a careful schedule of expedition movements above Tukche for optimum acclimatization to prepare us for living above nineteen thousand feet. We struggled to weave string onto metal snowshoe frames, a task so straightforward it brought cries of rage and frustration. Minor diversions became major projects.

Everyone knew that Morrissey intended to appoint a deputy leader to oversee climbing decisions and the coordination of our effort on the two routes, so a little politicking, spurred more by the boredom of waiting than real interest in the job, took place. Read had originally had the job, leaving a vacuum when he dropped out of the team, unable to obtain leave from his State Department position. There was only very vague general agreement on just what role a deputy leader would play, since there was already considerable leadership from the ranks. Peterson clearly wanted the job, Duenwald said he didn't often enough to suggest that he did, and Langbauer said he "would do it if he had to" in a way that meant he really didn't want it. Bech, just getting to know the team, wasn't sure he wanted any part of its loose organization; Reichardt was clearly capable and available. The rest were either unknown, not interested, or knew that the job would give them less rather than more control over the expedition's destiny and their own. Partly because the job was so poorly defined; partly because there was no obvious choice to fill it; partly because Morrissey still had a vague reluctance to delegate the necessary authority, and partly because we were enjoying the discussion, a decision was deferred.

Our medical oxygen system consisted of medical emergency bottles that Morrissey had bought in the United States, and veteran regulators and masks that were borrowed from friends. The system was adequate but a little heavy; a "Medical E" bottle weighs about eighteen pounds and holds only 600 liters of oxygen. Peterson discovered that the recent British expedition to the south

Porter, 1973 expedition. Woman, Tirke. Man, Dana.

Women and children, Kathmandu.

face of Everest had left seventy British bottles (also weighing eighteen pounds, but with a 1,200-liter capacity) in the Solu-Khumbu region, and that the newly constructed Japanese tourist hotel there was desperate for oxygen equipment, having lost some clients recently to pulmonary edema. We bought the bottles from the British and resold fifty of them to the Japanese for what we had paid for the lot, thus upgrading our oxygen system to greater capacity for the same weight at no extra cost. That meant we could sell any unused British bottles after the expedition for a profit, and we could sell the Medical E bottles to RNAC. The hotel owners were surprised to discover that the oxygen equipment they so desperately needed had been stored not far from their hotel. Perhaps we had learned a few tricks from our contacts with The Business World. Peterson relished the successful negotiations: "high profile with a minimum of detail work."

After a week or so of eating only food prepared by our Sherpas, climbers began to break training for secret feeds at Boris Lissanovitch's Yak and Yeti hotel. No story of Kathmandu is complete without reference to Boris, a Russian émigré who left the ballet stage for the hotel and restaurant business after World War II. In 1969, the climbers had stayed in Boris's Royal Hotel, an elegant palace once owned by the Rana family. Shortly after, Boris lost the hotel and landed in jail for his dealings in the national art treasures market. But fashionable Kathmandu society could not function without him as its most genial host, so he was released, rehabilitated, and allowed to open the new Yak and Yeti in a different palace. By 1973, the restaurant was thriving and plans were afoot for a new hotel. Knowing of our worry about local water-born diseases, Boris blithely promised Bech that he'd hang his cook if anyone got sick.

The fluid situation in Kathmandu reinforced the idea that our loose structure relied on men of good will wanting the expedition to work, and that in fact it could work. But we were becoming impatient waiting. On February 25, after a week of hoping for some hard information concerning the shipment, Fear, Duenwald, and Morrissey flew to Calcutta on a rumor that the ship had docked. Fear went along because he had shepherded supplies through India for the 1971 Austrian Dhaulagiri II Expedition, and presumably could do it again. Duenwald, an old farm boy, wanted to kick the ship to see if it were real, and Morrissey wanted to kick somebody, anybody, to see if the supplies could move. Both kicks were rigorously, if figuratively, applied, both with positive results. The ship was there and our containers were sitting in a congested alley, one of them broken open for use as a bedroom and kitchen by part of the Calcutta street population. A glowering presence often produces results, and when the shipping agent realized that they did not intend to leave his office until the containers were on trucks ready to roll north, he expedited our freight. Morrissey returned to Kathmandu on the twenty-seventh, while Fear and

Duenwald stayed to ride with the nine trucks through India to Pokhara. Fear, rarely perturbed and always looking for the good in any person or situation, wrote about the truck ride in his journal: "I'm sitting or lying on top of the truck riding along with the wind blowing in my face feeling free, and the expedition has started! This evening the stars came out and beautified the night. Flying along with the wind in our faces with the stars flashing by as the trees go over—the feeling of freedom and peace. I slept as we honked and wandered through the night." Duenwald, not so free with praise, merely characterized the trip as "grim." The progress was interrupted only by brief stops to visit the drivers' girl friends along the way.

Most of us were in Pokhara by April 3, and the last truck from India straggled into our campsite by Pokhara Lake on April 4. The circus was in town: we were reunited with our goodies. The containers were unloaded and used to make a wall around the bustling camp. Pande proudly produced police officers and dogs, but the camp was actually guarded day and night by our Sherpas. Ngawang Samden, the assistant sirdar, sobered up after waiting in Pokhara for us for three weeks, and Ang Namgyal, the cook, built an efficient kitchen, using two freight containers and a stack of boxes. Lines of boxes grew in the camp while equipment and food consultations droned on around long tables ringed with director's chairs. Shirtless, we baked in the tropical sun as we sorted, repackaged, and packed within sight of Dhaulagiri, pausing only to drink quantities of cool Heineken beer. In the mornings, when it was chilly, we obeyed our doctors' injunction against swimming in the lake, where deadly microbes of all descriptions supposedly lurked. In the afternoons the heat put precautions in their customary place, and we swam: no one died of cholera, but Lev did cut his foot on a beer can. We played a little football, and discovered that the Sherpas could kick the ball better than some of us could throw it. Urchins and townspeople watched, waiting for the spoils that would be left when we moved on. The expedition community was infused with the healthy life of purpose and interaction; passers-by stopped to question or to help; we planned and laughed and dreamed.

Organizing for the airdrops, we had to separate the stacks of boxes for French Pass and the northeast col, and we had to mark the boxes by priorities within each group. If air-to-ground radio communication failed, and our visual signals proved as confusing as they looked on paper, Skow would still know what to drop, when, and where, provided he could still decipher the jumble of code numbers on the boxes. We scheduled the drop on French Pass for March 20 and on the northeast col for April 1. Advance parties would push ahead of the main body of the expedition to mark drop zones and receive the drops.

Parodying the activity of the expedition, our nearest neighbors were a small herd of pigs. They had a pen and a large wallow close by, and they freely ambled through our camp to root in our garbage or chew on tents. Their presence bothered some more than others; Smith was often seen war-whooping across the rice paddies, ice-axe in hand, chasing a brood sow or a gang of delinquent shoats. One night, after dinner, as we sat around our long table under the glare of gas lanterns, sipping Jack Daniel's sour mash whiskey, the tenor of Morrissey's administration was revealed. Morrissey is a ladies' man, always suggestively polite, so he set out with Rennie to escort two visiting American nurses back to their quarters in Pokhara. They moved through mounds of expedition paraphernalia to the edge of the circle of light and suddenly, with a roar of surprise and outrage, Morrissey disappeared from sight. He surfaced sheepishly and looked up to see a Sherpa, candle in hand, grinning from his freight container house, and hear us choking with laughter. "That guy just watched me walk right into the pig hole!" he said in disbelief. The event eclipsed all others in Pokhara, and was elevated to legend as The Night Morrissey Fell Into The Pig Hole. The nurses made their way home alone.

Three days were enough to finish the sorting and packing, to store supplies that we would need in June, and to trundle the airdrop boxes to a small mud house near the airstrip. On April 6 it rained heavily in the morning, flooding us awake, and we trooped around in foul weather gear, loading trucks, feeling like old campaigners in muddy trenches. We remarked on how well rice paddies hold water, just as we had noticed how flat they were for tents a few days earlier. We left the lake in the afternoon of the sixth by truck, riding through the two-mile-long Pokhara bazaar to a campsite on the Yagahdi River, and a meeting with the sixty mules that would move us to Tukche. Ordinarily, one walks through the bazaar, but we felt silly enough about the size of the team without parading like a minstrel show along paved streets. We were off—not far, but it was progress.

We awoke early the next morning to Pinzo's bright smile and the cups of hot tea that always seemed to be present. We were with very little reluctance growing accustomed to the amenities dictated by the British Army style of the Sherpas. As we wandered off, we carefully failed to notice each other shifting parts of our already light loads to the backs of nearby mules or porters.

Walking days centered on the lunch stop, always a pleasant affair. The first day we stopped by a spring to read, write, drink beer, and watch the loads go by, while Ang Namgyal fried *chopaties* and cheese pancakes. Although Ang Namgyal and his assistants were last out of camp in the morning and after lunch, they always passed us, sometimes at nearly a dead run, to be found organized and cooking when we arrived at the next stopping place.

Two wandering minstrels found us near Pokhara and followed us, playing when we stopped to rest. They thought we would like their song about Tenzing Sherpa climbing Mount Everest, but were pleased when Anderson, translating for the rest of us, encouraged them to play other things as well. They used four string *sarangis,* instruments about eighteen inches long, carved from single blocks of wood, which are played with a bow. They sang two parts, one sometimes putting aside his *sarangi* to keep the rhythm by snapping two fingers of his right hand into the palm of his left. Fear remembered them from 1971, and Rennie had seen them on a trek to White Peak. When Bech arrived, he greeted them as old friends; he had known these minstrels for years, and considered them among the best in the country. They knew more than four hundred songs from all parts of Nepal, many of which Terry had recorded and transcribed. Bech bought one instrument. He was uneasy about taking an instrument from a master; he had worried about it a long time, finally deciding to buy it as he was about to leave Nepal. When they sensed that all of our spare rupees were gone they moved on to entertain other travelers.

It was difficult at first to tell how liaison officer Pande managed on the trail. His first meal with us, back at Pokhara Lake, had been a disaster. Pande took one look at the dehydrated beef in his rice and excused himself. Chips of desiccated beef are not very appealing at best, and it wasn't at its best as Ang prepared it. Pande was doubtful: if it was pork, as we told him, he didn't like it; if it was beef, as he suspected, it was forbidden him by religious law; if it was cardboard, as it appeared, he didn't think he could digest it. He apparently came to a clear decision then, because he never shared a meal with us again. We rarely saw him during the day and he did not camp with us, but he would appear from time to time in clean expedition-issue clothes and Nepali cap, with his packet of official papers. We knew he was not pleased with his assignment, and certainly he was not at ease with any of us. He worried about his poor English, and he was not sure of proper protocol, or of our status vis à vis his own. He seemed to think we gave the Sherpas too much freedom, clearly a dangerous thing. Eventually we learned that he traveled very early in the morning to avoid the heat; he rode a horse if he could, walked only if he had to, and had personal porters to carry his belongings. He rested or slept at midday and, as an important government official, was fed and housed without charge wherever he went.

During the first day of walking, we stratified by rate of travel into levels of fitness which were an indication of how seriously each had taken the Scientific Fat Factor in training. Some dragged weary bones late into the lovely campsite at a pass near the town of Khare. Sherpas put up tents, a wood fire was made for cooking dinner, and the long table was erected. The Sherpas, as professionals, performed their tasks efficiently but without subservience, rarely using the traditional term "sahib" in addressing us, preferring the more egalitarian "member." The "members" relaxed with Jack Daniel's or beer and enjoyed the good fellowship of a groaning table. Someone invited two itinerant

French anthropologists to dinner, but our group was raucous and inner-directed; we were exercising our growing intimate knowledge of each other and of our purpose, to the flagrant exclusion of mere observers. We had been together long enough to develop a vernacular, and refer to jokes by abbreviations: further, we were past the stage where we felt inclined to explain ourselves to anyone. Our group should clearly have been of clinical interest to anthropologists, but the guests were overwhelmed, and retreated early.

As dessert was handed around, Thompson began a short dissertation on Morrissey. Morrissey's honorific and official expedition title was *Bara-Sahib,* or head sahib; during his stay in Tanzania as a Peace Corps physician and big game hunter, he had been called *Bwana Mkubwa,* or great master. He was accustomed to nurses scurrying after him in the intensive care unit, addressing him respectfully as "doctor" meaning "Doctor, Sir," but on the other hand, he had irrevocably defined a role on the expedition by falling into the pig hole. None of his titles seemed quite appropriate. They were foreign to our tongues, and were altogether too formal; they lacked the irreverent affection we had to express. Our American heritage of comic books, Jack Daniel's, and caustic wit conspired to corrupt all Morrissey's honorific titles into a single one: the *Bumba.* "Bumba" caught on and soon the expedition renamed itself "Bumba Goes to Nepal," as we imagined Morrissey leading his troop of clowns ever upward beating a bumba drum. Occasionally Sonam Girmi even managed to call Morrissey the Bumba, or Bimbo in his pronunciation, with a straight face.

The next morning we were roused by shrill tones of argument between a firewood seller and Ang Namgyal. The Sherpas are wise in the ways of the road: Ang had been lonesome the night before, and had sought the company of the wood seller's daughter. Expeditions will pay for a Sherpa's food, clothing, and fuel, but that's all, so Ang had asked for money to buy a huge pile of firewood, knowing that the old lady would reclaim the unburned wood as compensation for the services of her daughter. The haggling was for dramatic effect, to give us at least some entertainment for our money; Ang knows the value of a rupee.

We traversed the hill from Khare along a boulder-strewn and densely vegetated stream bed of a trail to the neat, cultivated terraces at the Gurung village of Lumle. From the rust-and-earth-colored, oval mud houses of Lumle we continued traversing the hill to a village where there is an airy view of Machha Puchhare (22,900 feet), the "Fish Tail," a holy mountain on which climbing is proscribed, and then dropped steeply down to the Modi Khola River. Most mountains in the Himalaya have religious significance, but Machha Puchhare is apparently sacred to someone in office. Police in Bhiritante, a town

Man, Kathmandu.

Man, Tirke.

just across the river, checked our trekking permits, and we walked a short way up a canyon to have lunch at a swimming hole beneath a series of waterfalls. After lingering to wash dirty clothes and sweaty bodies, we continued on up the canyon to Tirke and a welcome early camp on a yard in town.

At Tirke the trail rises steeply out of the canyon and climbs several thousand feet to Ghorepani Pass (9,300 feet). The trail is so steep for the first two hours that it is made of stone steps, a truly formidable obstacle. It was here that Fear developed, in the language of a ski instructor explaining a new style or a sex therapist cataloging natural events, his Himalayan walking technique, which included two basic positions. Himalayan Position Number One is supine, rear end on the ground, with a pack; the feet can be raised or not, the head is back, and the eyes, which are glazed over, look skyward. Himalayan Position Number Two, a quickie, is prone, face down, under a pack. Masters recognize several more positions; we studied avidly. Fear summed up the trek in a diary entry: "Life is so good now with no responsibility, but soon we will have to climb the mountain. Now, nothing but enjoyment. There's nothing to do tomorrow but walk to the next camp and sleep ten hours; then the same thing over again."

Roskelley and Lyman overshot the lunch spot and almost missed camp; more conservative walkers never strayed far from the cooks. However, staying with Ang Mingyur could be dangerous too. Langbauer recalls an afternoon when his well-paced meditation was interrupted by the sound of Ang Mingyur crashing up behind him. Ang Mingyur was carrying eighty pounds, so Langbauer stepped back to let him pass. "After you, sahib," Ang Mingyur said with a mischievous grin. "The little bastard," thought Langbauer, "I'll show him." Langbauer knew he was caught; the rest of the afternoon was a grim competition as Ang Mingyur chased Langbauer up and down hill, neither giving an inch. Ang Mingyur laughed, and Langbauer asked himself why he was racing. On the last hill, Langbauer resolved to rest at the top, competition be damned. They steamed up the trail in lock-step pace, until Ang Mingyur collapsed in laughter at the top. Gratefully, Langbauer collapsed too. The next day, by chance, he delivered a long monologue on the virtues of the Sierra Club rest step hiking style, in which one pauses slightly on each stride.

We mounted the steps to Ulleri with resigned determination. In the Ghorepani forest, the blooming rhododendrons, orchids, mosses, and the dense, moist enclosing vegetation above old snow and a muddy trail were a refreshing change from the hot lowlands. The cool forest was filled with gnarled old trees. We slipped down the west side of the pass, through muddy troughs of trails, to a camp in a small glen near the town of Chitre. In clear weather Dhaulagiri's

Morrissey dispenses medical advice along the trail.

Porters above Windy Corner.

Tukche and the Kali Gandaki valley, looking south from the trail to Windy Corner.

south face and southeast ridge are visible from Chitre; but, mercifully, the weather was unsettled, close to rain, and we could see nothing. It was a little too soon to be faced with the intimidating magnitude of our objective. Rennie and the Bumba slept on a hill above the glen, hoping to make dawn photographs of Dhaulagiri, but at dawn the sky was still cloudy, so they retreated, and we began the precipitous descent to the Kali Gandaki River.

We crossed the river on a steel suspension bridge, walking north to Tatopani, a town known for its hot springs and popular with trekking westerners as a place for open-ended stops. Ang Namgyal had picked a miserable, fly-infested courtyard in town to cook a meager lunch, passing up a fine swimming hole-lunching place on the river not far back. The food committee was learning some things about feeding an expedition; our carefully constructed menus were ignored as Ang Namgyal raided food boxes for goodies and fed us Sherpa style, with huge mounds of rice covered with a stew-like slop of cabbage and only a hint of meat. The Sherpas thought our fare too heavy on sweets, with too little starch, and we found it difficult to adjust to their high volume eating. The sahibs began grumbling about the food—climbers will probably always grumble about expedition food—but this time it was justified. Morrissey began an investigation, and was righteously outraged to find the Sherpas eating canned meat spread while the members had soup and crackers. The Sherpas were confused; they found the meat spread revolting, and thought that they were doing us a favor by not serving it. Morrissey demanded an end to such favors.

At stops along the way, Morrissey and Rennie dispensed medical care to villagers and expedition members alike. They were a good team: Morrissey's surgical energy and optimism, thwarted by a dismal lack of surgery, being neatly balanced by Rennie's therapeutic nihilism. Most people who had anything wrong with them saw both, often at once, and so had a gratifyingly instant second opinion. They were then given the choice: ineffective drugs or stoicism. Since the medical supplies were almost invariably behind the expedition proper, the patient, deprived of the first choice, usually had to make do with a lecture on high altitude physiology.

We went a short distance up the trail in an afternoon thunderstorm, stopping for the night at a house in the village of Upper Dana. The house was a typical Nepali stone structure of two stories with an outside stairway leading to the second floor, mud floors, and a slate roof. A few Tibetan women from inaccessible Muktinath were on their way through town on a trading expedition so we consumed some excess energy and time in bargaining with them for their wares. Duenwald and Fear did not want to sleep in the dusty house, so they went down to the riverbed and pitched an eight-man Kelwood tent. As a design consultant for the tent, Morrissey had sent it to be tested in an industrial wind tunnel in Chicago; he now extolled its virtues loudly enough to court disaster. During supper, Ang Dawa burst into the room, laughing, to say that the tent had blown away down the river, bouncing like tumbleweed. After a chase the tent was recovered, and Duenwald and Fear spent a stormy night in it.

On the eleventh the expedition moved through the prettiest part of the Kali Gandaki valley, gaining almost four thousand feet from Dana, as we passed waterfalls and hiked through the rocks of Ghasa to the pine groves of Lete. There, on a gentle hill side, we made camp. Though it was only eight thousand feet, the evening air had a mountain-like coolness that reminded us of what we had come so far to find. While the valley sank into darkness, a pink light from the setting sun covered the austere Annapurna massif, eighteen thousand feet above.

It is half a day's walk from Lete to Tukche, and during that half-day, the nature of the land changes dramatically from monsoon-nourished larch and pine forest to high desert. Turning a bend in the river, one sees a wide flood plain with Tukche, seemingly close, crouched low against the steep hills at its end. At the point where the run-off from the southeast glacier enters the Kali Gandaki valley, the trail passes the monument to the dead of the 1969 expedition. Reichardt found himself weeping as he walked to the monument, a walk which took him back four years. From the monument he could see the southeast glacier, and feel a shadow come over him. As Reichardt stood in front of the monument, his consciousness flooded with its personal meaning, the focus of his eyes uncertain, Roskelley came up beside him. Roskelley paused, scanned the faded letters on the stone, then cocked his head and said, "Didn't get very far, did they . . ." The shadow passed; they walked on together.

Most of those who had not been there in 1969 crossed the river to avoid the monument, holding themselves aloof from too close a concern for history and for the memory of dead friends. From the trail we could see the mountain. The long southeast ridge towered above us as we came abreast of it and then passed it by: it was immense and seemed to have no end. Everyone looked up at the ridge, but few had much to say. Young remarked laconically, "Well, it'll be an interesting spring."

Tukche has an architectural integrity unlike any other village in the valley. It is an old city that stood for generations in its arid, windy place as a major commercial center on the trade route between Nepal, Tibet, and China. Since the Chinese invasion of Tibet and the subsequent closing of the border, trading interests have shifted south to India. Tukche is no longer a wealthy center of activity, but it retains an air of grandeur. Tukche's flat-roofed buildings, carved wooden windows and doors, inner courtyards, mangers, and rough cobbled streets are conditioned by the dusty, harsh landscape. Grain is threshed on the flat roofs that are edged with neat stacks of cured firewood which repeat the horizontal elements of the buildings. A rust-colored wash discretely sets off the predominant sandy tone of the houses and temples. In the spring, apricots and almonds bloom in an orchard concealed on a bluff above town. Since the town's earliest days, traders, men of affairs, and expeditions have clattered into the square with their mules, to camp surrounded by curious children. Maurice Herzog was there in 1950, and we sensed our repetition of an old pattern as our mules, with their bells and gaudy head ornaments, were unloaded while we sat on stone benches in the shade of a pipal tree.

A cheerful little man trotted up to greet us. He wore western clothes of reasonably good quality, and an ingratiating smile. He approached a group lounging in the shade of the pipal tree, and started, in broken English, "Good afternoons, gentlemen, may I . . ." "Ah," cut in Rennie, who had appeared to be sleeping, "You're Doctor Moghul Singh, M.D., Lhasa Veterinary Technical School, 1948. You're the 'doctor' in this town, and you'd like us to give you some of our medical supplies as a gesture of good will and charity, so that you can sell them at outrageous prices to people here, who don't need them and can't afford them." The man was nonplussed. "I am Moghul Singh . . ." he stammered. Then, ". . . You've been here before . . ." Rennie, archly: "I have." That was enough. Moghul Singh shrugged: he was a businessman, and quackery, like any other business, has its ups and downs. He could write off this expedition, but Rennie's reaction at least meant that he had been well clipped on a previous visit; there was some satisfaction in that.

At Tukche our route climbed steeply out of the valley, so we paid off our mule drivers and piled their loads in an empty house for the porters to bring up the hill. During the afternoon of the twelfth we rested, sorted our belongings, drank beer, and amused the urchins in the square.

On the morning of March 13, we stored our lowland tropical clothes and, a few at a time, started up the dusty trail through the orchards, yak pastures, and cliffs where hawks soared toward a campsite at twelve thousand feet. Sonam Girmi arranged for the 150 loads to follow us in successive stages. Only Bech, Morrissey, and Thompson were left in the Tukche square to take care of final details, when the low altitude porters approached Sonam Girmi and announced that they would carry no more loads. Some shouted interchanges ensued, the gist of which was that, having seen the wealth of expedition equipment and been given only a small part of it, they wanted better clothes for the high altitudes. Sonam Girmi would not appease them: all agreements had been fulfilled and they were adequately, if not lavishly, prepared for the work ahead. Representing them, he had overseen our purchase of their food and equipment in Kathmandu. Now, as their chief, he would see that they too played by the rules. His attitude was scornful because he did not consider their claims reasonable, and because they had found it necessary to drink a great deal before making their demands. Sonam Girmi addressed the porters in calm, quiet tones, listened to them alternate between sullen silence and drunken shouting, then turned and walked over to the sahibs. Bech was philosophical, Morrissey was furious: "The little bastards, bring them all the way from the Solu-Khumbu, give them a job, and this is what we get!" The same square had seen Herzog's porters strike in 1950 before the French ascent of Annapurna and many porter strikes since. Since we would not yield, the porters had little choice but to stage a walk-out, and it looked as if they were going to leave town. Bech went to find Pande, who intended to go no farther than Tukche himself, and had him alert the local police. If the porters quit, technically they would be fugitives and illegally in possession of expedition goods. Meanwhile, Tukche porters anxious for a job were watching like hawks; Sonam Girmi needed to do no more than say the word to have all the scab labor he wanted. He did not seem worried about settling the strike, and he clearly did not need three sahibs there to assist him. He calmed the bara-sahib's anger, assured him that all would be well, and sent them on. As the sahibs plodded up the hill, Sonam Girmi calmly walked back toward the knot of angry men.

Meeting the Mountain

In the almond groves five hundred feet above Tukche, the easy steps and obvious paths ended in a wall of cliffs. Everyone agreed that the yak pastures must be somewhere above, but no one was quite sure how to reach them. The cliffs were not too steep to support trees and grass but steep enough to hide any route. Picking likely gullies which seemed to lead straight upward, we started climbing. Smith drifted too far to the south and disappeared for the rest of the day. Langbauer and Harvard drifted north to a cul-de-sac high above the Kali Gandaki. Making their way back to try again, they spotted Ang Namgyal struggling up below them. Delighted, they went to meet him. Surely he would know the way, and he probably had a bit of lunch with him. As they approached he collapsed under an enormous load, obviously glad to see them. "Porters strike, not carrying now," he groaned. "I have all the kitchen." Langbauer and Harvard groaned too: the news of a strike was bad enough, but the immediate sight of Ang's immense load was worse. Without enthusiasm, they divided the load and labored up toward the pastures.

It took all day to gain the four thousand feet to the high pasture land above Tukche, although the distance on a map is less than a mile. Most of the sahibs were carrying heavy loads, and were not yet acclimatized. The campsite at twelve thousand feet later seemed like sea level, but on the first day everyone had headaches and the going was slow.

At the top of the cliffs the angle of the terrain lessens enough for the hill to be called a pasture. Scrub trees give way to mosses, grass, and dwarf shrubs, and wind begins. Here the wind is not just a variable aspect of the weather as it is below in Tukche, but a constant physical presence. Gusting, it drives dust into hair and eyes, and whips little eddies in the dirt of eroding yak trails; leaning heavily, it patiently carves the rocks and shapes the trees. It can always be felt, it can always be heard, and, in the landscape it has molded, it can be seen. The wind is born in the north over the desolate high plateau of Tibet, but it explodes on the pasture as if it comes from all directions at once. It suggests a pure force, something that has always been there, and always will be: shrubs grow; small alpine flowers bloom, die, and bloom again; rocks crumble away, but the wind remains. Sometimes the wind stops, and the sudden calm is shattering: the silence is an interruption for which the returning wind brings relief. Dhaulagiri, the mountain of storms, taught us much about wind, and the lessons began here.

It took more than an hour for everyone to admit that there was no shelter from the wind and no obvious campsite. As sahibs, Sherpas, and finally porters straggled up, the confusion increased. Everyone deferred judgment, so no one was doing anything. Finally Ang Namgyal built a little rock wall and managed to start a fire. We took the hint and tried with comic lack of success to pitch some tents. The wind was so strong that it was hard to walk and so cold that our fingers were numb, but we knew we couldn't hide from it until we put some tents up. Bech, the old Nepal hand, announced that the wind would die down at dusk and retired to his sleeping bag with a bottle of Jack Daniel's to keep him warm. The first attempt at setting up a tent ended when the tent, a four-man Kellwood, caught wind like a spinnaker in a gale and tore off toward the Kali Gandaki. Five men dove for the tent and stopped it just short of the cliff; Fear, who had been inside, emerged safe but shaken. We fell back and regrouped.

This was the first big test for the Kelwoods, our Base Camp tents, and it was starting to resemble the incident at Upper Dana. They were Morrissey's tents, so he took a proprietary interest in getting them safely pitched. He pirated cord from packs and boots to reinforce weak guylines; he theorized on aerodynamics to a skeptical audience, and at one point he raced around gathering rocks to build a protective wall. No one became excited—there was Bech's alternative, of course: drink until the wind either died down or didn't matter. "All we need is a stone wall about five feet high and thirty feet long," Morrissey clucked. "That may work on the boy scouts in St. Louis, but here . . ." cracked Langbauer. We finally managed to get three tents pitched in a cluster, tied together and heavily anchored with rocks. The noise they made was terrible; in the right wind conditions light cloth makes a noise like rifle shots and keeps it up until the wind dies or the cloth explodes. Watching the three tents undulating rhythmically together in the wind, linked by interdigitating cloth tunnels, Lev christened them "humpies," a name calculated to spark imagination. No one in the humpies really slept that night. The thought of imminent disaster so early in the expedition didn't bother the sahibs, but the inconvenience of crowding, noise, and constant motion kept us awake. The Sherpas were oblivious of these minor irritations, but the prospect of blowing off the cliff kept them sitting up holding on to the tentpoles. The tents lost pieces of frame throughout the night, but were still standing in the morning. We survived our first night off the main trail and our first serious wind, so we could consolidate the camp and move on.

We devoted the next two weeks to moving the expedition to the base of the mountain. Our rate of advance was a compromise between the desire to take plenty of time for acclimatization and the need to meet our airdrop deadlines on French Pass and the northeast col. Extra porters, hired for the carry from Tukche to the snowline, members of the local Takali clan, balked and would not carry as far as they had agreed to. Ngawang Samden tried to reason with them, but gave up in despair: they were not Sherpas, so his control over them was limited. It looked like another delay until Craig Anderson arrived in Windy Corner from a carry. He was furious when he saw the group of squabbling porters at the edge of camp. He harangued them in Nepali for bad faith, wondering at the top of his voice what kind of man would break a bargain: the dispute was heated, but Anderson's voice could drown out the porters' and they slowly picked up their loads and went up. We spent two more nights at Windy Corner, the understated name we gave to our first camp above Tukche, devoting the days to carrying loads up through the snow-patched pastures on stiff, grassy clumps of sod and lichen-covered rocks toward a 14,500-foot campsite.

To make the new camp, we cut out two large platforms on the side of a snow-covered ridge protected from the wind by a cornice, or lip of wind-packed snow. It was a beautiful campsite with the Kali Gandaki valley and the Nilgiri and Annapurna ranges on one side and a clear view of the east side of Dhaulagiri on the other. We occupied Cornice Camp as an acclimatization camp and a base for carries toward French Pass. It was our first camp on snow, and we were very glad to be there. Lev and Fear searched the porter loads for their skis and tore up the nearby slopes. Fear, a downhill racer, and Lev, one of the best off-track skiers in the business, managed to make skiing look easy at an altitude where most of the climbers were content to sit quietly. Anderson is probably one of the few beginning skiers to have taken lessons at over fourteen thousand feet. Lyman started to dig a snow cave and with the finesse of Tom Sawyer got Morrissey to do the wet inside work.

Life was good at Cornice Camp: the carries higher were hard but not exhausting, and we shared almost euphoric optimism now that we were on snow and close to the mountain. We still had beer from the valley, and, alas, plenty of rice and cabbage. There was trouble in finding a common ground between our desire to eat the meat, cheese, candy, and other goodies we had brought and Ang Namgyal's desire to serve us only the huge platefuls of rice and cabbage he cooked for the Sherpas and porters. Our food seemed to have a low priority, while loads of rice and dahl were always the first to appear. Ang's position was unassailable: he was the cook. We could give him all the

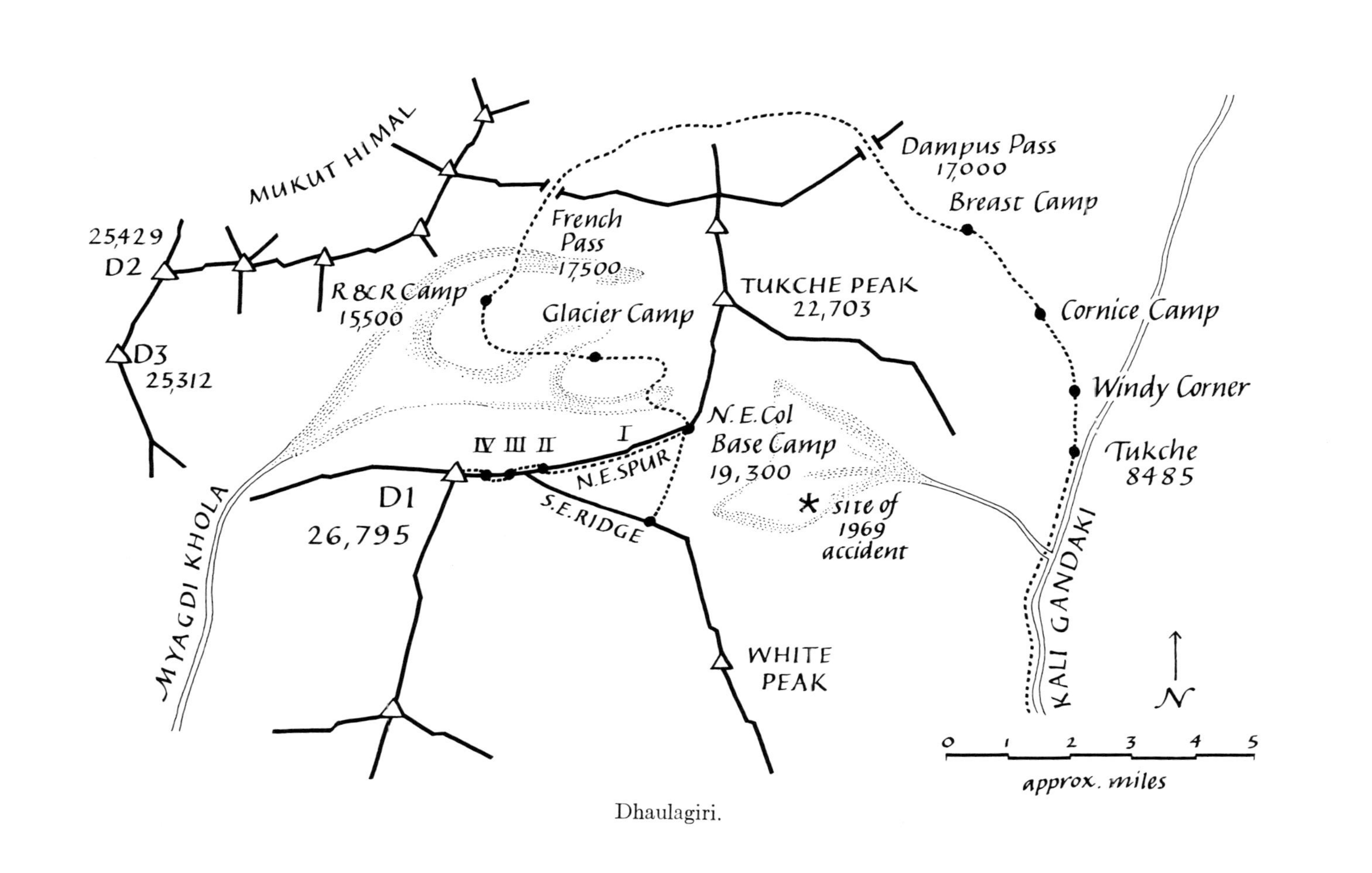
MUKUT HIMAL
25,429
D2
D3
25,312
R & R Camp
15,500
French
Pass
17,500
Glacier Camp
TUKCHE PEAK
22,703
Dampus Pass
17,000
Breast Camp
Cornice Camp
Windy Corner
Tukche
8485
N.E. Col
Base Camp
19,300
site of
1969
accident
IV III II
I
N.E. SPUR
S.E. RIDGE
D1
26,795
MYAGDI KHOLA
KALI GANDAKI
WHITE
PEAK
N
0 1 2 3 4 5
approx. miles

Dhaulagiri.

directions we wanted to, but he would cook what he felt like cooking. We began to dream of the days when we would be up the mountain away from our cook.

We carried loads up a thousand feet of snow and scree to a promontory, then began a long, rising traverse on the northeast side of the Yamkin Khola, crossing a series of snow ribs on the way to a cache at 16,200 feet. Each day we carried a little more and felt a little stronger doing it. People acclimatize at different rates, but everyone was making some progress. When Rennie pushed himself a little too hard, he experienced what he described as a "touch" of pulmonary edema. He subsided queasily onto a rock, gasping pathetically at Langbauer, who was nearby. Langbauer happened to be carrying an oxygen bottle, but the regulator was in another load, so he helped Rennie back to camp. The latter made a dramatic, staggering entry and retired to his tent; he showed distinct signs of recovery in time for a hearty supper that evening.

A common problem in acclimatization is a temporary loss of balance. When Duenwald told Thompson to rest because he was obviously ataxic, Thompson threw him in a snowbank and pointed out indignantly that he obviously couldn't stand up either. They both decided to take a rest day.

Our days at Cornice Camp were relaxed. It did not seem incongruous that we sat on chairs, at a table, and drank beer in a snowstorm at nearly fifteen thousand feet with views of Annapurna, Tibet, Dhaulagiri, or the plains of India to choose from: we were in the Himalaya and life was easy.

Sonam Girmi never told us how he had solved the strike of the low altitude porters, below in Tukche, but he did tell us that a Japanese expedition to Annapurna, which had been unable to hire Sherpas in Kathmandu, was prepared to offer our striking Sherpas bonus equipment and inflated wages to defect. He sent most of the porters up to Windy Corner before they found out about the Japanese offer, keeping only the few most trustworthy ones in Tukche to help him finish tasks there. We knew Sonam Girmi was a fair and efficient administrator, and we knew he was a kind and decent man, but it was not until we saw him work with the porters on snow that we really began to understand him. His authority as sirdar was absolute; he was the leader and the judge of the Sherpas and porters, and he could have commanded obedience by virtue of his position alone. But his leadership went beyond that; because he led by example and judged with fairness the obedience he received was more like devotion, built on trust and respect. The expedition team gained the strength of Sonam Girmi and his Sherpas by accepting them with the same trust and respect with which the climbers treated each other. Morrissey was one of the last to arrive at Cornice Camp; looking around for a place to sleep, he found room in Sonam Girmi's tent and asked if he could move in. Morrissey saw nothing special in his request; a tent is a tent, and we recognized no particular distinctions between the sahibs and Sherpas on the team, but to Sonam the request was unprecedented. He had been on eighteen expeditions and had never before been in the same tent with the leader, the bara-sahib. If our team functioned at all, it was in large part because the Sherpas worked with us, not just for us.

Morrissey had special reason to be glad he was Sonam Girmi's tentmate the night he discovered that rum and high altitude are a volatile mixture. One snowy afternoon Morrissey appeared in Reichardt and Lev's tent with a bottle of Ron Rico from the U.S.A.I.D. commissary in Kathmandu. He stayed on into the night with the bottle, as other members drifted in and out. As a good bottle should, it loosened our tongues; we talked of friends, of wives and loves, of climbs, and jobs, and dreams. In animated reverie Morrissey, the Irish wrestler, beat up a famous British climber for the crime of being Welsh. Fortunately, the hapless Briton was ten thousand miles away at the time. There was a brief intermission while everyone tumbled out into the snow to watch Lev, avalanche expert, wade up to the cornice above camp to knock off the new snow. The deeper he went, the more he laughed and the more the audience cheered. Morrissey finished the evening with a soliloquy on motherhood, and, draining the bottle, he disappeared into the darkness in the direction of his tent. Sonam, who was anxiously waiting with a light in the window, found Morrissey trying to crawl uphill through deep powder snow on his hands and knees. With remarkable delicacy, considering that Morrissey is twice his size, Sonam carried him home and put him to bed.

On the other side of the ridge from camp, there was a bare spot in the snow which exposed a slope of scree, the broken chunks of rock that collect at the bottom of a hill. The east side of Dhaulagiri was unobscured, so both routes to the summit were clearly visible from the scree patch. One morning Morrissey called an expedition meeting there to discuss once again the priorities of the two routes. We sat on the scree in a semi-circle like students in a lecture hall, with Morrissey, the lecturer, in front of the panorama of Dhaulagiri. From our perspective, a ski pole waved in the air could trace routes on the mountain background miles away. We went over the familiar ground: safety, fixed ropes, the wind, weather, extending our lines. The southeast ridge was ominous with its endless peaks, cornices, and towers. The wind blew a plume of snow out from the crest that was a half mile long. Duenwald spoke for the ridge. Young called for the option of throwing total effort behind the spur route if the ridge proved unsafe. Reichardt echoed the sentiment: risk was expected and acceptable, but must be within reason. Langbauer, Harvard, and Thompson spoke against a traverse of the mountain from the southeast ridge to the spur, a favorite idea of Morrissey's. The meeting droned on without resolving any of the problems. As the testimony continued, whispers, and then a stir of interest, crept through the seated group. In front of us, hidden in the rocks, was a rare sight: there was no mistaking it. Something we had not seen for weeks—a healthy, solid, perfectly formed human stool! Dhaulagiri was dwarfed in the background. None of the team was particularly preoccupied with bowel movements, but this signal change in habit caused a lively interest. Nepalese water and unfamiliar food, regardless of how careful we were, had prevented the production of one since leaving New York. Whose was it? Was it safe from Morrisey's boots? Could it have been produced from rice and cabbage alone? With suitable modesty Rennie claimed it, but others disputed the claim saying that as an idol, its origins should remain obscure, its conception immaculate. The discussion came to a close, and we shouldered loads for the day's carry. The afternoon storm brought heavy snow: clouds hid Dhaulagiri, and a blanket of new snow covered everything on the hillside.

During the early days of acclimatization and carrying, Morrissey decided to settle the nagging question of who should be deputy leader. The expedition could certainly function without the official designation of another leader, but almost everyone agreed that decisions could be made more efficiently by a sort of "administrative foreman" than by increasingly lengthy group discussion. We would soon have daily decisions on climbing questions and rotations which could take up a lot of time if they weren't handled somewhat arbitrarily. Morrissey wanted someone to take over the daily running of camps and selecting of teams for carrying, trailbreaking, leading, and supporting, while he directed the overall progress of the expedition. Most of the members wanted the decisions to be made by someone with more technical climbing experience than Morrissey had. We also had to consider the expedient of designating a responsible successor in case Morrissey, like Everett in 1969, was killed. The job was likely to be important because the deputy leader would have to make quick decisions which could have long-term effects on the expedition and its members. It was not likely to be much fun because it involved the mechanics of trying to satisfy as many members as possible within the framework of expedition goals. In theory, decisions on the mountain would work hierarchically: the group would agree to climb a route; the leader and his deputy would decide the general direction and anticipated rate of progress; the leader would pick the day to begin; the deputy leader would then consider the technical problems involved and designate teams to work on the route each day, and, finally, the men actually working on the route would decide on the details of the exact route pitch by pitch, the equipment to use, how much rope to fix, and where to place caches or campsites. Obviously, the deputy leader's role in deciding the general route and designating the climbers for the work could greatly affect the character of the climb. Morrissey had to select someone whom the rest of the team would listen to and whom he could trust.

Characteristically, a number of the members could have filled the job, and, not surprisingly, none was anxious to have it. For several days Morrissey caucused with the members of the expedition, and they caucused with each other. These were leisurely days, and the politics provided a little entertainment. Morrissey did more listening than talking, eventually narrowing down the possibilities: some didn't have the technical climbing qualification, or were judged to be too young, or were not willing or able to organize a group, or just did not seem to inspire trust. Morrissey finally asked Jeff Duenwald to take the job. The team reacted with general approval: "If it has got to be anybody, it ought to be Jeffrey," was a typical response. Duenwald himself was not enthusiastic; his diary notes: "I am not a very good choice for deputy leader because of my inability to get along with certain members. I'll have to avoid petty squabbles, hold my tongue to save my power for decisions on the mountain. It could be a job directing logistics with not much climbing—that would piss me off." Duenwald's volatile temper was legendary; but, like snoring or bad puns, it was a failing the team could live with.

The steady, almost relaxed pace of carrying from Cornice Camp was ideal for effective acclimatization, but it was not quite fast enough to ensure meeting our deadline for airdrops at French Pass. We had to push ahead to French Pass to mark a drop zone and receive the drops. By meeting the drops, we would be running into, rather than away from, our supply train. The constant problem of an expedition like ours is the capability of the climbers to get ahead of their supplies, to "outrun our logistics" or "stretch the snake," in the phrases we used. At Cornice Camp we were already far ahead of loads still at Tukche. By meeting airdrops at French Pass and the northeast col, we would keep our supply resources abreast of our progress. We were gambling heavily on the success of the drops: if we went to meet the airdrops and the drops were delayed, we would be overextended and would have to draw back; if they failed to take place or we lost the supplies, the expedition would fail.

Fear, Anderson, Smith, Peterson, Ang Dawa, Sonam Tsering, Nang Tenzing, and Gyaltzen set out on March 20 for French Pass. They were all strong and acclimatizing well and they had one cache already stocked on the way. They carried tents, food, and fuel for five days, enough to wait for the drops and to retreat if necessary. Sahibs and Sherpas accompanied them the first day, carrying loads for their first camp and an emergency cache. Bech, carrying one of the loads, couldn't bring himself to turn back at the cache, so he stayed with them until an afternoon storm prevented his returning to camp. Like everyone, he was a little impatient to move on, and he was very anxious to see if the airdrop plan, for which he was largely responsible, would work. He had traveled the route after his 1971 reconnaissance, so he led the party to French Pass, enjoying the trip immensely despite the fact that he didn't have a sleeping bag. Fear skied while the others took turns breaking trail in knee-deep snow for three days to reach French Pass. They bivouacked and traveled quickly, relishing the freedom of a small group in a new world, feeling once again like mountaineers and less like part of a flock. The deep snow and uncertainty of the objective made the trip hard but exciting.

Early on March 20 Ang Namgyal in Cornice Camp yelled "Yeti, sahib, Yeti!" and pointed to a plane winging up the Kali Gandaki. It passed high over the camp, then over the string of climbers and porters carrying loads toward the cache, and finally over the advance group still struggling to reach French Pass. We were confused: the plane was a day early. A day late would have been no surprise, but a day early was a cause for alarm. Circling over the advance group, Wick dropped a mailbag and continued circling, obviously waiting for an answer. Bech exploded as he read the notes in the bag. We were informed that RNAC had been told by their insurance company that our drops would require special coverage. Their insurer was a Paris firm connected with Air France, the airline which provided "technical assistance" to RNAC. Someone in Paris put the Pilatus, French Pass, Emil Wick, and Dhaulagiri together, and remembering the 1960 crash of the Yeti, blew the whistle. They were demanding a premium of five thousand dollars, an amount that would double the cost of the airdrops. The note from RNAC politely asked if, in view of this additional cost, we still wanted the drops. Extortion! It was too late, and we were too extended to consider any alternative method of supplying ourselves. Al Read and John Skow, whose faces we could see in the plane that day, had tried their best to move the airline bureaucracy in Kathmandu, without success. Morrissey threatened murder and mutilation when he heard; Bech just pointed out that this was, after all, Nepal. He signaled to the plane that we still wanted the airdrops.

Two days later the main body of the expedition moved from Cornice Camp to a camp near the cache at 16,200 feet, a long day's march from French Pass. From there we could support the advance party if the airdrops failed or move up quickly if the drops were successful. Some called the new camp "Breast Camp" in honor of a unique snow formation which reminded them of things they were beginning to miss. Others called it "Cabbage Camp" after the same lump of snow which seemed to them to suggest that mysteriously persistent ingredient of Ang's dishes. Actually, it was a rather neutral pile of snow, neither as good nor as bad as the names suggest.

The campsite was flat and well protected by the breastwork which proved to be an excellent hill for skiing, not steep enough or high enough to be exhausting. As the sun set we sat or stood outside, too tired and happy to let go of the day. We were already thinking beyond French Pass to the routes. The place, our optimism, and the promise of the mountain were an elixir.

When the sun sets in the high mountains, it gets cold very quickly. Not many men were still outside when a solitary figure appeared on the horizon moving toward us from the direction of French Pass. The figure was an hour away at least, plenty of time for speculation—an accident? Sickness? Had the advance party run out of food? The figure was tall, with a heavy load; his pace was slow but steady. We guessed it must be Peterson. Men went out to break trail, to carry his pack, to do anything rather than just watch his agonizingly slow progress. Lev, on skis, was the first to reach him. In a terse radio message, Lev reported that it was Peterson and that everything was O.K. Peterson came into camp and was welcomed with a warmth that reflected good will as well as relief that his purpose was only to make the seemingly redundant report that no airdrops had taken place that day. It was only later, in the quiet darkness of a tent, that someone ventured to ask him why he had really come back. What he told Morrissey then, as he had told Lev out on the snowfield, and as he had told the four others at French Pass, was that he was on his way home. Peterson later recalled: "We got up early—it was a beautiful, queer morning. I hadn't really seen Dhaulagiri up until that point and it was just incredibly fucking big. I'd never seen anything like it; even Everest is dwarfed by the mass Dhaulagiri presents. I was totally overwhelmed and my reaction was: this isn't where I'm supposed to be."

The next morning we awoke to the sound of a plane heading for French Pass and to the spreading news of Peterson's decision. That news was deadening because Peterson was a strong and resourceful friend. That day was agony for Peterson as he publicly tested his decision. Lost in his own thoughts, he had been almost surprised to find us at Breast Camp. Twice he readied himself to leave, and twice he resolved to stay. His final decision to stay was cathartic; it brought him relief, and he threw himself back into the expedition. He explained that altitude and fatigue had affected his judgment, and never mentioned it again. As friends, most of the climbers had shared his initial, emotional decision. Unfortunately, his subsequent vacillation drained that ability to respond with sympathetic emotion, leaving a residue of hostility and suspicion around him that took weeks to dispel. We were never again the same team. Duenwald and Rennie argued over the significance of Peterson's behavior so hotly that they never fully understood each other thereafter. Duenwald tried to force a confrontation between Peterson and Morrissey, which Morrissey felt compelled to avoid. Morrissey was bitter about Duenwald's handling of the question and rightly worried about its effect on his control of the team. Peterson had made a private matter a public concern but had then made his final decision without reference to Morrissey's leadership. Some were shocked, some

Dhaulagiri from the ridge at Cornice Camp. Southeast ridge is left skyline, northeast spur is just right of center, Pear route is just below right skyline.

Rest after a carry, Cornice Camp.

felt hurt, most lost trust. Even as we closed ranks it was clear that the foundation of the expedition, our ubiquitous but indefinable group strength, had been shaken. The effect was really beyond the scope of Peterson's cause. Optimism comes and goes, and enthusiasm cannot be kept at the high pitch we were trying to maintain. There were other problems, other tensions too: the next advance party was selected for the col, a routine decision made difficult by everyone's impatience to get on, and route priorities were discussed uneasily. When the sun set at Breast Camp on the day of our first successful airdrops, it was coldly beautiful as it had been the previous night, but the enchantment of that day was gone.

The day of building tension and anxiety at Breast Camp saw rejoicing and boyish release of energy at French Pass. After three days of waiting the advance party woke to the sound of the airplane. The success of the expedition hung on the success of the airdrops, not at all a certainty. The party was out in front, alone and unencumbered. They relished the freedom of traveling and working as a small group alone in the mountains, freedom normally taken for granted by climbers, sorely missed on a large expedition. Peterson's leavetaking, an emotional event the day before, was forgotten in the excitement of the approaching plane. From their little camp on the south side of French Pass, they listened to the drone of the plane's engine increase as it approached. The morning was clear and still; the noise of the engine abruptly ceased as Wick wheeled north to make his approach. From the south side of the pass, the silence was ominous. Suddenly it was broken by a shrill whistle of wind which preceded the plane as Wick cleared the pass by less than twenty feet. Boxes fell from the bomb bay as the plane dipped and passed the camp barely clearing the tents. The noise of the engine only caught up as the plane passed the camp and dove toward the Myagdi Glacier. Surrounded by the peaks of the Myagdi Gorge, Wick slowly circled to gain altitude and flew back over the pass for another run.

The snow was hard, so most of the boxes split open as they landed. Food bags burst and scattered their contents down the slopes. A plastic jug of kerosene cracked and lost most of its contents. Tent poles were bent and stoves dented in the drop, but nothing was lost. The mess was awful to behold, but the drop was successful.

The success seemed miraculous. In Alaska some of us had experienced airdrop losses of up to 25 percent; we had heard rumors that the army, presumably expert in such matters, routinely allows for 50 percent loss when dropping on a glacier.

On his second run Wick came so close to the camp that a sixty-pound box

Dhaulagiri from the air. Northeast spur is right skyline, southeast ridge curves upward in center of picture.

The camp at French Pass.

of food crashed through the cooktent, scattering pots, pans, stoves, and Sherpas in the snow. It was a direct hit on the single center pole which supported the tent. Thereafter, the tents were emptied and flattened before the drops. Wick was able to complete three trips from Pokhara to the pass that morning, making three drops each time, before the regular Dhaulagiri fog closed in. The advance party spent the rest of the day cleaning up the drop zone, happily rounding up the scattered goodies. Fear cornered the supply of crème-de-menthe mints; Smith collected a prodigious hoard of wild cherry sours. The food was cached in a huge snow pit, disorganized, but intact.

The success of the drops meant that the main body of the expedition could move to French Pass. The expedition was leapfrogging: tents and supplies were abandoned at Cornice and Breast Camps for new equipment dropped at French Pass. The supplies along the route would be used by our porters bringing in medical and scientific supplies we didn't airdrop, by our mailrunners during the time we would be on the mountain, and finally by the team retreating at the end of the expedition. Drops continued for two more days at French Pass, and kerosene was dropped at Dampus Pass, where deep powder snow softened its landing, preventing breakage.

The route between Breast Camp and French Pass is long, crossing the few final ribs and bowls to Dampus Pass and then turning directly west, following the lower flank of Tukche Peak to the pass. With heavy loads the trip was exhausting but the route offered us fresh territory to survey in the minor peaks clustered around remote Hidden Valley. French Pass is a 17,500-foot niche between Tukche Peak (22,430 feet) and Makut Himal (21,780 feet), the eastern end of the main section of the Dhaulagiri massif.

On the following day, March 26, the French Pass airdrops were completed. Wick obviously enjoyed himself as he buzzed the camp and circled below the pass demonstrating his skill. It looked like so much fun that we wondered if we shouldn't be flying small planes in remote and dangerous places instead of climbing. On the last pass Skow dropped a mailbag, two bottles of wine, and a live hen. When Smith picked up the hen, he found it blinking in amazement and apparently breathless but otherwise unhurt. The wine, safely wrapped in a foam tent floor, was set aside to rest, and the mail was devoured on the spot.

The expedition was split again later that day as an advance party of Duenwald, Lev, Roskelley, and Thompson left to establish a camp on the northeast col, where airdrops were expected to begin on April 1. Those who remained devoted the day to cleaning up the airdrop debris, repacking the split and scattered food boxes, and repairing the damage to stoves and hardware. Climbing equipment was sorted, ropes were cut to length from long spools, boxes checked, repacked, and marked. Langbauer, who knew the equipment system, once again found himself in the middle of a pile of boxes. He eventually sent his helpers away when it occurred to him that they were unpacking more boxes than they were packing. Harvard, Rennie, and Fear foundered waist-deep in the snowhole of food, eventually managing to substitute mere disorder for total chaos. The hen, immediately at home in the cooktent, spent the day stuffing herself on Ry-King and sunflower seeds.

Young and Lyman, among the few members who admitted to having been professional guides, held a seminar with the Sherpas on glacier safety techniques and general mountaineering skills. For our own safety and for theirs, we wanted to be sure that we all shared basic ideas on rope handling and crevasse rescue. We knew that the Sherpas had varying experience, and we wanted to learn what to expect of each of them. We learned. When Young laboriously demonstrated a bowline-on-a-bight, a useful knot for mountaineering, but not one used often by American rockclimbers, Nang Tenzing watched in confusion. He strained to follow Young's complicated movements but couldn't. He asked to see it again, and again was baffled. As Nang turned the finished knot over, shaking his head despondently, his face suddenly brightened. He took the rope and in a single, smooth, twist-and-flip motion, produced the same knot. "O.K., sahib?" he asked, eyeing Young. Young spent the rest of the day practicing the knot.

The advance party carried loads down from French Pass at 17,500 feet to the Myagdi Glacier, where they established a camp at 15,500 feet on the site of the 1960 Swiss base camp, then reconnoitered the route up the icefall towards the northeast col. That part of the route was the first real unknown and the first potential mountaineering problem. The icefall rose steeply, was broken, unstable, and heavily crevassed. It filled a narrow chute between Tukche Peak on the left and Dhaulagiri's Eiger on the right, both potential sources of dangerous avalanches. Late in the afternoon, when the temperature of the snow was stable so avalanche potential was likely to be low, Thompson and Roskelley hurried to the base of the Eiger to have a look. They found that by going up a short couloir, or gully, behind a black ice block and staying close to the base of the Eiger, crossing avalanche cones, that the route was easy and straightforward, with relatively little objective danger. The pressure was off; making the col would not be difficult. They returned to camp, announcing that the route was a "piece of cake," so they could sleep late in the morning.

The next day everyone carried loads from French Pass down to 15,500 feet and Reichardt, Harvard, Smith, and Lyman moved down to occupy the camp. The carriers straggled into the camp sweating in the reflected heat of the sun: few places in the world can seem as hot and as bright as a glacial bowl at high altitude on a cloudless day. Sunbathing was an attractive but dangerous idea. Most succumbed to the temptation and paid for it that night. A glacial pool with painfully cold water offered a chance for bathing. We had a new concentrated biodegradable soap solution which we were to test for the manufacturer: the nearly frozen water seemed an ideal trial. Duenwald tried some and found the stuff so concentrated that he turned blue before he could wash it all off. His endorsement of the product was obscured by chattering teeth. We were all proud of this contribution to protecting the ecology of the Dhaulagiri massif: we might have to leave five tons of surplus food, rope, and equipment on the mountain, and our garbage would be freeze-dried for posterity, but by God, our soapsuds were biodegradable.

The scale of big mountains is deceptive: while most of the team basked in the sun or carried loads across the wide landscape, Young and Roskelley went to look at a vertical crack in a rock wall at the edge of the icefall. It appeared to be a fine Yosemite-style rock-climb of delicate proportions, and it seemed close. It was neither. When they reached it after a long walk they found a gaping chimney, a very wide gap in the rock. The thin fissure they thought they had seen would not even have been visible from the camp.

For the next few days we settled into a pattern of stretching the expedition to meet the northeast col airdrops. Duenwald, Lev, Thompson, and Roskelley slowly worked their way to the col using an intermediate camp at 17,500 feet. Reichardt, Harvard, Smith, and Lyman with Ang Dawa, Sonam Tsering, Gyaltzen and Nang Tenzing carried loads behind them from 15,500 to 17,500, then from 17,500 feet to the col, while the rest of the team lived at French Pass and carried down to 15,500 feet.

The camp at 15,500 feet was clearly a transit camp: to pass through it quickly became the goal of most members. It seemed out of place, out of sequence. Two thousand feet below French Pass and four thousand feet below the col, it was like a sea-floor trough untouched by the momentum of waves passing above it. Even the name, Rest and Recovery Camp, which hinted at some future use projected during a past planning session, was absurd when everyone was healthy and straining to get on the mountain. The same restraint applied as before the French Pass drops: the main body could not move up until the airdrops were safely under way, but now, as if reserves of patience were spent, people were edgy and anxious.

To the people at French Pass, R&R was a place to avoid. Young delayed his move down there because "the place is too low, it's unhealthy." Men made ascents of the little peaks around the pass for acclimatization exercise rather than make the carry down to R&R. To the advance party it was the nagging link between their small, efficient group and the ponderous mass of the expedition soon to follow. To those who occupied it, R&R was a slough of despond. The breakage of some stoves during the French Pass airdrop and the stretching of supplies in anticipation of the col drops kept the camp undersupplied. When the support party occupied it, there was a fuel shortage; when they moved up, there was fuel but no stoves for those who followed. Morrissey remembers trying to eat noodles still raw after an hour over a fire of garbage soaked in kerosene. There were never enough pots, and despite elaborate efforts to prevent it, the Sherpas managed to smuggle vast quantities of cabbage and rice into the camp. At Cornice Camp we had waited; at R&R we seemed to be stalling.

Morrissey in particular was depressed at R&R, as he struggled with a problem which had increasingly bothered him since leaving the valley. There was among the members of the team a genuine enthusiasm for the project, but it was not expressed in the same way as it had been in 1969—it was colder, more calculated; no one would call it childlike. The seeming loss of momentum made the size of the team oppressive. In forming a large team, we had gained apparent strength and depth, but the price was clearly the spontaneous and unquestioned common enthusiasm, itself a source of strength, that comes so easily to a small party. Climbing once more from R&R, Morrissey decided that as the team was larger, slower moving, and more diffuse than it had been in 1969, the rewards of participation would have to be more subtle, slower to be realized, and, in the end, larger.

As the team spread out we began to experience the troubles of isolation on an expedition: each party in each camp knows that it is doing its job and that it is linked with other parties in other camps doing theirs. Intellectually, everyone knows that everyone else is pulling his weight to the best of his ability and understanding. But invariably, insidiously, the thought creeps in that somehow, one's own party is working harder, or is more uncomfortable, or is more important than the others. Rarely spoken but always recognized, this hint of paranoia haunts communication between groups in support of each other. Little misunderstandings over brief contacts are brooded over and nurtured into grievances which seem silly later. Despite the fact that progress was made smoothly and according to the timetable, the rear party thought that they were being slighted, and in turn, were thought to be carrying too little and too light. The support party thought it was being overtaxed in front while undersupplied from the rear. The forward party thought it was being pressed for time while carrying the burden of advance; they thought that they were poorly supported, while everyone else thought that they were unreasonably refusing close support.

As the group split we began to make use of our radios. We opened the boxes as a child opens a Christmas gift when he knows the contents are not clothes or books, but a toy. The radios were shiny and new with intricate mysteries of complex electronics, and, as a bonus, they were useful, so we could play with them without feeling guilty. And play with them we did. Everyone resurrected scraps of radio language from a murky background of old movies and occasional jobs; parts of the Ten Code, some authentic and some imaginary, even emerged. In time, distinct radio personalities developed. Bech and Anderson were drafted to do Nepali broadcasts, a job for which each recommended the other; Lev's Forest Service training gave him the most polished style; Lyman was mysteriously attracted to the medium and became the most efficient and enthusiastic operator. Reichardt never managed to keep his finger on the transmit button while talking or to keep it off while listening, a problem which was suspected of having an editorial, rather than technical origin. Rennie, who found transmitting a challenge to his literary imagination, could make a little Panasonic crackling out a conversation about the weather sound like a four-foot-high Philco broadcasting "Search for Tomorrow." But the star was Morrissey. No one could match his soulful repetitions of "This is Dhaulagiri Base Camp. Do you read me? Do you read me? Over." followed by "If he doesn't come on the air, I'll cut his balls off!" In the early days when our camps were separated by passes and peaks, through which the radios could not transmit, the hills echoed with the lonesome static of unanswered calls in the void. At R&R Morrissey had to climb a small hill in the pre-dawn cold to make contact with Reichardt, Smith, and Harvard because they couldn't raise their antenna without getting out of their sleeping bags. Our evening radio contact time briefly coincided with the Japanese expedition's broadcast on Annapurna across the valley. They used the same radio frequency, so our conversations interrupted each other. One night, in frustration, forgetting that he held the microphone on, Morrissey yelled, "Why don't those little bastards stay the hell off the air!" A short time later the radio crackled a faint "Hello? . . . Hello?"

As April 1 approached, the advance party slogged up to the col carrying their camp in two sets of loads. The support party moved up to 17,500 feet, and the men at French Pass finally moved to R&R. The porters made carries between Dampus Pass and R&R under the supervision of Ngawang Samden. The carries were long and exposed to the wind, but they moved the remaining gear up without complaint.

Sonam Girmi arrived at French Pass to direct the movement of supplies just in time to save the hen from becoming a dinner. Without emotion, but with obvious concern, Sonam told us that it would be inappropriate to kill anything on a mountain one is about to climb. His tone of voice was patient; the proper action was clear to him, but long experience had taught him that sahibs are often unaware of such simple precautions. The chicken went to Tukche with the mailrunner, and rice with cabbage was served for dinner.

Wick approaches airdrop target on French Pass.

Wick circles over Dhaulagiri.

The night before the first group of Sherpas entered the Myagdi icefall was dark. A chanting sound from their tent grew into a leader-and-chorus response hum. The Sherpas, four of them present that night, were praying. For Sherpas, no phase of life is separable from another, so religious observance and climbing procedure are interrelated. Before the expedition began, lamas had instructed Sonam Girmi to make an offering at the base of the mountain to Guru Rinpoche, the spirit associated with Dhaulagiri, from the best of the expedition supplies. Pasang Tenzing erected a small, stone altar and presided as Ngawang Samden gravely poured a quart of Jack Daniel's to the goddess for the safe conduct of the expedition.

Carriers cross below the Myagdi icefall en route from French Pass to R&R camp.

Carriers move into the Myagdi icefall above R&R camp.

The Southeast Ridge

After a thirsty night at 17,500 feet where a miscalculation in loads had left them without a functioning stove to melt water, Lev, Roskelley, Duenwald, and Thompson slogged toward the col. The route was not difficult, but the altitude, the sun, and lack of water made the walk painful. The two weeks during which the airdrops took place, March 23 to April 5, were weeks of clear, calm weather. The sun was bright, and the glacier became a desert. Dehydration was an acute problem: the greatest chore was melting snow for the five liters of water a body needs each day. The sun made it too hot to wear heavy clothes but scorched any flesh left exposed. Optimistically applied sun creams mixed with sweat to invade squinting eyes and run in gritty drops off the tips of noses. On the thirtieth, just before the col airdrops began, Thompson wrote in his journal: "During the two-thousand-foot loadcarrying slog to the northeast col I made a short stop to drink the last few ounces of water in my water bottle. Collapsed in the snow, I reflected on the meaning of being deliciously wasteful. One must be seriously dehydrated in an environment that is alternately zero degrees and ninety degrees, breathe so hard to get enough oxygen that one's lips are cracked and swollen, and have a tongue that is swollen and sunburned because of necessary open-mouthed breathing. Then, knowing the exact value and texture of each drop of water, to allow the last few drops in the bottle to drip into the snow."

The advance party, tired and drained by the new altitude, nauseated from the smell of the kerosene they carried in unsealable jugs, moved along the gradual rise to the col for the first intimate view of the southeast ridge. There was considerably more exposed rock on the face section of the ridge than anyone remembered from photographs. They studied the face in front of them, almost a mile away across a gently sloping snow bowl. The obvious route turned the lower section through an hourglass series of ice gullies and ribs through a narrow gap between rocks on the right and a hanging glacier on the left. The face appeared to be two thousand vertical feet high, or about twenty pitches of forty-to-fifty-degree ice. The route then traversed along the almost horizontal ridge to the main body of the mountain. There were places on the face where the layer of ice over rock was terribly thin, and the ridge itself was frighteningly broken by cornices, towers, and seracs of ice, snow, and rock. The ridge joins the main body of the mountain at about 24,500 feet; the route then eases off, joining the Swiss route at the top of the northeast spur, a thousand feet below the summit.

The four climbers, the eyes of the expedition now, inched their way up on the col, like snails carrying their homes upon their backs. Each step showed them more and more of the southeast ridge, a wall growing up in front of them. All that had been written and spoken about the awesome stature of the southeast ridge was transformed from public relations puff to grave truth. Here are eight thousand vertical feet of some of the hardest climbing ever attempted above nineteen thousand feet. The southeast ridge had the clean integrity of difficulty and beauty. The single most striking feature of the ridge, cause for unspoken apprehension, was its intimidating length. It is about two miles from the point at which the route gains the ridge crest to where the ridge joins the mass of mountain.

On March 31 in their two small tents the team on the col rested. The Dhaulagiri expedition had many beginnings and climaxes along its way, but the tiny stirrings on the col were a prelude to the coda. The expedition existed to expend itself on the southeast ridge, and that expenditure, the crux of the expedition, was beginning.

They awoke early on April 1 to a thick coat of hoar frost inside their tents and crawled out into the bitter, pre-sun cold to wait for the sound of a plane. Lev, the snow scientist, measured the temperature of the snow at minus eleven degrees Fahrenheit, colder than any he had measured and dangerously cold for feet. They stood by the little tents near the crude "X" they had stamped in the snow, jumping to keep warm, nearly frozen in their heavy down suits. Duenwald had slept with a radio and now warmed it inside his down jacket hoping to need it soon. A faint buzz preceded Wick's popping into the large east bowl of Dhaulagiri. The tumult began: civilization was scattered into the wilderness.

"The drop zone looks good. Any messages, any messages from Dhaulagiri Base Camp?" Skow radioed from the plane. "You're beautiful, baby, you're really beautiful! Do you have anything for us?" was Duenwald's excited reply. "Al got your butter, beer, and Calcutta beef, and there is some mail. Any messages?" Skow returned.

"Does this camp look big enough to generate messages?"

"It will be soon enough; watch out!"

Wick made his approach from the northeast to make full use of the glacier's gently sloping run out toward the southeast ridge. At 6:30, the edge of morning sunlight had not quite reached the drop zone, so Wick's depth perception was not good and he came in slightly high. At forty feet and on target, the bomb bay doors opened, dropping the boxes that had been piled on them. The boxes made large craters in the deep, soft snow, the heavy ones sinking quickly, the light ones bouncing, spinning after the plane. Apologizing for the height of the first drop, Wick made a long approach, giving Skow time to stack more boxes on the doors, then deftly flew in at ten feet off the snow. Boxes bounced higher than the tail of the plane. Once accustomed to the light, Wick put most boxes within a minute's walk of camp, and even rolled a few right up to the growing stack. They danced ecstatically as the boxes fell. The flying was flawless, the snow perfect: the airdrops were an unqualified success. We had carefully nursed these boxes from the beginning; we could relish their final delivery. On the way back to Pokhara for another load Wick demonstrated his virtuosity, his precise awareness of Dhaulagiri and his joy in his own control by flying to the edge of the snow bowl, then making a wing-tip dive down the steep southeast glacier.

In three trips from Pokhara, making three drops each trip, Wick and Skow put sixty boxes on the col the first day.

Altitude oppresses the unacclimatized. The climbers collapsed with severe headaches at noon when all the drop had been gathered and organized. Lev sighed, sat on a box, and gobbled a half-pound package of Australian butter. By afternoon it was snowing. A daily weather pattern, a harbinger of miserable climbing conditions, was developing: clear mornings followed by afternoons of snow, wind, and little visibility.

Early on April 2, Duenwald made it into frozen boots and out of the uncomfortable tents just in time to make contact with Skow before the first run. "People in Kathmandu are saying that two Sherpa women were killed during the approach of the expedition. Is this true or false?" Skow asked from the plane.

"What the hell is going on? Maybe some were killed in the icefall and we haven't heard," was Duenwald's alarmed aside to the others; then he broadcasted, "No, John, that report is false! I repeat, false! False! FALSE!"

The plane flew out of radio range as Duenwald hurled his last ejaculations at it. The climbers looked at each other in mute alarm. The accusation made them feel defensive and vulnerable for a moment. They relaxed; the expedition had hired no Sherpa women.

"I wonder how we were supposed to have done them in?" asked Lev, a glint in his eye.

Wick made four drops that day, the last in tricky cross winds. He was obviously in control and having fun. In the afternoon, Reichardt, Young, Lyman, Smith, and Harvard moved to Base Camp from Glacier Camp. The hints of misunderstanding and rivalry which had flickered during the days of isolation vanished as easily as they had grown, resolved in acceptance and camaraderie. More housetents were put up and eight-man cooking and dining humpies were staked out behind protective walls of boxes. A city grew.

We were at last ready to start climbing, and although there was tension between the climbers who identified themselves with the ridge route and those who favored the spur, we held back from argument. The ridge would be started the next day and the mountain would define our subsequent actions more precisely than we could. Roskelley and Thompson were chosen to start leading on the ridge in the morning, with Young and Harvard to carry loads and break trail in the deep snow of the mile or so to the bergschrund at the bottom of the face.

During a lull in the airdrops on April 3, Harvard, Young, Roskelley, and Thompson walked south down the unbroken glacier toward the ridge. The morning was sharp and clear, an auspicious day to begin. The climbers neared the ridge, a silent part of the natural world, indifferent to their approach and the meaning which they attached to it. The climbers were elated: the beginning was new, the object in sight, and confidence came easily. Base Camp was in miniature across the bowl, and Wick's Pilatus was a lazy, methodical gnat. He spotted them, realized that the climb was about to begin, and flew toward them, banking at the last minute to fly belly-up in a graceful arc along the ridge. As they neared the ridge, the little camp on the col receding behind them, they felt themselves breaking new ground for the first time since their arrival in Nepal. The snow was deep and the steps were difficult, but they were steps to savor.

They rested and cached their extra rope and hardware where the glacier steepened to reach the bergschrund, in sight of the Nilgiris and Annapurna. From the cache, it was a half-hour up the slope through deep snow to the lip of the 'schrund, across a small gap from the face itself. Young sat at the cache, Harvard kicked the last steps to the 'schrund; as the sun rose over the Annapurnas, the sharp line between silver-white and gold-white retreated down the glacier to meet them.

Roskelley and Thompson strapped on carefully fitted crampons over boots, holstered their alpine hammers, adorned themselves with slings and hardware, and roped themselves together in observance of solemn starting ritual. The dangling paraphernalia which sheathe the climber, the highly personal badges of his activity, are merely the thoughtfully designed tools he uses. The only effective resources at a climber's disposal are his calm and his imagination. These are the things which can make him a bold, graceful climber. Strength is secondary and equipment is peripheral. Happy to be at work on the problem of the southeast ridge, they flipped a can of smoked baby oysters to decide who would lead off.

Roskelley made a long step across the bergschrund, hacked away a piece of its overhanging lip, and swung up onto the face. The first pitches were easy snow, at an angle of about forty-five degrees, pockmarked here and there with rocks that had fallen from above. Roskelley speeded up his lead, dragging two ropes, one a nine-millimeter climbing rope which led to Thompson, the other a line that would be fixed to the slope and left for later ascents and descents. His feet plunged ten inches into the snow—nothing difficult there—so he quickly reached the end of the rope, stopped, and placed a two-foot aluminum snow picket to secure his belay and anchor the fixed line. Thompson followed, took the hardware from Roskelley, tied the end of the next 150-foot piece of fixed line to his swami belt and took off.

They hungered for vertical feet quickly gained. The ridge climbing started two thousand feet above the start of the face, the route was long, and it was important to make a fast, dramatic start to erase any doubts about the ridge, to convince the spur route people that the ridge was possible. The support of everyone on the team was necessary, and a good first day would cement that support.

At the end of the fifth pitch the ice began. Thompson took the sixth lead, traversing diagonally up and left on moderate, forty-five-degree, rotten ice with a breakable, porous surface. Not perfect, but it was ice. Normally conversation between a leader and belayer is minimal and limited to "How does it look?" or "Do you think it will go?" which are purely speculative questions and rarely answered. The leader will sometimes ask "How much rope?" or "Is that a good anchor? (I'm about to fall off.)" which etiquette requires that the belayer answer in an approximate way with "Looks like about forty feet! Or maybe only twenty." Or "If your last piton holds the fall, and the directional pull on me is up, the anchor is O.K." Roskelley became very conversational during the beginning of the sixth pitch.

"That looks really nice. How's the ice?" Roskelley began.

"O.K."

"Looks like it gets a little steeper up above, then traverses left over that thin stuff with the exposed rock."

"Yeah."

"Are you getting tired?"

Roskelley knew that it was late in the day, that the sixth would be the last pitch, and that the rotation of leaders would probably mean that he would have to wait a few days before being up again, and he was anxious to lead some ice.

Thompson stopped short of the end, and belayed Roskelley up to finish the pitch.

They rappeled down the fixed ropes, sliding easily on a carabiner brake clipped to their harnesses, then trudged up the glacier to camp in time to meet Anderson, Bech, Langbauer, Morrissey, and Rennie arriving from Glacier Camp. It was a good day's work and foreshortening made it look from camp as though the ropes covered a third of the face.

April 4 began with Lev charging toward the igloo latrine only to fall flat into the drifted snow covering the garbage pit. There were sounds of boots squeaking on sub-zero snow, the clink of sorting hardware, Rennie calling for his bootlaces, the plane, and the whine of falling boxes. As tea was served, the Bumba blustered out of his tent to announce: "This is unreal!" The logistic snake of supplies moving on the ground still extended to French Pass. Some of the Sherpas had come up the day before, amused and amazed to find us actually climbing. We had had so much fun on the approach that some of the Sherpas suspected that we might be clowns, so they were surprised to see that we were indeed very serious about the ridge. Ang Dawa, who had been on Dhaulagiri with the Swiss in 1960, and who was not a particularly enthusiastic climber, said only: "sahib route" and shook his head. None of the Sherpas had seen a route like the southeast ridge attempted in the Himalaya, and they had no intention, nor were they expected to have any intention, of taking part in such a technically difficult ascent.

Duenwald chose Roskelley and Harvard to lead the next day. They left camp around eight o'clock, preceded by Reichardt and Lyman, who broke trail. The fixed rope on the first pitch now hung directly over the lip of the bergschrund, making it necessary to climb ten or fifteen feet of free hanging rope. Roskelley struggled up first, the rope digging its way deeply into the wet snow of the lip. As Harvard followed, he jammed his jumars up into the snow around the rope, but succeeded only in freezing them in place. The harder he struggled, the deeper the rope cut into the snow. Hanging nearly upside down, turning slowly in the open bergschrund, neither coming nor going, and gasping for breath, he looked at Reichardt, who eyed him dubiously from below. "Um . . . ah . . . there is probably a more elegant way to do this . . ." he said. "Yes," said Reichardt, "I suppose there is." By the time they reached the high point, the weather was deteriorating. Roskelley led the seventh pitch, which was rot-

Airdrop at the northeast col.

9N-AAZ

ten, forty-five-degree ice like the sixth, and they rappeled off the route in foul weather.

We had been talking about reaching the ridge crest after that day and possibly a short additional day, so the progress was disappointing. Fear and Peterson arrived at Base Camp from R&R during the afternoon.

On April 5, the last day of airdrops, Wick dropped a contraption for mail pickup, inadvertently striking a vulnerable chord in the psychological makeup of the team. For many, mail means normalcy and contact with familiar, human things. On a mountain, as at home, people wait for the mail. Usually, one of our two Sherpa mailrunners left R&R each week, and the other arrived from Pokhara. Flurries of concern surrounded these comings and goings, the interest growing daily from indifference to obsessive worry as the day for mail delivery neared. Mail was a link with what one left behind, with the past, and as such it was a bulwark against the strange and sometimes horrible immediacy of the present. Wives, children, and future plans could obliterate climbing problems and make any present drudgery bearable as it changed from present to past. Once painlessly past, that mountain experience retold in stories is itself a bulwark against the coming present. Letters were also an important vehicle for emotion. Climbers who had to live together could complain about each other's habits in a letter home, or present tensions could be exorcised over faraway subjects. While writing a letter, Roskelley once worked up a good, theatrical hate for the Spokane dogcatcher who had harassed his wife and dog.

When Wick flew over, Roskelley, Reichardt, and Thompson were roped to descend to Glacier Camp for loads, and Lev and Young, whose turn it was to lead on the face, were being chided for a leisurely start. Activity in camp stopped abruptly as people dove for tents to dig for aerograms and frozen pens. Roskelley, who was already on his way out of camp for the carry, exploded in disgust, then went back to his tent to write. Harvard said he'd never seen such nonsense, and said that the mail service here was better than in the states.

We set up Wick's crooked bamboo poles with a long loop of Nepalese manila cord slung between them. As the time for the last drops neared, everyone scrambled to finish letters. Letters complete, the business of the expedition was resumed as the mailbag was reverently tied to the cord. With a mixture of hope and skepticism, we watched for the plane's return.

When Wick came back for the last run, he had Kathy Reichardt, Lou's wife, aboard. He had always wanted to know how high the plane would fly, so he flew over Dhaulagiri's summit, cheering as the plane reached twenty-nine thousand feet. Kathy joked over the radio with Lou, who was at Glacier Camp by then, about reaching the summit before him. The plane circled for an ap-

Base Camp on the northeast col, southeast ridge in background; the approach to the ridge crest was through the prominent hourglass on the face.

proach to Base Camp. Skow let a grappling hook down through the open bomb bay doors. The population of Base Camp assembled to watch as the plane came by too high on the first pass. Wick circled slowly to try again as we joked about the trial run. With heightened anticipation, we watched the second miss. Again, Wick flew south, circled slowly, passed to the north, disappeared, then came toward the camp, very low. Self-assured nonchalance was gone; all eyes anxiously followed the trailing hook. The hook caught, the bag jumped and then the cord snapped, leaving the precious mailbag in the snow.

Clouds were coming in quickly as Lyman cut a few feet of nylon from a large spool. Climbers ran through the deep snow to replace the rope as others heard Wick curse the winds over the radio. The weather was changing; he had to leave the mountain. The mailbag went down the mountain with the mail-runner, its rightful guardian.

Interference with the progress of mail was almost as universally suspected on Dhaulagiri as U.S. Postal Service prying is in the United States. Liaison officer Pande, comfortably ensconced in the valley, once commandeered a mail-runner to take his progress report to Jomsom north of Tukche, for transmittal to Kathmandu. The mail was delayed two days as a result, and the married climbers consumed whole evenings in the dining humpy at Base Camp, thinking of macabre ways to punish Pande for that transgression.

The same storm that had driven Wick away was giving Lev and Young a hard time on the face. Heavy snow was falling by mid-afternoon. Ice breaking off from the hanging glacier to the left of the hourglass made ominous noises, but it thundered harmlessly down the gullies alongside the route. Breaking cornices on the ridge crest above were also a threat, but an unlikely and unpredictable one. New snow accumulated and then sloughed regularly down the route, however, and it was in these powder slides that Lev and Young were climbing. Young led up over thin fifty-degree ice from Roskelley's high point to the bottom of the hourglass. Lev made a very fine, short lead, the ninth, over a fifty-five-degree bulge into the center of the hourglass. Climbing conditions were bad. They climbed between slides that swept over them, plagued by wind which blew spindrift snow in all directions. But this was the climbing for which they had come so far, so, oblivious of everything but the immediate task, they kept on. It was dark when they finally descended, and the trail back to Base Camp was covered with fresh snow, so they started to dig a snow cave at the cache for a cold night's bivouac.

At Base Camp over a dinner of Calcutta Beef Peterson, joking speculation about their absence grew into serious concern for their safety. Two parties left the comfortable tent armed with headlamps and hot tea to retrieve the lost climbers. The rescuers stumbled around in the darkness and fog, anxiously calling to each other over the wind, tripping on equipment, tying into the wrong ropes, generally providing more immediate excitement than the distant rescuees. Some who went out returned exhilarated by the night's beauty; others were exhausted by its fierceness. Those who remained in camp sat with candles at the door of the eating humpy, alternately cynical mountaineers and fathers with teenage daughters out late. They made hot tea to revive the sufferers, but drank it themselves.

Lev and Young arrived at camp under heavy escort, making laconic, understated comments about the day's climbing. They demonstrated the requisite nonchalance of climbers who have just been forcibly rescued. Morrissey articulated his relief in a shower of criticism for staying out late, mixed with lavish praise for a job well done. Both rolled off tired ears. Leisurely starts and the daily increase in the length of fixed ropes were leaving little time for climbing before the daily storm. Duenwald mischievously eyed the next day's team: "Tomorrow, you get up at three." Peterson gave him the finger, and Harvard choked on his tea, but nobody disagreed.

We considered the establishment of a camp at the cache below the ropes to reduce approach time, but, though half the face was finished, we were still only on vague terms with the ridge, so we maintained a tentative, waiting posture until our assurance and intimacy should increase.

The momentum of our expectations, built on nine days of mercurial activity, was suspended the next day by heavy snow. The day was devoted to reading, writing, talking, eating, or sleeping, all conducted at the same slow pace and low level of emotional involvement. Occasional harried trips were made to the drifted-in latrine on the edge of camp. Running to the latrine, Anderson fell into the garbage pit. Appearing at the door of the communal tent, his hair, beard and clothes thick with powder snow, he said, "Hah! I didn't know there were any pigs up here." Morrissey, inside the tent, returned, "Yeah, well . . . they dig holes all over the place, you have to watch out." It snowed three feet during the day.

The southeast ridge people, the climbing technocrats, quietly discussed the objective danger of the route, that danger over which a climber has no control. The danger on the face, mostly from rockfall, was not excessive, but appraisal varied according to the safety-mindedness of each man. A few were prepared to take great personal risk for the sake of the route; others found serious risk unacceptable. In any case, willingness to take understood personal risk was not the central issue. The varied backgrounds of the team meant that nearly half of the members did not have the big mountain experience to judge the danger for themselves, but would be exposed to it repeatedly in carrying loads to Camp I at the ridge crest. What might be an acceptable amount of rockfall for an alpine ascent when one is exposed to it only once, could be unthinkable for the repeated exposure of loadcarrying. The length of the ridge and the projected number of camps dictated that about two hundred loads be carried up through the hourglass to a site for Camp I. As the season progresses, the route deteriorates and rockfall increases, endangering the heavily traveled fixed ropes. Perspectives from the Himalaya, the Andes, Alaska, the Yukon, and the American west were focused on deciding what was justifiable risk for the expedition as a whole.

The night of April 6 was clear and cold enough to make skin draw tight. Good weather held during the next day, which we spent studying the face to learn how it disposed of new snow. It appeared that there was no avalanche danger from snow accumulation on our route on the face. Most new snow slid off immediately in the form that had bothered Lev and Young. Because it was a good day, camp puttering was rampant. Tents were dug out, food organized, spools of rope cut to length, and kits made of basic items to establish camps.

While the weather was good and the food and equipment were accessible, Duenwald, Langbauer, Harvard, and Thompson made photographs of Products-In-Use-On-The-Mountain. Bech and Anderson performed as product users with genuine zeal; they babbled with delight, gasped with satisfaction and grinned with mindless ecstasy over cans of fruit, cans of beer, cookies, meat, and cakes. It wasn't clear what they were up to until the camera work was over and they were still eating. Lev wandered around in sunglasses and grey, one-piece, itchy-scratchy underwear, offering to pose with the flap down for his favorite sponsors.

This promotional activity particularly amused Ang Namgyal, at least so it seemed insofar as we could determine how he felt about anything. We posed for food ads in front of Ang's cooktent, an assortment of cameras draped around our necks, parka pockets bulging with film, lenses, and light meters. Ang came over at inappropriate times helpfully pretending to pour tea from a pot into a box of crackers. His expressionless countenance, cultivated as shelter from a succession of insensitive sahibs, wrinkled with a barely perceptible smile; he would grunt a short, possibly disdainful laugh from deep in his chest when we tried to organize him to do the right thing. If Ang Mingyur, Namgyal's extroverted assistant, saw anything silly in pretending to fill broken stoves from a jug that had no kerosene in it, he did not say so.

At three on April 8, the austere, reflected light of the moon cast grey shadows on the faces of Dhaulagiri. Scattered clouds gusted through the bowl. By morning the expedition was paralyzed again by storm. Unseen thunder crashed and high winds made visibility less than thirty feet. Fortunately, the cooktent was not far away.

The bamboo poles left over from the aborted aerial mail operation were pressed into service as an unconvincing Base Camp flag pole. The two sections were bound together with a red rag. Naturally, as a rallying point and assertive symbol of our presence in the wilderness, the flag pole flew our National Geographic Society flag. We placed the same faith in the flag as we did in the society itself; having been to the highest mountain and to the deepest, dark ocean, the flag gave us reassuring contact with an enduring tradition of exploration. That foul morning we were saddened when the flag came away from the pole and disappeared into the storm. Luckily, we had another.

Although it was the third day of inactivity, we were not concerned; on the contrary, we felt that days of decisive, successful climbing were imminent. We lay around, enjoying a soporific base camp life. Groups formed and reformed in the dining humpy, which was high enough to stand in and offered a comfortable arrangement of boxes to sit on. As the snow built up around the tent, it was an awkward step down through a triangular zippered door on to the burlap bags which covered the floor. The yellow tent was littered with walkie-talkies, tape recorders, camera equipment, books, candle ends, used paper towels, a red tool box, open jars of cashew nuts, and dirty utensils from the previous meal. A second tent sat behind, communicating through interlocking tunnel entrances; an adjacent, smaller tent served as the kitchen. One had only to call to the kitchen and a two-gallon aluminum tea pot heavy with a steaming mixture of sugar, milk, and bitter Indian tea appeared in the door.

Storms can make men reflective and drive them into themselves; if a storm lasts long enough, it will make a man talk of his most closely guarded concerns. While the gale force wind rattled and swelled the tent, we turned to speculation. Rennie and Duenwald, who lead complex, specialized professional lives, saw the expedition as a simplified version of the world they knew at home, affording them the rare luxury of contemplation. Duenwald saw simplicity as an absolute good. "I feel very, very good," he sighed. "There have been few times that my life has been so pure and simple as the last few days. The absolute simplicity of life is becoming my goal." Harvard suggested that contemplation should not be solely the province of old men and that even idle musing had a place in a busy life. Duenwald told him to wait until he had a wife and kids. Smith thought that was all very nice, and said that the expedition gave him the only real opportunity in a very balanced existence, other than weekends of course, to follow his "avocation" of climbing. Lev thought that too much reflection was unhealthy, and would only admit to being on the trip for fun. He pursued the theme of simplicity to say that a man has a greater chance to operate as a successful human being in the simplified context of the mountains than in the "outside" world. Fear, meanwhile, wrote in his diary: "The peace, the stillness, the beauty—the basic life. A time for learning and a time to think! To the north is the border of Tibet; to the south roll the plains of India; to the west is an old friend, Dhaulagiri II, and to the east is Annapurna! The Himalayas, my love! Mountains are my only trouble besides women."

Reichardt poked around between the food boxes looking for a chess piece that Fear had lost.

Thompson prodded the topic from simplicity to happiness, announcing that happiness is the unachieved goal of everyone. He called it bovine stagnation, and said that as a goal sought by all the world, happiness is a pimpery. Duenwald accused him of devaluing everything that wasn't painful. Rennie said that happiness was important to him, but identified two kinds: the blithe happiness of the ignorant, and the disciplined happiness which rises above pain the way the fourth movement of Beethoven's Ninth Symphony grows from the previous movements. Smith started to hum the movement; Bech said it was the wrong piece, and Fear said it sounded like boogie sung by a schoolmarm. Searching for an example in literature, Rennie decided that few writers understood happiness, or were capable of expressing it. Bech was reading Mann at the time, so Rennie began to hold forth on Germans as a bad example. Lev, remembering that he had once been a Mann scholar, challenged Rennie more on principle than on conviction. Apart from literature, Lev identified happiness with selflessness, saying that happiness increases with responsibility. Langbauer, who had read almost all the books in camp except the Mann work under discussion, began to characterize the rest of the expedition from the book he was reading, *Tom Jones*. He claimed relevance on the ground that in the context of adventures even more implausible than ours, apparent tragedy was thwarted by ascendant wit, a stylistic approach we would understand. He bogged down on the problem of who was a better Squire Weston: Morrissey or Duenwald.

On afternoons like this one, the Sherpas wisely stayed clear of the sahibs' tent. They probably sensed that once inside, they might never emerge again. Tea was served through the door. As the conversation lazily continued, the smell of popcorn drifted into the tent. We all ignored it for awhile, then Morrissey stirred himself, walking stiffly toward the door of the cooktent. Startled Sherpas looked up to see the Bumba, face set and arms folded across his chest, bigger than life in mock anger. "I didn't know we had any popcorn left. THE SAHIBS LIKE POPCORN VERY MUCH," he said slowly, distinctly, emphasizing each word. Then he turned and stalked back to his corner. A bowl of popcorn appeared. Then another, and another, then pots and bucketsful—finally we cried mercy amid cheers from the cooktent.

That evening, with all sixteen climbers wedged into the dining tent for dinner, talk turned again to the conflict about the routes. Fixing the route to the ridge crest occupied two men at a time, leaving almost everyone else idle and impatient. Anderson and Bech were especially anxious to start carrying loads to the site of Camp I on the spur. Duenwald argued that working on the spur then

Del Young climbs through the hourglass on the southeast ridge route.

Telephoto of two climbers, halfway up the fixed ropes leading to the southeast ridge crest (arrows indicate position of climbers).

124

would waste energy that would be badly needed in a few days on the ridge when loads would have to move to Camp I on the crest. Behind his argument was the fear, held by most of the ridge group, that working two routes at once would drain too much manpower from the ridge effort. The route up the ridge was obviously going to be arduous, starting with a long, exhausting carry of about twenty pitches of jumaring. Once the spur route was begun, it might become an easy alternative by comparison. It was true that some of the strongest members of the team were not working on the face, but they would be critically important when the carrying began. It was generally agreed that we could start the spur later in the month and still reach the summit before the monsoon drove us from the mountain. As a compromise, April 15, six days away, was set as the day to begin work on the spur. That meant that by then, the route to the ridge crest must be secured for safe carrying, and a campsite on the ridge crest must be ready for occupation. No one really doubted that it could be done in time.

The morning of April 9 was clear. Duenwald and Langbauer went to the face to assess the post-storm objective danger and observe the new snow conditions. They were supported by Anderson, Bech, Reichardt, Smith, and Young, who optimistically carried loads to the cache. Roskelley, Thompson, and Harvard stayed at Base Camp while Morrissey, Rennie, Fear, Lyman, Peterson, and Lev went down to Glacier Camp for loads. Travel in all directions was trying in the deep, new snow. The face seemed safe immediately after a storm. The bergschrund was mostly filled and easier to cross, but some equipment that had been left there was lost in the snow. Lyman, working like a spelunker, dug a hole twenty feet deep searching for the equipment, but found nothing. He and Thompson were to lead the following day; Harvard and Peterson were to carry loads and break trail for them to the 'schrund. Assuming the ridge crest would be reached, Langbauer and Duenwald were to jumar up later in the day with the equipment to establish Camp I.

Shaken by the prospect of a 3 A.M. start, Harvard woke up at fifteen-minute intervals throughout the night to check his watch, but was finally asleep when the alarm went off. He had drawn the short straw, so it was his job to wake the others, a difficult task on top of the strain of waking himself. The wind was blowing at over fifty miles per hour, and appeared to be getting stronger. The tents were being drifted in quickly, some were almost buried. There was no visibility, and it was impossible to tell just where the swirling snow in the air became the drifting snow on the ground. Storms always seem worse when contemplated from a sleeping bag, so Harvard got up. Outside, the storm was bad. He headed for the cooktent where a faint light glimmered between blasts of snow. "What the hell," he thought. "I'm up, the others might as well be up too."

Watchers in Base Camp follow progress on the ridge route.

Climber on the seventh pitch of the southeast ridge route.

As an afterthought, "Besides, the weather might even get better." Bent over by the wind, he plodded around to the others' tents.

"Lyman, you awake?"

"Sounds like just the wind, Tom," came Smith's voice inside the tent.

"Shut up, Lowell. Yes, I'm coming. Thanks."

The stark light of headlamps was reflected from the ice crystals that coated everything inside the tents. Fully clothed bodies emerged from frozen sleeping bags, then shivering hands groped in the lukewarm depths of the bags for boots and mittens. Anything left out at night would freeze, so boots, socks, sweaters, water bottles, batteries, even pens and tubes of sun cream vied with bundled-up bodies for sleeping bag space.

At the edge of camp, Lyman noticed the rattling skeleton of a dead four-man sleeping humpy. The wind had knocked it apart, he supposed; frame parts were scattered everywhere. Walking on, he hoped its occupants had found shelter in other tents.

One by one, Harvard, Peterson, Lyman, and Thompson took shelter in the dark, frigid dining humpy. Frost covered everything in the tent. Three or four candles were lit and headlamps switched off. Ang Namgyal was busy next door making breakfast, which Ang Mingyur soon handed in. The four ate a breakfast of chocolate, tea, and porridge in silence. They wanted to go down the glacier to the face; it was their turn that morning, and it was to be up before dawn to climb in grizzly weather that they were on Dhaulagiri. But the weather was worse than grizzly, so they could not go.

"Whorish wind; we're not going anywhere today," Thompson dramatically announced from behind a steaming cup of tea.

"Damned perceptive, Todd," agreed the others. It was not yet four o'clock. The climbers warmed as the tent slowly thawed. At last, when wool mittens could be removed, Harvard set up the chessboard, his numb fingers barely able to feel the pieces. Lyman, normally a taciturn man, recited snatches of Robert Frost's poetry as the thick tobacco smoke of Nepal Gold Flake cigarettes began to mix with the haze of steam and condensation that filled the tent. The others added what lines they could, then plumbed for other poets. Then they sang. Playing chess by candlelight while the ground blizzard howled outside, they sang English ballads of tragic love and American country-and-western songs of the road. Lyman's north-country voice led as the haze became a jumble of gypsies and lovers, Vancouver towboats, barrooms, Tennessee horses, and always a lonely truck stop. The morning was a climbing failure, but there was freedom to be found in that tent on the mountain. It was the best of mornings, and new climbs came into being.

More sahibs drifted in; by nine the tent was full, and the early risers were cramped in a corner. The singing tapered off. Sonam Girmi, who had arrived at

Base Camp late the day before, came in at ten with a disgruntled look on his face, clicked his tongue, and said, "Much wind," with a sweeping backhanded gesture toward the mountain.

The day turned out to be comfortable, but inactivity had begun to breed tension. When the wind subsided at ten, early in the day but too late to get up the fixed ropes, the prospect of a wasted day suddenly seemed unacceptable. In frustration, Roskelley demanded action; in equal frustration, Duenwald lectured him on patience. Ironically, returning bad weather quieted the argument but underscored its cause.

The same team set out on the eleventh, with an even larger support party set to prepare the route for loadcarrying by chopping steps in the ice at difficult places. They rose at 3:15 to a clear, moonless night. It took one hour to go from camp to the cache by the uncertain light tubes of our headlamps. The hard, eight-inch-wide base of the trail, well-packed after many crossings, was hidden by new snow. It was marked every few hundred feet by three-foot bamboo wands, barely visible at thirty feet with a headlamp. The first man had to feel along for the trail. If he stepped off, he plunged in to his thigh. When he stepped off, if he could not find the trail again in one step, he had to struggle back and forth until he did. Those behind tried to avoid his mistakes.

The pre-dawn light caught them at the cache where they stopped to put on crampons and drink hot chocolate from a vacuum bottle. A full half-hour was required to reach the bergschrund, and another two hours to jumar the nine pitches to the high point. The jumar is a spring-loaded clip which slides up, but not down the rope. A sling runs from the jumar to the climber's seat harness, or swami belt, to catch him if he slips. Jumaring requires patience and desire, or perhaps only insensitivity to pain, because it is dull, hard work. On the first five pitches of easy snow, one jumar handle was sufficient, but two were necessary on the steeper ice above. If one has a strong upper body, he can pull up the ropes and not worry much about what his feet are doing. If one is weak or, what amounts to the same thing, has lived at high altitude for long, he will be forced to rely on a combination of arms, legs, and style to get up the ropes. Starting from an anchor is the most irritating part of jumaring. The spring on the jaw of a jumar handle holds the jaw firmly against the rope, so a small resistance is necessary to slide the handle up the rope. There is not enough weight of slack rope below a jumar at the start of a pitch to provide the resistance, so one must use a free hand, or knees, or elbows, or even teeth to hold the icy rope still while pushing up the jumar.

Two people do not jumar on a single section of fixed rope at the same time, so Thompson reached the high point first, and stood on one foot in a small step to tie himself to the anchor. He cleared a jumble of ropes left there by Lev, and called down to Lyman to come up. While Lyman jumared up, Thompson cut a six-by-ten-inch platform for him and prepared to belay him up the next lead. Lyman arrived, adjusted his load of pitons, slings, carabiners and rope, caught his breath, and began to climb the fifty-degree ice pitch, cutting occasional steps. The main danger on the route seemed to be falling pieces of ice cut by the leader. Langbauer, working directly below on the eighth pitch, was cut on the forehead by some of Lyman's ice. Fear, on the snow slopes below, later noted in his diary: "Rocks and ice were coming down around us all day—dangerous, but I love it!"

Meanwhile, Del Young conducted a climbing seminar on the bottom fixed ropes of the face for the expedition members who had not done much technical climbing of this type. In the guise of an afternoon lark, he taught them new ways to jumar and rappel and get along on a big face. Rennie, who had always used body rappels in which the rope passes over the shoulder and under the crotch, announced, "My God! My balls are no longer in jeopardy!" when he learned about rappeling from a carabiner brake system attached to his seat harness. The Sherpas made a carry from Glacier Camp to Base.

On the face, Lyman ran out of rope, stopped, and set up a belay. Thompson made the eleventh lead up easier ice. One more pitch each exhausted the day. Four pitches were substantial but not decisive progress. The ridge crest looked close, perhaps only another day away, but the climbing was consistently difficult, and we had already underestimated some of what we had had to do. All who worked on the face felt that it was a fine, demanding route, fully worthy of our sweat. A number of smaller routes of the same difficulty had been completed outside of the Himalaya, but we could only think of rare instances when ice so hard had been climbed at over twenty thousand feet in the Himalaya. The southeast ridge pleased us deeply, but we were becoming nervous about our rate of progress.

Reichardt and Young left for the face at 3:30 on April 12 in marginal weather conditions. Harvard and Lev carried loads to the bergschrund, then followed up the ropes carrying additional rope and hardware to support Reichardt and Young, with hopes of leading part of the way to the top. Though the fifteenth had been set as the day to begin work on the spur, so many were impatient and idle that the first carry was made up easy snow to the site of Camp I later that morning. As usual, the bright morning quickly deteriorated into storm. High wind and cold made movement slow; whirlwinds of snow made climbing on the ridge uncomfortable.

While the team on the face struggled to reach the ridge crest, Anderson, Bech, and Peterson reached the site of Camp I on the spur. Morrissey, Rennie, and Smith stopped and made a cache about halfway to the campsite. Morrissey was furious when he returned to Base Camp, his crampons had fallen off six times, and he had made some unplanned sitting glissades while trying to get them readjusted. Rennie was euphoric; he reported that he had photographed Morrissey in compromising positions on his backside in the snow. Smith had fallen up to his waist in a crevasse while trying to stop Morrissey from sliding down the mountain during one of the scrimmages with his crampon straps. Anderson, Bech, and Peterson were annoyed at all three for not making the full carry to Camp I. Langbauer asked Morrissey for a sponsor's endorsement of the crampon straps as he cut them off. As he replaced the cloth straps with neoprene ones, Morrissey suggested aberrant clinical procedures for the manufacturer to perform with his product.

Young made two consecutive leads up forty-five-degree snow and snow-covered ice, leading continuously from a six-hundred-foot spool of rope. Progress was slow, and the storm grew worse. Lev and Harvard nearly froze in the slings at the belay point. As they waited at the anchor, half-standing, half-hanging in slings, Lev and Harvard could watch the easy progress of the roped carriers a mile away on the spur. They stood quietly as powder avalanched around them, as the afternoon storm built up, happy to be where they were, but envious of the sunlight that still covered the spur. In terrible winds, Reichardt, wanting the top, made the third lead. They were close, but did not know how close, and they had to get down. Yet another day was needed to reach the crest.

"Oh! Sherpa, dai!" [Oh! Sherpa, my brother!] Bech cheerfully called when he returned from the spur to the Base Camp, hoping Ang Mingyur or Pinzo could produce some thawed beer. The northeast spur people were happy to be engaged, finally, in some satisfying activity. We had had a little trouble with the airdropped beer. We discovered that partially frozen beer which has been suddenly taken to 19,300 feet erupts violently when its top is popped. The only alternative to soaking a sleeping bag or down clothes is to take the whole can in the first explosive overflow. A fully frozen can can be opened completely, offering a large, starchy white popsicle and a small residue of alcohol. Ang Namgyal headed a Sherpa combine in the business of warming cans for a 50 percent drinking fee. The beer was soon gone, leaving only whiskey and rum.

After Bech got his beer, dinner was served. The menu included freeze-dried pork chops, soup, sauerkraut, strawberries, peas, corn, noodles, and hot buttered rum. Those who had carried on the spur were boisterous; a good day of exercise, an optimistic beginning, and measurable progress. In contrast, the team from the ridge was silent; tired and apprehensive, to them the tent seemed noisy and crowded, almost hostile. Rennie was in good conversational form because he had trumped Morrissey on the day's carry. He regaled us with the story of a highly sophisticated urine collecting device that he had wangled from NASA to test for possible use on Dhaulagiri. Rennie said he had decided to test the thing at an Explorers Club dinner held at the Waldorf Astoria in New York. With secret joy he pissed as the wild gorilla meat canapés were handed around, only to discover that there was a leak in the system.

He touched on a serious problem. The cold and discomfort of the high mountains are seldom so apparent as when one has to leave a warm sleeping bag in the middle of the night. With a high-volume fluid intake, amounting at times to forced fluids, to combat dehydration, not to mention the advancing age of some of the climbers, nights could be very long indeed. In Alaska, a three-dog night is a cold night; on Dhaulagiri, a three-piss night was even colder. Some braved the winds as a matter of principle, but most resorted to the expedient of a can or bottle, safe inside the tent. By fortunate coincidence, we had a large number of quart cookie cans with tightly fitting plastic lids. Smith was one of the first to use one, and almost the last. He was horrified to see the can filling blood red. In hurried medical consultation, the doctors found no reason for the obvious internal hemorrhage. Only later did Smith discover that he had cut himself on the rim of the can.

There was no refuge for defecation, and no matter how calm the day might appear, spindrift always managed to fill one's pants with powder snow. Ang Namgyal's cooking never let us forget the gastro-intestinal problems of the Kathmandu valley. Morrissey woke up suddenly one night with the thought that he needed to get out of his tent in a hurry. He found the zippers on his sleeping bag, the tent and the tent fly, but at the last moment, he reached on the wrong side of his red one-piece angora underwear for the flap zipper. As he sat the next morning washing the flap in a dish pan of hot water, the denizens of the cooktent sent Reichardt to ask respectfully that he not wash his flap in a dish pan. We could hear the cry of, "I haven't studied medicine for thirteen years for nothing," as Reichardt dove for cover. Harvard, who had an identical set of underwear, solicitously gave Morrissey a regular "zipper drill" thereafter.

Lev's snoring was the only sound in camp that otherwise clear and quiet night. Langbauer and Roskelley were to start early on April 13 and attempt to reach the ridge crest. Duenwald was to go up after them and make a final judgment on the objective danger that affected the route. Some climbers still expressed grave doubts concerning the feasibility of the route because of the danger. The fixed ropes, only ten days old, already showed serious signs of wear. Ropes come under harsh scrutiny during a rappel, when the climber must watch and feel the rope as he slides down; we were noticing cuts, occasional crampon holes, and an unexplained flattening of the rope sheath. The crucial variables on the ridge were the weather, the imminent arrival of the monsoon, and the objective danger. The ridge fanatics were anxious, uncertain, hopeful, and vulnerable. Doubt crept in.

Langbauer and Roskelley started early on the thirteenth. Driven by an urgent sense of mission, they reached the top of the sixteenth pitch by nine o'clock. Roskelley led off on the remainder of Young's six-hundred-foot spool going two hundred feet on forty-five to fifty-degree ice, then led the eighteenth pitch, which steepened a few degrees toward its end, within eighty feet of the ridge crest. While the members and Sherpas who remained in Base Camp watched them closely, Thompson noted in his journal: "I stand in Base Camp and watch the figures struggling competently high on the route and see that they are fragile. They are like our puny notions of honesty, beauty, and the free act juxtaposed with the simple mass, the resistance, and negation of this mountain. The resistance of the mountain to our efforts, even the wind alone, deny us as incisively as clods of earth landing on the top of a coffin deny life. I stand in Base Camp amidst the negligible material implications of an idea and know the hiatus between the concept of the southeast ridge route and physical possibility; between the line the eye follows on the mountain, and the gradual 150-foot sections that mark a day's work."

Langbauer led the last bit, which tilted back to just over fifty degrees, to the ridge crest at 21,500 feet. His hands in snow-clotted Dachstein mitts gripped the narrow ridge as easily as they could the back of a chair; he looked over and thirteen thousand feet down the other side. The south face dropped away at sixty-five degrees; suddenly, he was very tired. He chopped a two-foot-square platform on the top of the ridge for his belay anchors, eased a leg over, and straddled the ridge. The ridge crest was sharp, steep ice, corniced here and there, as far along it as he could see in both directions. Tired and dejected, he thought he heard laughter. The smile and the irreverent laughter of David Seidman loomed in his consciousness. It was a surprise: he had not thought about the 1969 expedition, or of his friends who had died on it, while working on the ridge. Suddenly he felt better, and even managed to smile back at the dancing figure above the ridge. Later he wrote: "I had to appear serious when John came up, because he hadn't known David, and wasn't aware of my sense of his presence." Roskelley and Langbauer stayed a few minutes on the crest, then started the long series of rappels. On the way back to Base Camp, they paused at the cache to pack the personal belongings stored there; they knew that they would not be back again, that we could not climb the southeast ridge of Dhaulagiri. It was a long, slow walk up to the col.

As Langbauer and Roskelley walked into camp, we noticed that they had large rucksacks, and carried much of the stuff that climbers on the face were in the habit of leaving at the cache. Questions were asked: "What is the crest like?" "Is there a good campsite?" They cast their eyes down, avoiding our anxious looks, then glanced at each other. No, there was no campsite, not even a place to chop one out. The ridge was fantastically steep, and all hard ice with a rotten surface. It was possible that a campsite existed under a huge cornice about five pitches farther along the ridge, but it would take all of the expedition's hardware to fix those pitches properly for loadcarrying because they would be horizontally traversing pitches. Anyway, nineteen pitches was almost too long a day at that altitude with only a light load of climbing equipment; a twenty-five-pitch carry with heavy packs was probably not realistic.

We did not want to believe that we could not climb the southeast ridge. Without the ridge, the expedition made no sense to many of us. We were cast adrift. Duenwald asked Harvard and Thompson to go to the crest to assess the route themselves; Lyman volunteered to go with them. Roskelley and Langbauer would have liked to have been proven wrong.

The weather was not stable enough early on the fourteenth to go to the ridge, but loads were carried to Camp I on the spur as they had been the previous day. Quiet, vaguely desperate meetings took place in tents around camp. Some members were so committed to climbing the ridge that they began to consider establishing a camp under the cornice and climbing and living on the ridge as long as possible: if there was to be a failure, let it be a glorious one. Thompson, Lyman, and Harvard decided to try making the five or so leads along to the ridge crest to the cornice when they went up for their assessment.

At three in the morning, April 15 was unusually clear. They walked to the cache by headlamp. Great balls of snow clung to their feet, making each step an uncertain landing on a slippery plane of changing angle. They did not talk. Their measured breathing, their steps, and an occasional curse that followed sliding off the trail into deep snow were the only sounds in the dark bowl. Dhaulagiri squatted benignly on their right; the dawn would come from their left.

The three climbers paused a few minutes at the cache to savor the pre-dawn light and suit up for the long jumar. Lyman and Harvard left quickly to begin the leads on the ridge; Thompson lingered to chop unnecessary ice pitons out of the ice to be used in fixing rope along the crest.

Jumaring on steep ice without steps puts tremendous strain on ankles, calves, and crampon bindings. On the tenth pitch, Harvard's left crampon broke, popped off, and bounced down the face. He crashed against the ice, caught his balance, swore, then started a slippery, frustrating descent.

Lyman and Thompson continued on. The weather went to hell at midmorning but they jumared along, tied together with a 150-foot rope, unable to see each other most of the time. The wind increased as they neared 21,500 feet; energy and will eroded away. The goal became simply to reach the crest, look around, and get out before the new snow started sliding off the route.

At the top, they straddled the ridge face to face, dangling a foot on each side, as if playing on a seesaw. They were worn out. It was cold, and visibility

Climber above the hourglass on the southeast ridge route.

Crest of the southeast ridge, looking downhill.

was less than a hundred feet. They could only see a little way down the south face. They agreed that it was an exposed, spooky place, and that Langbauer and Roskelley were right. After taking a few pictures they rappeled down, throwing off the extra ropes and hardware that hung at the anchors. They wanted to leave the route as clean as possible. A few snow slides swept over them. At the end of the last rappel, standing on the bottom lip of the 'schrund unclipping his carabiner brake from the rope with gloveless hands, Lyman looked over at Thompson, who stood a few feet away, and tried to joke. They both felt very empty. A powder avalanche hit Lyman and built around him before he was free of the ropes; then he was free, and moved out of the slide.

Thompson wrote in his journal that night, "And so, after a confrontation with the ridge crest, and knowing that we had already done some of the best high altitude ice climbing in the Himalaya, my attitude changed. The climbing itself is very fine, but cannot be supported. A camp at the crest, if one could be made, would be ridiculously exposed. A twenty-five-pitch carry to a camp at the cornice would be unreasonable at that altitude on that terrain. As I rappeled down those nineteen pitches, I was not sad nor angry nor disappointed nor even chagrined any longer by our dramatic failure. Only a better reconnaissance before the expedition would have been to the point. The route is pithy and beautiful. Knowing that it is not our failure to climb well, one can accept the ridge's greater-than-usness that is unrelated to expedition politics, and be on."

Harvard's brief entry was "The ridge won't go . . . I think we should follow it for a little way anyway, but I am alone in thinking that—the expedition has rightly focused on the spur."

While part of the team reveled in the progress on the spur, the other part languished. It was not easy at first for the men who wanted so much to be on the ridge to work on the northeast spur with enthusiasm. It seemed ridiculous to have thirty-two people and tons of airdropped equipment at 19,300 feet in the Himalaya to make a third ascent of a straightforward route. "It seems to me that the third ascent of a mountain by the old route is hardly worthy of comment. Well, at least the publisher won't be able to use 'Ascent of the Impossible Ridge' as a title for the book; that's one consolation," Duenwald said. "Maybe they won't want a book at all," someone added hopefully.

Young and Harvard climbed the ropes to the ridge crest on April 17, a rare good day, ostensibly to photograph the ridge in optimum weather conditions, but really because they wanted to see what was there. They picked up more hardware, and threw down more ropes. Young wanted to cut down all the fixed lines as a matter of form, but by the end of the day, altitude, exhaustion,

Climber on the crest of the southeast ridge looking toward the summit.

The future of the ridge attempt is discussed in the communal tent at Base Camp.

and imminent bad weather sacrificed form to expedience. Cutting the ropes would have been a symbolic ethical act based on the desire to leave no trace of their passing. They started down, remembering an obscure warning from a forgotten Ibsen play, "Lack of oxygen weakens the conscience." Their ascent was only a footnote to the ridge attempt. From the high point, they could see a long line of carriers to Camp I on the spur trudging slowly along, bent under their loads.

Duenwald studied the situation in a letter to his wife: "Darkness is descending on my tent and the wind is still blowing and drifting snow around. The whole knowledge that we can't climb the southeast ridge will not sink home for several days. What it will mean to me in future years is inestimable now, but my guess is that I will most remember my homecoming, answering the boys' questions and just being the farm boy that I know in my heart I am."

The realization that we could not climb the southeast ridge was a severe blow but not a completely unexpected one. The ridge had, after all, been called impossible, and we had recognized its potential difficulties. We had approached it as an unknown. During the months of preparation and research before coming to the mountain, we had ignored the one possible source of information which might conceivably have saved us the trip to the ridge crest, a detailed reconnaissance by air. On a close flyover we would have seen the sharp angle at which the two faces form the ridge, and perhaps have seen that load carrying on the crest itself would not be feasible. Reason might then have dictated a change in objectives . . . but we would never have known for sure.

There was no clear line between success and failure. We seemed to fail, yet there was much more in the event than simple failure. We wanted to climb the ridge, but we did not need a heroic ending. If anything, anti-heroism was the attitude we found most comfortable. We had tried more than we could do; that was enough.

The Northeast Spur

Carries up the spur continued while the work on the face of the southeast ridge withered to a conclusion. Within a day after Langbauer and Roskelley reached the crest, the shift of attention to the northeast spur was complete. The realities of the ridge swept away the conflict about the routes.

The route on the spur would be done in the traditional Himalayan style, with careful logistic planning, patience, and endurance the components of success. We began work on the spur with virtually unlimited supplies and a great depth of manpower. In fact, we had too many strong and healthy climbers. The only real threat to speedy progress was bad weather, but it appeared that we would have ample time to wait out storms. On April 15, we still had more than a month of pre-monsoon climbing time, even allowing for the early departure that our long retreat route would necessitate. After the face, the spur looked easy: a "walk-up" where thirteen years earlier the Swiss had easily put eight men on top without oxygen. Morrissey announced that we would "get all sixteen Americans and eight Sherpas to the summit in four weeks." He pointed out that, with the abortion of the southeast ridge attempt, our suddenly oversized team would look silly if we didn't try something more than a simple ascent. Morrissey felt strongly enough about this to withhold news of our failure on the ridge until he could report progress on the spur. The idea of a mass ascent was plausible; we conjured up the image of a crowded parade up the mountain led by Morrissey playing the bumba drum.

In a flurry of enthusiastic speculation, we made our plans. Bech, Reichardt, and Duenwald plotted the logistics for a large assault on the spur, adapting the original plan of a small party ascent in support of teams on the southeast ridge to the new situation. The route dictated four camps above Base, at 21,400, 23,500, 24,500, and 25,700 feet, on or near the sites used by the Swiss in 1960, the Japanese in 1970, and the Bechs in 1971.

In good weather, it was conceivable that we could put as many men on the summit as stayed healthy and acclimatized during the next month. If weather kept us immobile on a third of the days we had, our chances of a mass ascent would be cut in half. But really bad weather, on this mountain of storms, would reduce our chances still further, and could turn our walkup into a struggle to get even one team to the top.

A heated discussion over whether we should shoot one team quickly to the summit, or work slowly toward putting a large number of climbers on the summit ensued. The issue was subtle: as a team, where success was to be shared equally as the work was shared, a single pair to the summit meant success for the whole expedition on that route. Himalayan routes are always dangerous; an expedition can never be certain of an ascent. Concentrating on one team would give us the best chance of success while minimizing risks. Duenwald summed it up: "Since getting our bacon home intact is as important as reaching the summit, there's no point in really hanging it out for the third ascent of a standard route. We have to put a team on the summit, but pushing for more is begging for trouble."

On the other hand, group satisfaction isn't everything, and when the goal appears to be relatively easy, that potential satisfaction may seem small indeed. Most of the members wanted a personal chance at the summit if possible, and some had virulent summit fever. The summit of any big mountain is worth a struggle, and it appeared that we could put a number of people in a position to realize their ambitions.

The impulse to make a mass ascent is at once as ridiculous as the urge to jam a record number of fraternity brothers into a telephone booth and as respectable as the drive to break the four-minute mile. A mass ascent would offer both collective and individual fulfillment: perhaps more important, it offered us a way around the problem of picking a single summit team.

We decided in favor of a multi-party attempt. The logistic requirements of the effort kept us all busy, and resulted in well-stocked camps that would give us a needed margin if bad weather slowed our progress. Peterson worked out the logistic system to supply the four camps we would need above base; eight loads to Camp IV at 25,700 feet meant over fifty loads to Camp I at 21,400 feet, at the bottom of the pyramid. Reichardt developed a climbing rotation system designed to give everyone high work for acclimatization, while ensuring efficient movement of loads between camps.

Duenwald, deciding that he preferred to be an opinionated private citizen rather than a titled bureaucrat, resigned as deputy leader, declaring that the need for the post had ended with the southeast ridge attempt. Morrissey wouldn't accept the resignation, possibly because he had more fun contemplating wringing the neck of a deputy leader than of a mere member.

The expedition settled into a pattern of daily carries to supply Camp I on the spur. The route is not technically difficult. It follows a gentle slope through a short crevasse field just above Base Camp, then up the spur. It is one of the ironies of a big mountain that at altitude easy terrain is often very hard going: most of the route offers no protection from winds that can blow a man down, and where a contour does provide protection, deep powder snow accumulates. An easy slope allows a rapid gain of altitude, which drains strength quickly above 20,000 feet. A carry was just enough work to fill a day comfortably, breeding good appetites and sound sleep. Bech, speaking with the authority of experience, marshaled the routine: tea at dawn, followed by a good breakfast when the sun hit the tents, a late morning start, and back just as the afternoon storm closed in. Loads varied, the net probably averaging forty pounds, a respectable weight at twenty thousand feet. Carrying teams were roped as a precaution against the few crevasses. The route was marked by bamboo wands to show the way in whiteout conditions, and measured by resting places of growing familiarity. Fear and Lev even skied down the route from twenty-one thousand feet, entertaining the climbers, amazing the Sherpas, and exhausting themselves as they carved beautiful turns in painfully slow motion.

Camp I at 21,400 feet was occupied on April 17 by Bech, Anderson, Langbauer, Rennie, and Gyaltzen and Nang Tenzing. The camp was a cluster of tents on a platform cut in the snow on the east face, the leeward side of the northeast spur. The camp was in a beautiful place, an expanse of clean snow sculptured into sweeping curves by the wind. From below, its beauty was enhanced by a lacy plume of snow which sometimes swirled across the face. Once at the camp, the party discovered that the lovely plume could quickly bury anything, a tent for example, that the wind could not flatten or blow away. The first night was miserable. The Sherpas were frightened. Everyone was cold and wet. The noise and confusion in the tents was reminiscent of the first night at Windy Corner; the tents seemed particularly small and uncomfortable, with snow piling on the uphill side and wind snapping the nylon on the downhill side. Cooking was a chore, the more so because the climbers, pampered by the cook at Base Camp, were now out of the habit of cooking and melting snow for themselves in a small tent.

Rennie's broadcast at radio contact that night was a happy mix of deadpan reporting and defiant resolution. The camp survived, to be dug out and strengthened the next day. Langbauer went down to Base Camp with a breathing problem mysteriously labeled by the doctors as "frostbite of the inner ear," and Lyman replaced him. Lyman likes nothing better than working on a snow cave, and Camp I needed nothing so much as a cave for protection against the snow blowing across the face. The cave that was created under his direction became the kitchen, dining room, supply cache, and rest area of Camp I.

It grew more elaborate as time went on, and became a warm, cozy, and above all, quiet place to hide from the weather.

Work on the route to Camp II began immediately. Bech and Anderson reconnoitered to 23,500 feet, the site of the old Swiss Camp IV (the Swiss began their camp numbering from seventeen thousand feet, the site of our Glacier Camp). Bech rejoiced in the discovery of the tattered remains of a tent left by the Japanese in 1970 and used by him in 1971, then chastened the Sherpas when they honored tradition by tearing it to shreds. The route went up the spur crest at a smooth incline of thirty degrees. Then it steepened a few degrees, went through a short, slightly crevassed area, and continued up a crest that was roughly pockmarked by the wind. Moving up was trying, because the consistency of the snow changed frequently. The route moved out on the east face in the last few hundred feet to avoid rock on the crest.

Duenwald, Roskelley, Reichardt, and Peterson moved to Camp I on the nineteenth. During the next days, eight three-hundred-foot ropes were anchored on the top half of the route to Camp II, to be used for support on the way up and for hot hand rappels on the way down. The slope was not difficult: the ropes were carried up with the loads, then anchored and strung out on the trip down. Carries to Camp II began. John Skow, his airdrop tasks over, trekked up from Tukche to join the expedition at Base Camp. By the twenty-third, Harvard, Thompson, Lev, Young, Ngawang Samden, and Sonam Girmi were in Camp I, and Camp II was almost fully stocked. On the twenty-second, the six icefall porters had made the last carry from seventeen thousand feet to Base Camp at 19,300 feet, and on the twenty-third they took over the task of carrying from Base to Camp I. They had been specially picked by Sonam Girmi for the work on the Myagdi Glacier and had performed well there. Assignment to the Base Camp–Camp I carry, which was easy and free of objective danger, gave them high altitude experience which could mean a better job the next year. The new assignment, officially recognized as work above Base Camp, brought them a small bonus in pay and equipment, and a great boost in status.

Camp I grew like a suburban development, blossoming into a tract house village boasting a communal snow cave and two "streets" of tents precariously perched on the slope. Each morning the residents politely grumbled at each other as they cleared the night's snow away from their tents, like homeowners digging for their cars after a New England blizzard.

After one particularly bad storm, Fear wrote: "This lady above me just doesn't want our feet up there to stand on her—she just wants the wind, clouds, and snow for her friends." Mountains, like ships or the sea, tend to be female, possibly because climbers, like sailors, tend to be male. When the climber endows a mountain with human qualities, he does so in order to comprehend it in the familiar terms of mood, character, and motive. He talks to a mountain because he must: he needs to confront, to caress, to share, to convince, to know; to learn to balance the proper combination of deference and control. Though he comes to meet the mountain as part of a group, the climber talks to the mountain alone: he draws strength from his companions, but he seeks understanding and solace in the mountain. If the climber can talk to the mountain, then he has a witness to the triumph of a hard move or to the injustice of too heavy a load, a companion on an exhausting carry, and an explanation for an unexplainable avalanche. The mountain is a silent mirror which, in the vagaries of its terrain and weather, shows as many moods as a man can show and more than he can fathom. The climber may howl at the tedium of a long slope, argue with the wind, rhapsodize about the beauty of ice and snow, whisper seductively to a difficult rock, or banter with a dubious snow bridge. In response the mountain can be dull as well as brilliant, instructive or misleading, excited or dispassionate, charitable or cruel.

As for the female character of the mountain, the anthropomorphism has become automatic, its roots found in a tangle of male psychology and mountaineering tradition. The usage varies, the climbers' approach to the image is personal. Fear's sweet lady and delicate lover is Morrissey's siren, whore, and bitch: only the eyes of the beholder are different.

In context, Fear would not really expect the lady to wish to be under his feet, but he would want to be up among her friends. Morrissey, in threatening cramponed footprints and a thousand pitons, is really seeking the same thing. Whether the climber sees himself as warily stalking a coy virgin in the garden of a convent, or lusting after the wisest old madam in town, the tribute is in the attention paid. Familiarity and acceptance turn derogatory terms into terms of endearment. The spur route started for the team as the "three-dollar whore," but the market price eventually rose by popular demand to a classy seven dollars. When Roskelley started up the spur, sighing "Well, let's climb this pig," he was calling on an image not of the barnyard but of a college freshman mixer. Seidman, killed on Dhaulagiri in 1969, separated the specific mountain from the recurrent image, bringing with him to each mountain an arcane pantheon of the Great Whore of the Mountains and several lesser whores. For the Sherpas, a particular mountain does not itself have human attributes, but its spirit does; Dhaulagiri's spirit is female.

Bech, Anderson, and Reichardt moved up to the site of Camp II late on April 24. A mixup in communications in the morning led them to expect the loadcarriers that day to set up tents for them: those who carried were unaware of the plan, so they dropped their loads and retreated in the face of the afternoon storm. Bitterly disappointed, the three struggled to pitch tents in a growing storm. They found two tents defective, and finally pitched a third on a small, sloping stone platform built by the Swiss in 1960. The platform was smaller than a single tent, but it was nearly level, and comforting to have. Somehow the tiny pile of stones, perched on the great mass of Dhaulagiri and exposed to daily gale force winds, had survived for thirteen years. The antique and tenuously placed iron pitons to which the tent was anchored provided more psychological than physical security. Camp II is at the apex of the north and east faces, where the northeast spur joins the massive summit block of Dhaulagiri. It is exposed on both sides to high winds which can be intense enough to wither anything in their path, and make frostbite a constant hazard. From the camp, one can look across to the top of the southeast ridge, and down along it to the expedition's high point. The sun highlights the texture of the ridge crest and the face. From below, the crest looks like a line of little towers gracefully rising toward the summit; from above, it is a fat saw with broken and jagged teeth.

The following day, Peterson, Roskelley, and Nang Tenzing joined the first three at Camp II. They pitched two tents on more comfortable but no more secure sites. A network of hand lines, utilizing anchors of 1970 or possibly 1960 origin, linked the tents as a token gesture to safety. A challenging outhouse was established by hanging a loose rope between two rock outcrops over the windy north face.

After a rest day, the men at Camp II began carries to Camp III. The route climbs the east face for several hundred feet of ice and crusted snow, then follows a snow crest to a series of rock bands, in the middle of which is a comfortable platform. That day and the next they anchored fixed ropes on the lower part of the route, the east face snow slope, but found them unnecessary in the rocks above.

Ang Namgyal, the cook, officially designated Camp I as the center of expedition activity by installing himself in the ice cave there. Everyone suddenly felt compelled to carry elsewhere. Sonam Girmi and Morrissey moved in. As the remaining sahibs and Sherpas arrived, sickness forced some to descend to Base Camp. Lyman was plagued by a neurological problem in one leg which made loadcarrying impossible so he went down for a brief recuperation. Rennie was twice forced to return to Base Camp to recover from minor injuries and ailments. Smith and Fear were in Base Camp nursing bad colds. Fear had actually made the long trip down to Rest and Recovery Camp to spend a few days at a healthy altitude of 15,500 feet, the only one of the team to use the camp for that purpose.

From April 26 until May 1, carries continued from Base to Camp I, from Camp I to Camp II, and from Camp II to the site of Camp III. The days

Camp I on the northeast spur.

Nang Tenzing and Pasang Tenzing at Camp II on the northeast spur.

Camp I after a snowstorm.

were cold, clear in the mornings, and stormy in the afternoons. The weather was stable, but there was a perceptible daily increase in the strength of the winds. It was still climbing weather certainly, but the mountain was beginning to bare its teeth. The carry from Base to Camp I was drudgery, a route on which one counted the bamboo wands placed as route markers, but finally lost count because it was so dull. The pace of walking at altitude dictates to all levels of consciousness. The spectacular scenery did not relieve the chore, because, like gluttons after too long a feast, we were growing jaded and immune to the beauty around us—besides, there was always the thought that the beauty could be better appreciated sitting down.

The carry from Camp I to Camp II was grim. It was absurdly tiring for a gentle slope rising only two thousand vertical feet. The camp didn't even look far away, and there were no serious technical difficulties on the route. Yet the wind, the snow, and the altitude combined to make the carry an all-day project. Roskelley, spurred by anger one morning, made the carry in three hours, others took as long as seven, but whatever pace one chose, no one called the carry easy. Peterson, veteran of the Everest South Face Expedition, had voiced amazement at the technical difficulty of the route to the ridge, and was now equally shaken by the physical difficulty of the carries on the spur. Sonam Girmi, who has been over eight thousand meters several times in his career, thought the carry was the hardest he had ever made. Such expressions were rare: most climbers dully avoided thinking about the effort as they made it, and, as a depressing topic, avoided it afterward in conversation. Fear wanted to ski the route, so he carried his skis part of the way one day, finally leaving them tangled in the fixed ropes halfway to Camp II.

The fixed ropes were a useful, though not completely necessary aid on the way up, but at the same time, they were a nagging measure of the near helplessness of a climber at high altitude. One could not forget that they were only three hundred feet long, even a bit less, figuring for knots and slack. Snow and ice conditions varied, and balance was sometimes tricky, but little more than putting one foot in front of the other was ever required. Yet on the last two ropes, it took healthy men thirty frustrating minutes to move along only three hundred feet of rope! It was only after dropping a load at the top and beginning the sliding, tumbling rappel down the ropes that one could really be glad of their presence.

On this carry the one real casualty of the expedition occurred. It came not as the quick violent accident or brief painful illness so common and so expected in the mountains, but with the slow realization that Sonam Tsering, the youngest of the Sherpas, was physically incapable of high altitude work.

Wind hits carriers on fixed ropes below Camp II on the spur.

The southeast ridge from Camp II on the spur.

Sonam Tsering had worked before as a porter, but this was his first expedition as a high altitude climbing sherpa. He was quiet and somewhat shy, as befitted his status as a rookie, but he had worked very hard, always with a clear, ingenuous smile. He took boyish delight in discovering the mysteries of sahibs and their equipment. He was anxious to learn and very willing to work; his future was promising. In Pokhara, Doctors Rennie and Morrissey had noticed his slight build, narrow shoulders and sunken chest more because his clothes fit poorly than because they suggested disability, but at twenty thousand feet it became clear that a congenital illness had left him with lungs too small for acclimatization to high altitude. Hard work had concealed his small breathing capacity up to that point, but he finally reached his limit. Three times he struggled with a load up towards Camp II, and three times he had to tie the load off below the camp. A few of the sahibs, including the doctors who sadly pronounced him unfit, had to do the same, but they did not lose a career in the process. A Sherpa who cannot acclimatize cannot work. Sonam Tsering was a clan relative of Sonam Girmi's, and that relationship, which could have ensured good jobs in the future, now made his failure complete. Sonam Girmi had, in fairness, given him a chance: in fairness, he would not get another. There are other ways for young Sherpa men to make a living, and there are even non-climbing jobs for Sherpas in the trekking business, but all that means nothing to a man just out of boyhood who comes close to realizing his dreams only to find them blasted by something he cannot control, or even fully understand. Sonam Tsering took his disappointment with silence, while the sahibs railed at cosmic injustice.

The carry to Camp III was shorter and more interesting than the carry to Camp II; the lower half of the carry was partially protected from the wind, but the higher altitude made it a beat-out nevertheless. Camp III at 24,500 feet marks the altitude above which oxygen is normally used full time on eight-thousand-meter peaks, and men carrying there had no difficulty in understanding why.

As the supply of Camp III neared completion, we discussed the method of getting teams to the summit. The question was again whether to give priority to putting one team on the summit quickly, or to move up slowly en masse. Should the team out in front at Camp II move to Camp III, or should men at Camp I be rotated to Camp III? The team at Camp II was best acclimatized to the highest altitude, therefore best prepared to move to Camp III. Undeniably, that would give them the best chance for the first summit attempt, but would also expose them to the greatest risk of physical deterioration through staying too long at high altitude. They would bear the brunt of finding the route, but would have the satisfaction of being first. Since the route on the spur is well established, leading was not as important as it was on the ridge.

In traditional Himalayan practice, rotating teams establish camps, then descend to a lower altitude to rest and gain strength, and move back up one camp per day. We agreed instead that the most effective use of our resources would be to ascend continuously. Each summit team would move up as fast as the team ahead of it vacated camps. The system gave everyone a personal chance at the summit and assured a good acclimatization schedule. If good weather held, we thought four teams might reach the top. Morrissey and Duenwald worked out a scheme of camp occupation based on the estimated arrival of the monsoon. Agreement was possible in the common ground between the idea that a delayed advance meant a better personal chance for the summit, and the belief that it really was the most sensible way to advance teams.

Lev was the only implacable critic—he wanted to share in the route-finding —so Duenwald, still sporadically wielding his deputy leader's imperium, told him to go on ahead with the first party. Lev moved to Camp II and pitched in with the carries to Camp III. The Sherpas were baffled by our lengthy discussions; in their experience, expedition leaders did not tolerate collective decision making. And while they could accept the idea of getting a single team to the summit as a postulated necessity of the business, the thought of getting everyone to the summit seemed to them to be tempting fate.

While the carries continued, the wind, the exposure, and the cramped tents made life at Camp II uncomfortable while life at Camp I settled into an easy pace of cycled working, resting, and eating. The porters kept up mail service. Lyman, working in the ice cave, made an oven by placing a small pot on a pile of carabiners on the bottom of a big pot, then covering the big pot and setting it on a butane stove. His biscuits and fruit turnovers were a rare treat and a potent bribe to get people out of the sack. Sonam Girmi shared his carefully husbanded *rakshi* with Duenwald and Harvard one night. It took very little alcohol to turn the cold snow cave at 21,400 feet into the hilly woods of Washington, or the rocky hills of the Solu-Khumbu. Ang Namgyal sat in the corner of the snow cave, expressing his disapproval of the camp, and courting the Bumba's outrage by spitting on the floor and into the pile of snow for meltwater. The winds grew stronger, and heavy snows more frequent.

Long stormy days passed in a snow cave or a cozy tent are the gestation time for other climbs, other adventures. If it is cold, plans mention hot granite slabs, dry desert sandstone, and warm beaches; if the mountain seems big, the plans call for delicate short climbs on Alpine peaks; if it's a long time until the next meal, the visions are of roast lamb in a high Andean meadow, or trout in the Wind River range of Wyoming. Morrissey, Thompson, and Harvard planned a raft trip in East Africa; Young thought of rock climbs in Yosemite. Bech told of his idea for a trekking service in Nepal where he could employ the expedition's Sherpas. Fear planned a trip to South America for the coming months, listening to tales of the great tributary rivers of the Amazon, and talked of new routes in the Cordillera Blanca.*

Altitude and exposure began to sap the strength of the expedition. After a hard carry to the site of Camp III, Peterson, Anderson, and Lev had to return to Base Camp. Peterson was exhausted, Lev, poorly acclimatized, had a bad case of laryngitis which changed his lilting western drawl to a frustrated squeak, and Anderson had suffered superficial frostbite on one hand when he briefly removed a mitten to adjust a crampon strap. Wind, cold, and dry air made sore throats and sharp hacking coughs common. Rennie separated rib cartilages in his chest in a spasm of coughing; Young mistook sleeping pills for cough suppressant and took to his bed for three days to sleep off the mistake. Hemorrhoids plagued various members from time to time. Although theories abound, no one is certain why high altitude climbers are particularly susceptible to them, but they are a problem of legendary proportions in the high mountains.

Camp III was established on April 29, and occupied, after a day of storm, by Bech, Reichardt, Roskelley, and Ngawang Samden on May 1, with Nang Tenzing and Pasang Tenzing carrying loads. Duenwald, Thompson, Harvard, and Sonam Girmi moved up to Camp II as the second wave, in support of the team above. Camp III at 24,500 feet was far more secure and comfortable than Camp II. Camp III was exposed to the wind, but nestled among rock outcroppings instead of hanging over an abyss. The rocks provided an illusion of security if not real protection from the wind. The views, as everywhere on the mountain, are spectacular—we could see Tibet, the Annapurnas, southern Nepal and, far to the south, the plains of India, where the monsoon front was beginning to form. At an altitude low enough to appreciate such things, the site itself would be called an idyllic alpine setting, but at close to eight thousand meters, its beauty was austere and forbidding.

On May 2, while Nang Tenzing and Pasang Tenzing moved up to Camp III and the new team at Camp II rested, Bech, Reichardt, and Roskelley probed

* In late August of 1973, as this chapter was written, members of the expedition received the following note from Morrissey: "I had a call last night informing me that the greatest love affair I have ever witnessed is ended. Ron Fear has been secreted away by that harsh mistress death. How life could have allowed this to happen I cannot fathom. He loved her so. Was he not attentive enough? Was he not constantly extolling her virtues and recording for us her most secret places so that those who might not be so aware could share in his love? May his passing bring to us who knew him a new awareness, an increased sensitivity to that which he held most dear—Life."

Ron was lost, presumed dead, on the Urubamba River, not far from Machu Picchu in Peru.

Lyman straddles the crest of the southeast ridge.

Man, Kathmandu.

Woman drying grain, Bhiritanti.

Cornice Camp.

Porters, near Dampus Pass.

Breast Camp.

Carriers, near Dampus Pass.

Roskelley jumars across the bergschrund, southeast ridge route.

Morrissey sits in the ice cave, Camp I, northeast spur route.

Camp III, northeast spur route.

Ang Namgyal in the ice cave, Camp I, northeast spur route.

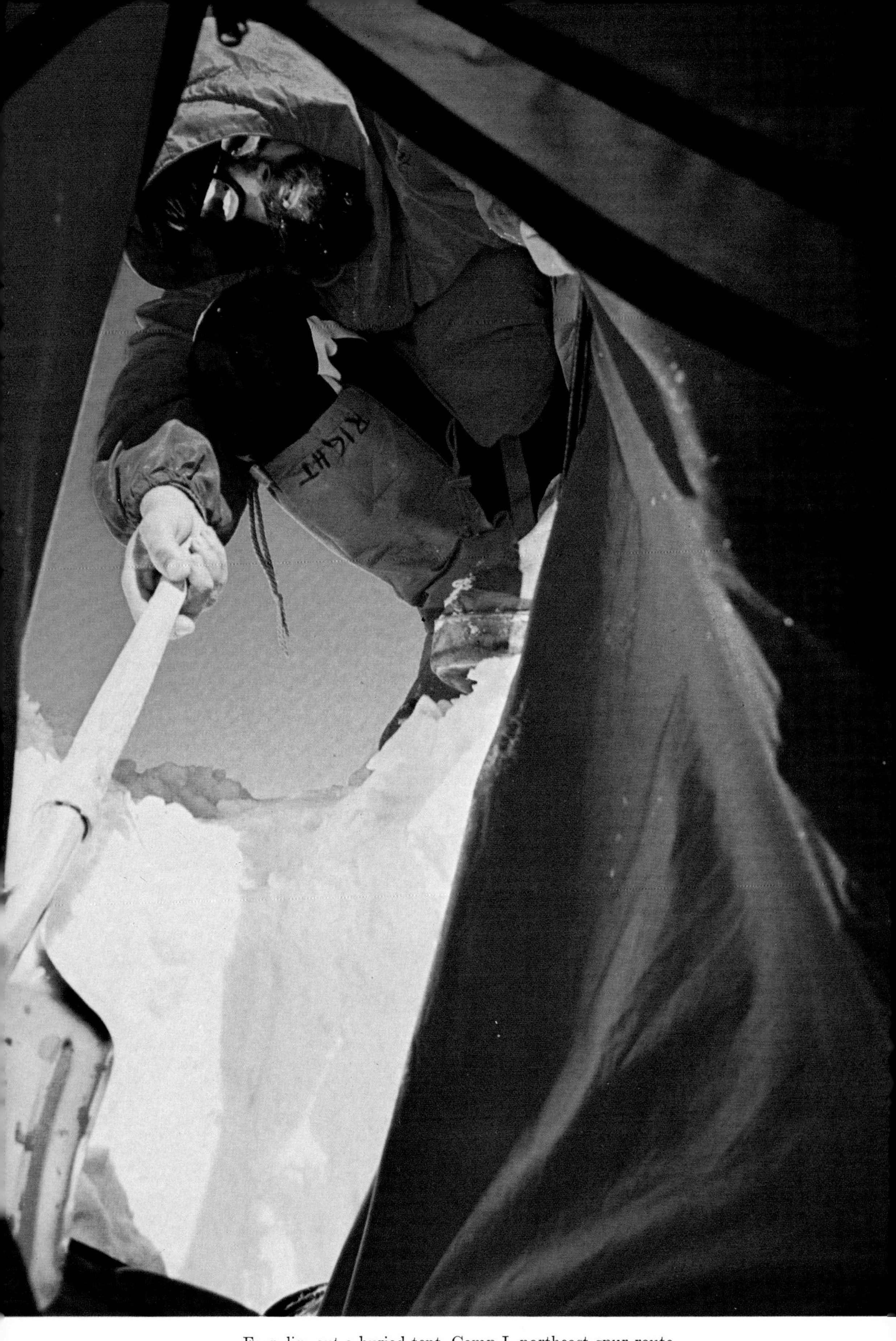

Fear digs out a buried tent, Camp I, northeast spur route.

Carriers approach Camp I, northeast spur route.

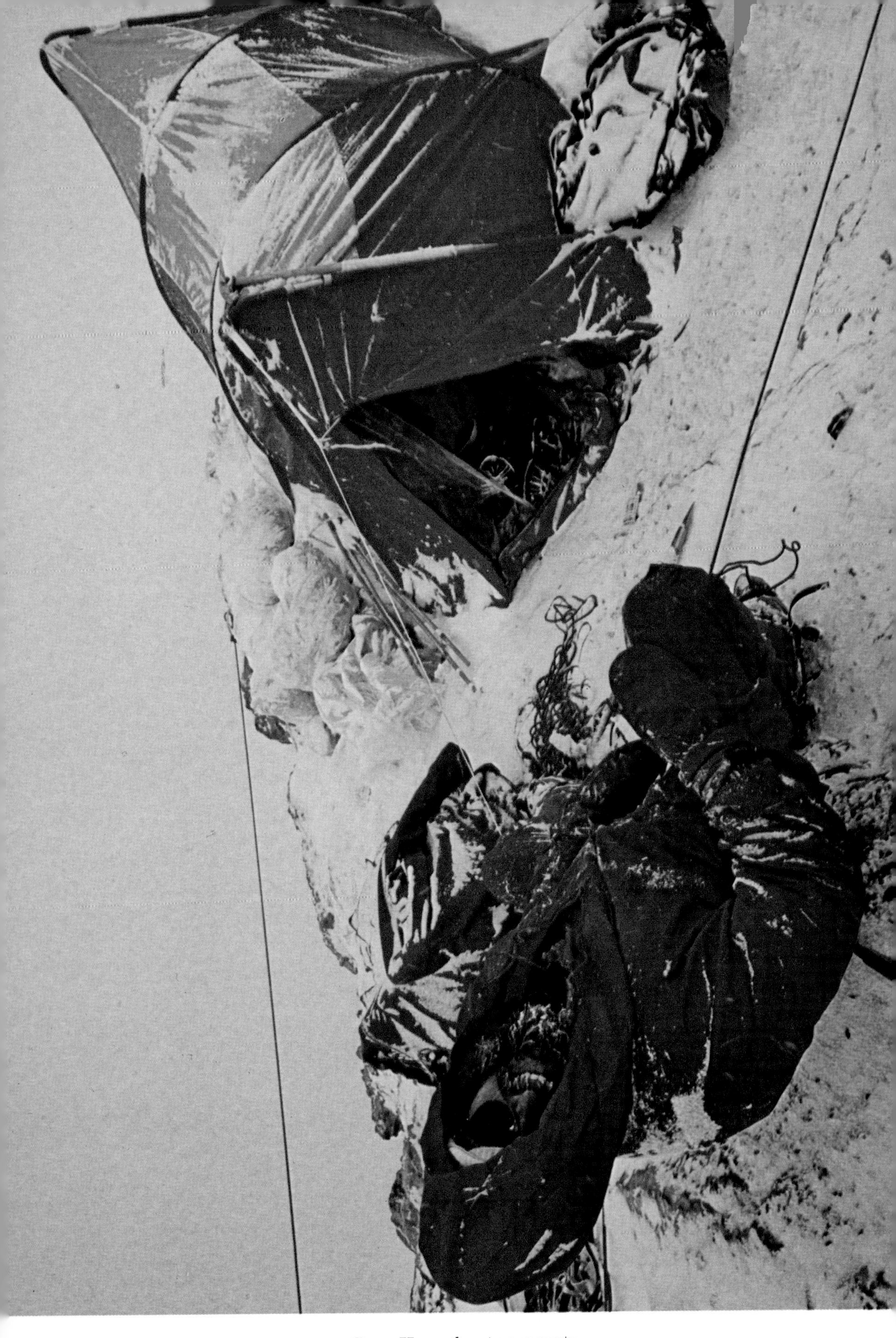

Camp II, northeast spur route.

Rennie treats Roskelley for frostbite after his return from the summit. Rennie compares the color of his hands, slightly blue from oxygen deficiency, with Roskelley's, pink from the sudden oxygen increase.

Dhaulagiri from below the icefall at dawn. The upper northeast spur is in highlight.

for the route above Camp III. "Immediately we chose the wrong route and wasted valuable hours trying to follow a ghostly rope fixed by a previous expedition. We decided that a better route had to be found," Roskelley recalled. He had tried one gully, then Reichardt tried another, finding the snow only a brittle layer over downsloping rock, and then wondered why earlier expeditions had gone that way. They ate a quick lunch, and set off again, dropping slightly below their camp to a snow ramp which led diagonally up toward the summit. Roskelley remembers the slope as "set for slab avalanche, loaded with wet snow." Bech and Reichardt fixed a few hundred feet of rope along their route, then returned to camp. They had covered a reasonable distance, but gained less than 150 vertical feet. The following morning was clear, with high winds. Over the howling of the wind, the climbers at Camp III heard the slope avalanche, clearing itself for safer travel. When the wind didn't die down, they declared a rest day.

At Camp II, Duenwald, Harvard, and Sonam Girmi prepared to make a carry. It was a clear, cold morning; windy, but not unreasonably so. After breakfast, the three sat outside the tents packing loads and strapping on their crampons. Suddenly Sonam Girmi looked up, alert, and then the wind crashed over them. First a shock, then just steady force all around them. The tents bowed, parkas filled, and the temperature dropped. Unable to stand, they crouched and blinked at each other. High above, puffy clouds drifted by unruffled. Four thousand feet below, at Base Camp, climbers were sunbathing. At Camp II, three crouching figures could not even stand, and the fourth, still inside, had to hold down the tent. Slowly, as their toes and fingers numbed, they realized that the wind was not going to die down while they squatted there, so they hung their loads on a piton and crawled back in the tent. The loads were to hang there a long time.

The two weeks that followed should have seen a steady, orderly progress to the summit, as successive teams moved up the mountain. Instead, days of high winds and storm made it the most frustrating time any of us had spent in the mountains. Dhaulagiri's weather froze us in place. Although the Swiss called it the mountain of storms, it had given them a respite in 1960. The Sherpas knew Dhaulagiri as the mountain with the meanest weather in Nepal; on the northwest end of the range, there are no big mountains to shelter Dhaulagiri from storms sweeping down from Tibet. The wind had been with us since Windy Corner; we thought we could deal with its power and unpredictability. But now, we ran up against the wind as a solid obstacle: it was intangible, we could not come to terms with it as a negotiable problem, but it stopped us like a blank wall across our path. It didn't come in swirling, gritty gusts as it had at Windy Corner, chopping at us with bursts of energy, but as a solid, steady presence of power and noise.

Life in the camps settled to a daily routine, beginning with an expectation of a change in the weather. In Camp III, Reichardt and Ngawang Samden, Bech and Roskelley, and Nang Tenzing and Pasang Tenzing shared tents. The simple tasks of cooking, eating, and keeping warm with the simple diversions of reading and writing suddenly were capable of filling whole days. Reichardt wrote home: "The major problem is keeping hydrated and fed. You just sit here feeling water and energy flow away. Wind permitting, I am capable of sleeping eighteen hours a day. I'm just amazingly lethargic. I'm definitely losing strength sitting here. I've got a cough, which is, I suspect, just the altitude, but I don't feel debilitated. In fact, it's quite comfortable here. Only getting out of the tent to handle bodily necessities is really nasty. Today I almost got frostbitten in a wind the velocity of which reached, I believe, two hundred miles per hour." Cramped and noisy as they were, the tents were a comfortable refuge; the security they offered was far out of proportion to the actual strength of their thin nylon walls. The tents were islands, isolated in silence by the noisy sea of wind. Though they were only a few feet apart, the occupants were remote from each other, and they communicated by radio when they couldn't shout over the wind.

The days of waiting were not days of physical stress, but each one took its toll of our health and slim reserves of physical strength. Camps II and III were above the altitude to which men can acclimatize, in the "death zone" where gradual physical deterioration occurs regardless of preparation or diet. In this zone, colds develop, coughs get worse, minor infections do not heal, climbers begin to lose weight, and altitude-linked neurological problems, like impaired balance, begin to emerge. Awareness of time changes. Days are made up of tasks, not hours, and the time tasks occupy has no relation to the time between tasks. The hour it takes to write a letter is longer than the three hours it took to decide to write it. Generally, simple tasks take much longer than they would at low altitude; putting boots on can be a thirty-minute job, alternately leaning forward to struggle with frozen leather, then straightening up to suck in huge, gasping breaths. Thoughts tend to be simple, but not necessarily clear or accurate. The line between sleeping and waking blurs. Time passes imperceptibly. Fear talked about whole days when he and his tent-mate could not remember a single thing they did. The commitment to climb increases as the climber's reference to physical realities diminishes. A man's will hardens as his body weakens, and as the distinction between dream and reality fades for a climber at high altitude, a remembered commitment is reassuringly concrete, needing no questions, no reasons, no thoughts.

In Camp III, as the days of wind wore on, Bech developed an ear infection; Reichardt lost his voice to laryngitis; Roskelley fumed at inactivity, and the Sherpas were silent. As the storm ate away at the time, and they ate away at the supplies, the expedition's chance of multiple ascents dwindled. Instead of being the first wave, they were becoming the last resort.

Camp II was not a comfortable place to wait. The tents at Camp II were completely exposed to the wind, and very precariously pitched, conditions which brought the weather indoors. Duenwald and Harvard occupied one tent, Thompson a second, and Sonam Girmi the third. There were stoves in Thompson's and Sonam Girmi's tents; when the weather allowed they ate crowded together in Thompson's tent. The schedule gradually changed from three short meals to one long one a day, to eliminate dangerous trips between tents. Duenwald and Harvard could crawl from the entrance of their tent and half-climb, half-slide down ten feet of rope to crash through the front door of Thompson's tent. Sonam Girmi had to put on crampons to jumar up the twenty feet from his tent. Meals in Camp II were important social events, though the sociability was briefly threatened when Harvard, whose digestive system had been disrupted by codeine cough syrup, developed an inability to hold his food down. He would eat voraciously, smile contentedly, and then throw the whole thing up into a plastic bag. Whoever was nearest the door would throw the bag out, signaling the end of the meal. It didn't bother Harvard nearly as much as it did those who had to watch, but he wasn't getting enough to eat.

In a safe, warm hole, a wind howling outside can be a soothing thing, but in a small, insecure tent, it banishes all hope of comfort. One is never at ease; there is a sense of constant interruption. One sits immobile, but does not rest. During an afternoon of wind watching, Duenwald wrote to his wife: "As I have said before, this is like putting in time in a jail—a very uncomfortable jail. I am sure that no one could design a system of confinement which could rival this for punishment." Seventy days earlier, on a truck crossing the plains of India, he had written, "No adventure is good unless you pay the price. Painful experiences make an adventure worth while." No one was ready to argue that this adventure was not worth while.

The exercise in getting to a meal, and the talk during it were as nourishing as the food itself. The high altitude food was disappointing; many of the goodies we sought down below were unattractive at altitude. There was for once too little starch, and not enough tea. We craved butter and we needed quantities of hard candy to soothe sore throats. We lived on soup, rice, cheese, and dry meat, with some puddings and chocolate. Canned cakes and canned cookies were the backbone of the diet, but they never lasted long. Fluids were a constant problem. Supplies of clean ice and snow within an arm's reach of the tent door were soon depleted, leaving the choice of roping up to forage or using off-color snow. Cooking was a protracted operation, and a dangerous one, because precariously balanced pots could easily be knocked over, and often were. There was little room and no flat space for cooking, so a delicate pot-on-stove arrangement had to be balanced on a rickety base and shored up by piles of equipment, held by hand, or both. If one opened the tent a bit for ventilation, spindrift snow poured in; if one left it closed, steam would condense heavily on the nylon and then rain inside. In compromise, we generally got both spindrift and condensation. Small, lightweight pressure cookers were a great help at altitudes where an open pot of water boils at less than 150 degrees, turning food to mush before it can cook properly. But a pressure cooker which blows a valve or is accidentally opened inside can create a blizzard of its own when the outpouring of steam condenses on the cold tent walls.

Huddled in the tent at Camp II, the climbers talked of everything but the mountain, and every kind of weather but wind. They hiked, sailed, cut trees, harvested wheat, dined on haute cuisine, drank heady old wines and planted new grapes. Sonam Girmi took them to Namche Bazaar, to his wife and sons and cattle. They listened to Sonam Girmi's tales of eighteen other expeditions, and of his dreams for his eldest son, destined for a post in Kathmandu's government bureaucracy. The wind drew them back to the Himalaya. Sonam Girmi told them of the spirits of mountains, of the power of mountains over men. He liked the Dhaulagiri region, because he had always had good luck there, on Annapurna and on Tukche Peak, but most Sherpas were suspicious of the place —it was too far from home, the weather was always bad, and the winds blew without reason. Dhaulagiri would let us reach the summit, he was confident of that, but why did we want to try for a multiple ascent? That he did not understand, nor did he think the mountain understood.

Each day dawned frustratingly clear; the features of the mountain were sharp, but the wind continued. The aluminum poles and fiberglass wands in the tents broke one by one, so the tents became amorphous bags of red nylon, alternately puffing out like balloons and slapping tightly down around those inside. On the days when the wind was strongest, Sonam Girmi did not leave his tent. The wind was deafening, but through its noise, Duenwald, Harvard, and Thompson could hear the chant of Sonam Girmi's prayers. His steady low monotone was set against the high erratic fury of the wind; the prayers had a patience and serenity that balanced the wind's aggressiveness.

In Camp I, the winds were not as high, but heavy snows kept everyone busy. It often took two men four hours to dig out a single tent after one night's snow. Movement between Camps II and III was impossible, but the carry from Camp I to Camp II was feasible, although extremely unpleasant. Rennie and Smith attempted it but were forced down short of Camp II; Morrissey and Gyaltzen made it, but arrived seriously exhausted. Morrissey pushed himself to reach the camp because he was worried about the health of its occupants, making one of the highest house calls on record. When he got there, his patients prescribed hot tea, a rest and immediate descent. Over the radio each night, optimistic plans were discussed for the next day's movements. We began to stretch our radio contacts, savoring the diversion as we built a network of highly independent broadcasters. Each morning, the terse reports from Camps II and III told of more wind, with little hope of movement. At Base Camp, Lev, Lyman, Young, and Fear convalesced, then returned to Camp I to watch for progress. Anderson, sidetracked by his frostbite, and Peterson, turning his attention to his clipboard, began to consider the logistics of a safe withdrawal down the icefall and across the passes.

On the night of May 5, the wind blew as it had never done before. It seemed to skin the mountain, and Camp II, exposed as it was, was literally blown apart. Sleep was normally an uneasy proposition there, but that night no one even tried to sleep. Duenwald and Harvard sat fully clothed and booted as their tent danced on its tiny platform, ominously close to the void. They were of course roped, but they were painfully aware of the weakness of their anchor. The other two tents fared little better. In the morning, the four climbers in Camp II were as exhausted as after a hard day's work, and the camp was a shambles—cooking was impossible. Thompson couldn't talk, Duenwald had headaches, Harvard was weak from dehydration and Sonam Girmi was ill-at-ease. The morning radio contact was brief, and discouraging: Camp III couldn't move, but would try if the wind died; Camp I was freshly buried, but had ample healthy manpower there; at Base Camp all was serene. Camp II was a blown-up link in the chain. The three sahibs and the sirdar conferred, and quickly, dully, agreed to go down to be replaced. Their role was support, but on the morning of the sixth, they were barely able to support themselves. They had all been strong proponents of the group goal, so the pain of retreating was not personally unbearable. Actually, the pain was nonexistent: when Duenwald asked, rhetorically, if everyone felt all right, Harvard replied, "Jeffrey, I don't feel a thing . . ."

The wind did drop later in the day at Camp III, so Roskelley and Ngawang Samden set out to probe the route above the May 2 high point. "The cold was extreme, but we had had enough of sitting in tents," Roskelley recalled. They rounded a rock buttress and climbed up the wide gully using the buried fixed ropes. From the ridge at the head of the gully, they began a long climb to the junction of the upper ribs of the southeast ridge and the northeast spur. They cached loads for Camp IV at the site of the Swiss high camp, a precarious rocky ledge, and investigated a site for Camp IV, a sheltered step about two hundred feet above, at 25,700 feet.

Their return to Camp III was joyous, but the joy was short-lived; the evening brought the return of the winds, and everyone was pinned down again. At Base Camp, the team just down from Camp II was set to enjoy a night of comfort, of actually lying down to sleep, of being able to take boots off, of warmth and silence and peace. However, a sudden night storm dropped two feet of heavy wet snow on the col, and crushed two tents before their sleeping occupants could react. Groggy climbers woke up to the weight of snow and wet nylon as the tents caved in, struggled for boots, pants, and mittens in a close darkness, then cut the tents open, dug themselves out, and staggered into the storm to look for other shelter. After a miserable search, they found a place in the frozen muck on the cooktent floor.

Morrissey returned to Base Camp with a bronchial infection, and an unexplained ability to cough up pieces of his pharynx. He would start to gag, and then work up a chunk of the stuff, roll it around in his mouth, spit it into his hand and proceed to examine it with clinical *sang-froid*. That was all right, but he insisted on showing it to his friends, and speculating on just what part of his respiratory system had produced it. He had his throat and the specimens photographed. He stored one piece in a film can for study after the expedition, but forgot about it, put a roll of exposed film in the can and sent the whole thing off with a shipment to *National Geographic*. Lyman continued to have trouble with his legs, a problem diagnosed as neuritis. Both Ang Dawa and Gyaltzen were under the weather, with coughs, headaches, sore throats, and general malaise, and Sonam Tsering was beginning to show the emotional strain of his physical disability. Above Base, the climbers were beginning to show clear signs of physical wear. Psychologically, most people were convinced that everyone else was slowly losing his mind, but that it would be a breach of etiquette to tell them so. The doctors recognized definite symptoms, but the only illness was altitude, and the only prescription would be: "Go down."

There were other hazards too. Late one evening in Base Camp, Lyman had just finished baking a double chocolate layer cake when one of the Bluet bottled gas stoves he was using ran out of fuel. The other stove stayed lit. To insert a new butane cartridge in the stove, the burner unit must be removed, then replaced after the new cartridge is in position. As the four others in the tent dumbly watched Lyman force the butane tank against the sharp point on the burner without sealing the junction, they wondered when he would realize his mistake. No one spoke, unconsciously carrying the important, and by now habitual, group-living expedient of minding one's own business to its natural limits. Suddenly a three-foot ball of flame erupted in the tent, jumping from the stove in Lyman's hands. Five men dove for two exits. Morrissey, who had been sitting in the center of the tent, was the first out, and spent the afternoon embellishing the story for the evening radio broadcast. "I guess I shouldn't have done it that way," Lyman allowed, as the five stood beside the charred alumi-

The route above Camp III on the northeast spur.

John Roskelley and Ngawang Samden on the summit of Dhaulagiri.

num and fiberglass superstructure, great chunks of melted nylon flapping in the breeze.

The storms continued. On the night of May 8, Langbauer woke at Camp I in a fit of coughing. He was sharing a close, stuffy tent with Smith; snow had piled around the tent, sealing off circulation. The coughing was followed by hyperventilation, which brought on coughing again. The cycle accelerated, and increased in severity. Prostrate, Langbauer perceived the symptoms of shock develop in himself; he was suddenly cold, and on the verge of blacking out. Smith called to Lev and Fear in a nearby tent. They brought an oxygen system from the snow cave, and Langbauer was given oxygen at four liters per minute to steady his breathing. No one was sure what the trouble was, but any therapy at high altitude includes oxygen, and Langbauer's gasping needed quick attention. He warmed quickly, and his breathing regularized as his cyanotic blue skin turned a healthier pink. He slept well on two liters a minute that night, and went down to Base Camp the next day. After a clinical conference which considered the problems of too much carbon dioxide (from the climbers), too much carbon monoxide (from the stoves), too little fresh air (the tent was nearly buried), and too little oxygen in the air anyway, the medical community of three physicians, a veterinarian, and an ex-army medic collectively shrugged: "It's the altitude."

On the morning of the ninth, Bech in Camp III woke again with a troublesome earache. It had begun a few days earlier as he sat waiting for good weather. He had tried antibiotics, but the pain became worse, and he now had to admit it was not going to go away. Bech, a concert violist, could not afford to gamble with his hearing. Resignedly, he descended to Base Camp, where he announced that he had come down in order to conserve supplies at Camp III while the bad weather lasted. On examination, Rennie found a severe middle-ear infection on its way from bad to worse. It was a painful disappointment for everyone, and a personal disaster for Bech: he had worked harder than anyone on the spur. His determination gave strength to others, and his cheer was an endless resource. He, more than anyone else, symbolized the efforts on the spur.

On the tenth the weather finally broke, with a warm, windless day. In Camp III, Roskelley, Reichardt, and Ngawang Samden made loads of sleeping bags, tents, and ropes; Pasang Tenzing and Nang Tenzing loaded up the Camp IV food bag, stoves, fuels, and ensolite tent floors and the five started up. Roskelley and Ngawang Samden, in the lead, followed the route they had found four days before to the cache at their high point. They reflected on the available sites for Camp IV, choosing a sheltered snow bowl, flat enough to pitch a tent in com-

Roskelley carried down from Base Camp.

Afternoon at Base Camp.

fort and reminiscent of the soft mountains of the American northwest. Reichardt, Roskelley, and Nawang Samden pitched a single tent while Pasang Tenzing and Nang Tenzing scurried back to Camp III in the face of the afternoon storm.

That night, they enjoyed the goodies in a special high altitude food bag: tea, soup, butter, mashed potatoes, and savory, if not particularly digestible, freeze-dried fruit, vegetables, and chili. Outside, the Dhaulagiri winds returned, and with them, new snow.

"The eleventh never dawned," Roskelley later wrote. From top to bottom the mountain was battered by wind. The three were comfortable in the tent, moving little, talking less: Reichardt was forced into silent reverie by laryngitis, Ngawang Samden is a taciturn man, and Roskelley was not inclined to monologue. Reichardt began to suffer a slight loss of balance. When he was not concentrating, he would lean slightly to one side. Imbalance made walking difficult, and it was a threat to the stability of teacups and soupbowls in his hands. That evening, Bech and Morrissey gave them an optimistic weather forecast based more on hope than conviction. The weather simply had to let them go; they could not wait at nearly twenty-six thousand feet for long. The good weather prediction was taken as gospel in Camp IV because that was the easiest way to take it. They went to bed early and slept well.

"Hooray! Hooray! For the twelfth of May. Outdoor screwing starts today!" Rennie cheerfully greeted Pinzo at Base Camp the next morning. "Tea, sahib?" ventured Pinzo, waist-deep in yesterday's new snow, as he looked down into Rennie's tent-pit. "They're going to make the summit today," said Bech from a neighboring pit. In a third, the Bumba argued briefly with Roskelley at Camp IV over whether carrying a radio to the summit would be an act of desecration; more to the point, thought Roskelley, a radio weighs more than a pound. Morrissey gave up, wished them luck, and sent them the blessing and hopes of the rest of the climbers in camp. Beyond that, they would be alone.

May 12 had dawned clear in Camp IV but, as always, windy. Reichardt, Roskelley, and Ngawang Samden got up at five to the routine of preparation followed every day regardless of weather. They cooked, melted snow, and ate breakfast between spurts of dressing, a difficult task in the cramped tent. Some time after seven, they unceremoniously piled out of the tent into a howling gale. The zipper on the tent froze open. Reichardt struggled to close it. Roskelley roped and took off, Ngawang followed, and Reichardt went third. Stiff muscles and empty lungs rebelled, but the warmth of movement and a slow pace quieted bodily complaints. The going was easy at first. The route rises to a hummock, an annoying obstacle that does provide some protection from the wind, and then follows a long ridge which grows rockier toward the summit. The ridge is narrow, dropping off steeply on both sides, with a series of tantalizing false summits. Clouds hid the glaciers below. There was some deep snow, and a few crevasses, but the route was otherwise straightforward. At the end of a moderate ice slope, they rested, then Reichardt took the lead.

Reaching one snow hump he was convinced would be the summit, Reichardt maneuvered the seventy-five-foot rope so that they could all climb the last few feet together. As the three reached the top of the hump, they saw "peaks that looked like the Sierra Nevada, with the summit out there among them." The scale blew up before them. Rather than standing on the summit, they found themselves dwarfs atop a subsidiary blip on a great ridge that rose magnificently before them. It was discouraging. It seemed to Reichardt like "walking from Lone Pine to Mount Whitney." The ridge continued in a confusing series of stubby spires with no identifiable summit in sight. Slipping back into the dull half-consciousness that hard work at high altitude brings on, they crossed a col, then climbed both on and off of the ridge. Winds made the going treacherous. At one point the ridge turned into a knife-edge of rock, so they moved along *au cheval,* straddling with one leg on each side. After turning a small buttress on its left side, they finally found themselves just below the true summit.

Roskelley took the lead. Spurred by a pressing desire to unrope and relieve himself, he stumbled up the last rock steps, climbed the left side of the summit block and dropped his pack. As Roskelley searched for a sheltered spot below the summit block, Ngawang Samden and Reichardt gained the summit. After five hours climbing from Camp IV, the three climbers stood squinting at each other in the wind at 26,795 feet, on an island in the clouds. Each was lost in his own thoughts, and his own understanding of where they were, how, and why. Ngawang Samden was silent, impassive; Roskelley was intense; Reichardt remote. Altitude slowed their emotions and isolated them from each other. Roskelley eyed Reichardt—a pensive silence or a staggering muteness? Reichardt saw the question, but only later understood it. He dropped a glove, which landed near Roskelley. "Why doesn't he pick it up?" thought Reichardt. "Why doesn't he pick it up?" thought Roskelley.

Mechanically, they started the obligatory job of photographing flags. A vestigial custom inherited from European alpine clubs of an earlier era, the practice of placing summit flags has survived its original purpose. Once a symbol of conquest with roots in the chauvinism of exploration, and in keeping with the man-over-nature approach to climbing a mountain, flags are now more a symbol of communion, of the spirit with which climbers and mountains briefly become as one, sharing secrets.

Photographing at 26,795 feet was painfully slow and difficult, but important as a universal rite of the mountains. That it was also a commercial obligation for the expedition would not have been reason enough for the effort. As Roskelley took the first picture, his camera broke. Reichardt took over, and superficially frostbit the tips of three fingers in the process. Each flag had to be dug out of a pack, and then held out in a wind that threatened to tear it apart. The wind further blunted motions already slowed by altitude. A tiny American flag was followed by a gigantic National Geographic Society flag; a bright Nepalese flag was added, making too great a handful. The Explorers Club flag remained crumpled in the pack. Though the wind was fierce, they managed to smile, or at least grimace heroically. National flags borrowed pride of accomplishment from the numbed climbers, but symbolically the most important was a Tibetan prayer flag which Reichardt had brought from the United States. Ngawang Samden translated the text selected for the expedition: After a series of invocations to the gods to hear the prayers, it stated that when it was flown from a high mountain, it would bring safety to all creatures beneath it in all directions.

They shared almost an hour with the summit, then left. Roskelley's feet were cold.

Reflections of the Mountain

The descent from the summit to Camp IV took two and three-quarter hours. Roskelley's feet had lost all feeling. Reichardt climbed slowly, laboriously balancing himself with each step, vaguely aware of his mild ataxia. More frustrating was his laryngitis, which made talking nearly impossible at moments when the emotional need to communicate was greatest. A few days later he dictated these recollections of the descent: "I had switched to down clothing for the first time and my suspenders had been of the wrong type: buttons not clamps, so I had no way of holding my pants up. The descent was very slow because of me. The combination of my balance and pants problems was lethal, and I was completely unable to talk. I was in no particular difficulty, but could not keep up with John's pace without falling quite often, so, as we were past the summit spires, I sat down, untied the rope, and said that I could proceed on my own. John was very reasonable although he probably thought he had a corpse on his hands and insisted that I tie in again. Anyway, I accomplished my major purpose, which was to go down at my own speed. I guess it was just crazy, but I might have been better off alone, because I would have stopped to fix my pants. I think I was the only person ever to come off Dhaulagiri with a bare ass."

Roskelley warmed socks over a Bluet stove and put them on his chilled feet during the night at Camp IV, allowing himself to realize at last that his feet might be seriously frostbitten. He did not sleep. Reichardt too was worn after nineteen days above twenty-three thousand feet. The physicians attributed his balance problems and an inability to distinguish left from right on the summit day and descent to a tiny hemorrhage on the left side of his cerebellum at the base of the brain: such hemorrhages are not uncommon with the increased capillary activity in the body's attempt to acclimatize. By comparison with his debilitated companions, Ngawang Samden was fit and apparently unaffected by the altitude, a strong, quiet man.

Early on May 13, Roskelley bolted for Base Camp before Reichardt and

Ngawang Samden were up. He later wrote a description of his descent: "My descent was rapid. The slope below Camp IV was avalanche prone and wind slabbed. I fell or slipped many times from exhaustion. I was weak and my load was heavy. The snow slope near Camp III and Camp II was horrible: I kept falling. Lowell Smith and Ron Fear greeted me at Camp II and I read some two-month-old letters from my wife that hadn't reached me up high. After resting I clipped into the line and continued the descent; the slope was easier and I felt better. At Camp I, I gave my pack to Sonam Tsering and continued on alone. I was warmer and the wind had died: things looked good. Just before Base Camp came into sight, I stepped up to my crotch in a crevasse, and continued a little shaken. Several hundred yards from camp, I could not hold my feelings any longer and I sat down in a peaceful spot and cried until I felt better. I got up and went over a small hill to see Terry and Jeff coming out to greet me. I couldn't have asked for more: I was down and the warmth of Base Camp cheered my heart. It was over."

Those in Base Camp watched him walk the last ten minutes to camp, down a little incline and then across the flat: a hero returned from an odyssey certainly, but like most modern heroes, he presented himself not as a conqueror but as an agent of circumstance. His first comment was an offhand compliment to Skow, whom he had not seen since Pokhara, for his work on the airdrops. The resident underemployed physicians jumped on their case. Roskelley was hustled inside, where his feet were placed in a basin of 105-degree water while he breathed oxygen at an extravagant five liters per minute. In seconds, the oxygen made him pink-skinned and healthy looking, showing the others how blue and cyanotic they looked. He sat in the dining humpy, an oxygen mask on his head, his pants and long underwear rolled up to his knees, reading old letters from his wife. The oxygen equipment hid most of his face, and his frame drooped from exhaustion, but his eyes sparkled under the canvas helmet.

People hovered near by, solicitously checking the water temperature and badgering him with questions about the summit. It is difficult to judge the extent of frostbite damage until a month or two after treatment begins, but Rennie was optimistic enough to say: "John, you have absolutely the longest toes I have ever seen. A half-inch off here and there shouldn't make the least difference!" Roskelley laughed, Rennie's remark echoed an old fear he and his wife had discussed during hectic days of trying to find boots large enough to fit Roskelley's size thirteen feet.* Rennie did not mention his biggest worry: the possibility of severe infection if Roskelley's evacuation from the mountain was not clean, rapid, and immediate.

* At this writing John Roskelley is climbing in the Canadian Rockies after losing one joint from one toe and two from another.

Ngawang Samden and Reichardt started the three-hour descent to Camp III at midmorning. Ngawang stayed at Camp III to talk with Pasang Tenzing and Nang Tenzing, descending later in the day to Camp I, while Reichardt continued alone to Camp II. On the face above Camp II, Reichardt met Fear, who was on his way to Camp III for the second summit try. They talked briefly; Fear offered to go down with Reichardt. Reichardt croaked that he could make it alone. Lev, Young, and Smith were in Camp II, also on their way up. Reichardt spent the night in Camp II, where Smith fed and rehydrated him.

On the next day, as the expedition's upward momentum centered in Camps II and III, Ngawang Samden and Reichardt reached Base Camp. Reichardt did not leave Camp II until afternoon, and would not have come all the way down had Morrissey not gone up from Base Camp to Camp I and led him down by moonlight. In the thick air at 19,300 feet, as Reichardt's voice returned, Reichardt and Roskelley could smile about the tension and isolation felt near the summit.

Roskelley was carried down to R&R in relays on the fifteenth. He was in great pain and had been given injections of demerol, a pain suppressant, but could not take his evacuation seriously and, he said, felt silly about burdening others. Singing snatches of "Sunshine Superman," he rode pickaback on a seat made of broken snowshoes, supported by a tumpline. Pemba Chotar and Hackpa Dorje, porters who had worked carrying loads up the Myagdi Glacier, did most of the carrying on the relay to seventeen thousand feet and said they had never carried a man more comfortably. Roskelley sneaked across several crevasses on hands and knees while ladder crossings were being set up for him. He was nervous about being carried over steep sections, so insisted on being slid down on his back.

Duenwald and Skow accompanied Roskelley to Tukche. There, they heard that a light plane was due in nearby Jomsom, a lucky coincidence. Skow arranged for space on the plane for Roskelley and Duenwald, saving Roskelley the pain of a long trip overland. In Kathmandu, on May 19, Roskelley was presented with a bottle of champagne by Ambassador Laise while he relaxed in the comfort of Al Read's house. Duenwald and Roskelley left for the United States the next day.

The expedition was still making an active drive for the summit, but the time was short as the monsoon approached. Smith, Fear, Young, Lev, Pasang Tenzing and Nang Tenzing were together in Camp III on the fifteenth for a summit attempt if the weather held. The following day, all but Smith and Young moved to Camp IV. Base Camp was a convalescent ward of dubious support value for the teams still on the mountain. Sonam Girmi, Langbauer, and Lyman descended to R&R on May 13 to join Peterson and Anderson in organizing the withdrawal.

The climbers still high on the mountain wanted to go to the summit themselves. A climber's motivations and ambitions are essentially personal, though in some circumstances, particularly on large expeditions, personal achievement, at least in theory, is subordinated to group goals, sublimated in the rewards of team effort. But those rewards can become very poorly defined, and frustratingly vague.

Morrissey made the painful decision to establish an evacuation date. The choice for the actual date was based on Sonam Girmi's and Bech's considerable experience of the monsoon weather pattern. If the expedition was caught high on the mountain in heavy monsoon snows, getting everyone off would be dangerous. At the time the monsoon was approaching, and conditions on the icefall below Base Camp and on the long route over Dampus Pass were deteriorating as the days warmed. More risk was justifiable for the first summit team than for subsequent ascents. Two days were required to move one load from Base Camp to R&R, where the pressure would be off: it was the familiar logistic boggle.

The decision to leave on the twentieth sat heavily on the expedition. With Camps III and IV occupied, the summit seemed assured, well within the grasp of the climbers there. At Base Camp, where the support team was in limbo, the climbers were inclined to leave, but as a second summit day seemed near, they talked of taking their coughs and infections up "in support," following the others to the summit. But the wind and the waiting returned.

During these days, the expedition was spread from the highest camps to the lowest on the mountain, with Duenwald, Roskelley, and Skow out in the valley. Since radios were line-of-sight walkie-talkies, we could not communicate directly between some of the camps, but had to relay messages. The daily radio contacts, particularly the evening one, seemed consumingly important, not so much for the content of the messages, but for their entertainment value and for the reassuring idea that we were indeed in regular communication, with the tacit assumption that someone, somewhere on the mountain, was in control. As the contacts became longer and longer, rhetorical styles grew florid. It happened that during these days Smith was at Camp II, the relay point through which Base Camp could communicate with Camp IV, R&R, Dampus Pass, or Duenwald in Tukche. Smith's precocious career on the radio had begun long before at Cornice Camp. As the advance party prepared to take off for French Pass, Smith, who stutters when he is not angry, reached for the radio. "Don't give him the radio," Fear had said, "we don't want . . . ah . . . any pauses . . ." his voice trailing off. Smith looked him in the eye: "There won't be," he said, and there weren't.

At the communication center, Smith became the moderator, and brought to the job remarkable zeal and admirable verbal agility.

"Tell the bastards if they don't carry through the icefall I'll kick their asses out of R&R," Morrissey would growl at Base Camp.

"Jim thinks you ought to carry down there," Smith would relay. "Fuck him. The mountain is falling down around us," would be R&R's answer to Smith, who would relay back to Morrissey, "They'll carry, but there's avalanche danger."

Smith would ramble on with the stamina and questionable humor common to late night announcers, while Morrissey's dinner got cold. Everyone waited to critique Smith's evening show: his enthusiasm as he monopolized the air time, chiding, lecturing, translating and interpreting, was a tonic. His weather reports listed three feet of snow as "some powder" and gale force winds as "a breeze." Lesser stars developed, and audience sophistication grew. Fear shied from over-complex discussions: he would turn his radio on, make a brief announcement of his intentions, and turn it off again. Morrissey mastered the technique of sleeping bag broadcasting, appearing some mornings to be a great blue caterpillar with a silver antenna. The antennae were directional, so if everyone stayed in the sack, or at least in a horizontal position, reception was good.

The quality of life at Base Camp steadily eroded. *War and Peace, The Decline and Fall of the Roman Empire,* Sartre and Aristotle retreated to frozen corners of grubby tents, giving way to *The Day of the Jackal, Thor* comics and even *Time* magazine. With two issues of *Time* in the mail, the Watergate affair invaded our mountain citadel. As gale winds blew outside the communal tent, we reclined in the squalor and detritus of two months' residence on the col, and read aloud of politicians running for cover back home. Their situation seemed absurd, ours quite reasonable.

As climbers descended through Base Camp from high on the mountain, Rennie clomped around camp in oversize white rubber boots emblazoned with a large "R" on each toe, ophthalmoscope in hand, peering into our eyes in search of retinal hemorrhages. His hypothesis was, roughly, that well-acclimatized people, such as all the members of the expedition, when climbing strenuously to high altitude, should not develop the hemorrhages that he had seen in unacclimatized subjects. Finding hemorrhages disproved Rennie's hypothesis, but he was not in the least upset by the results, gloating, rather, over the shape, size and color of the spots he photographed. At any rate, Rennie's lectures on physiology were good, and better when contested by Morrissey. A newly discovered hemorrhage was an event, and some of us learned to look for them; the retina is a wonderful thing to look at. For that matter, by then anything new was wonderful to look at.

The interesting retinae were photographed with the special camera in Rennie's humpy laboratory. Rennie made elaborate preparations for his appointments, which, in a vain attempt to avoid condensation in the camera, were only scheduled in certain weather conditions. He could be seen on clear mornings bent over a recalcitrant Tiny Tiger generator, damning condensation and apologizing for the noise and inconvenience of the whole business, which was slight, and nothing measured against its value as a diversion.

Weather prevented a summit attempt from Camp IV on May 17. Difficult as it was to believe, the weather was worse than it had been the week before. Nang Tenzing, who had stayed high for a chance at the summit, descended to Camp III, where Smith diagnosed frostbitten feet. He came down to Base and immediately put on the warm water and oxygen treatment. Only after his feet were in the water for a few minutes did we realize that the bluish color of his feet, thought to be a sign of tissue damage, was, in fact, sock dye. His feet were only numb, not frostbitten; his real problem was snowblindness, brought on by taking off his goggles in a whiteout during his descent.

With Sonam Girmi at R&R planning the Glacier Camp-to-Tukche section of the retreat, Ngawang Samden was in charge of dismantling operations above Base. He went to Camp I to see about digging out tents and sending selected loads down. Rennie went part way to Camp I to accompany him through the crevassed section on the lower half of the walk, then decided to return alone after he had untied and watched Ngawang Samden disappear upward in a low-visibility wind storm. He made his way down, the electricity in the air sparking from his pack-frame, and had to crawl over some troublesome crevasses without protection. He tumbled unexpectedly into the dining tent about lunch time, glowing with the light of terror, and told us about his adventure. Others spent the day inside making up loads of medical and personal equipment, throwing away what was superfluous. It brought tears to Morrissey's eyes to abandon sixty pounds of excess surgical equipment, but each additional load meant a dangerous carry in the icefall below. Climbers are not greedy, but they know the value of equipment, and fully expect to use things until they disintegrate. Many is the rescue party which has failed to find a body but has recovered climbing hardware.

The monsoon was in the air on the eighteenth, dumping three or four feet of snow on Dhaulagiri. The situation was like the one that stopped Ibañez, Watzl and Passang Dawa Lama in 1954. The new snow made climbing up unthinkable: the upward orientation of the expedition was over. Fear wrote

Crossing a snowbridge between Base Camp and R&R camp.

from Camp IV: "The eighteenth is here and we have to get down; there are six feet of new snow all over the mountain and all the members are worried about us up here. It is not so easy to leave when it takes fifteen minutes to put on one boot! Away we go at 12:30 P.M. (an early start), and we only have to get to Camp III one thousand feet below (hell, I could ski that in two minutes easy). Peter starts an avalanche in the first twenty feet that cleans the route most of the way: it was great. Then there is the downsloping rock section with three or four feet of new snow, and a long way to fall! Peter and I slip more than once; then Smith yells and we find the way to Camp III. Camp III is three people in a two-man tent with the wind trying to blow us off. All three of us have frozen feet, but when we put them on each other's chests they warm up!"

Young found shoulder-deep snow between Camps III and II on his descent. Across the valley, Annapurna had the same heavy snows; four Japanese and one Sherpa climbing there were killed in a snow avalanche that day during their retreat from a high camp.

The problem at Base Camp was not the wind but the danger of losing tents to the snow. Snow drifted quickly, and only frequent shoveling allowed those inside to breathe. Avalanches coming off the Eiger menaced climbers on the route to R&R. Large, wet snow slides crossed the trail to seventeen thousand feet, and although they generally came only at predictable times, before and after the heat of the day, they made everyone nervous about working there. A food shortage at R&R made the situation worse.

Young reached Camp I on the eighteenth and Base Camp the following day; Smith, Fear, and Lev arrived in Base Camp on the twentieth. Camps were abandoned intact; sleeping bags, radios, and oxygen were all that could be carried down; there was no hope of reaching the camps again in that snow. Lev called the northeast spur above Camp III "gorgeous." It reflects not a change in the mountain, but a difference in descriptive styles that neither he nor the summit team could find a troublesome rock wall and ice cliff detailed in the official account of the Swiss expedition. Fear said he had never spent three harder days in the mountains.

The icefall porters had been working hard taking loads down from Base Camp, and by the twentieth only about fifteen loads were left. We were ready to leave Dhaulagiri and high altitude living, yet we were still held by a strong attraction to it. R&R did not seem a pleasant prospect; we referred to it as "the pit," and felt that the food shortage, the pressures of daily carries under the avalanching Eiger, and its location on an ugly glacier made it an undesirable place to be. The last groups left Base Camp on the twenty-first and the

End-of-the-season snow on the moraine near Dampus Pass.

twenty-second, timing their departures to traverse under the Eiger after the heat of the day. Late in the afternoon the Myagdi Glacier was soft, showing many crevasses, and snow bridges over crevasses were weak. Crashing through snow bridges time after time; crawling along frozen ropes, squashed like bugs under heavy loads; staggering through wet drifts, the last climbers reached R&R after dark on the twenty-second.

While we had been deteriorating slowly higher up, the green things of lower altitudes did not occur to us, they never do. There, at a mere 15,500 feet, were mud, birds, and rich wet rocks oozing with life. To the onslaught of new smells, sounds, and textures, the seduction of our senses was quick, unquestioned, and complete.

The social climate at R&R was tense because the expedition was nearly over, because we were tired, and because the carries under the Eiger were a dangerous business. Nerves were jangled by the regular crashing sounds of breaking ice. Communication between the members was maintained not because we spoke the same language, but because we could all speak it with subtlety. Vast covert differences or antagonisms could be lost or accommodated in conversation so that living together and transacting the affairs of the expedition could progress smoothly. As a result, complicated interaction took place on a variety of levels. Tensions or hostilities could be expressed by non-verbal signals or shunted aside by conversational devices, while the main channels for communications were consciously kept open. It was not a perfect system, but it was a workable one.

Sonam Girmi devised a schedule to clear the icefall quickly so the members could leave. He called in support troops, the porters who had lived on Dampus Pass since early April as a sort of rear guard to keep curious trekkers out of our camps. As a matter of principle, we wouldn't leave until the last load was in R&R and the risk to any porters over. As a matter of tradition, the Sherpas insisted on one more load after our last one.

At 5 A.M. on May 23, a handful of members and seventeen Sherpas, including Sonam Girmi, some on a glacier for the first time, raced up to seventeen thousand feet and made a double carry to retrieve the final loads. It was a glorious morning, sunshine poured over the mountain, and, now that we were off Dhaulagiri, the wind stopped. The members, though they were almost useless in Sonam's mass operation, wanted to be the last off the mountain, but Sonam sent Nang Tenzing and Ang Shitah, one of the strongest of our porters, to eighteen thousand feet to recover a load that had been cached there the previous day. When the two Sherpas returned to R&R at the dangerous hour of one o'clock in the afternoon, we discovered that they had ascended beyond the cache to Base Camp on the col just to get some food to ease the pressure of low supplies. They carried down meat and canned fruits which they knew we preferred, and actually left some of their rice on the col.

We broke camp on the twenty-fourth to climb over French Pass to Dampus. What had been an arduous trek in two months before, was an easy stroll out. In the simple spatial terminology of mountaineers, we were thinking "out," seeing the distinctly different sections of the journey to Tukche, to Pokhara, and to Kathmandu. Dhaulagiri was no longer our immediate concern; cleaned of our baggage and plans, our abandoned camps absolutely buried, the mountain was aloof, untouched. We looked back at Dhaulagiri with eyes that saw more than when we came. Reichardt reflected on the summit: "All the work had gone before. It was such a team effort that I had more the impression of being kicked up the mountain than of struggling up it. Correspondingly, I felt no great elation on the summit, which was just putting the final stone on the top of a pyramid. Once we had dismantled the pyramid, Dhaulagiri was as remote from me as before the expedition. It was a strange sensation I carried away with me, of collective, not individual accomplishment." A song of life came to mind as someone mused, "Maybe we didn't beat the mountain, but we drank her beer for nothing."

At Dampus, where the porters supplied their campsite with food and firewood from the valley below, we drank cups of tea as the camp fell into shadow. We had not seen some of these porters since leaving Cornice Camp, but the bond of sharing work for an isolated objective now seemed very strong. The tea they served us had a pungency that was new to us on the mountain, but hauntingly familiar. Darjeeling? English Breakfast? Factory Lunchroom? We tried to guess where the tea was from. Tea flavored by woodsmoke figured in the earliest memories of the mountains for all of us, but somehow it took us a long time to pin it down.

The reunion turned again to parting. A small crew of Sherpas would accompany the sahibs to Pokhara, the rest would remain to move loads from R & R to Tukche, where mules could be hired. Sonam Girmi seemed to think nothing of calling the Sherpas outside in the after-sunset cold to announce who would go with us and who would stay. We lay in our tents listening to the meeting. Someone called out, "Hey, Jim! Do you think you could call a meeting after sunset and get us out of our sleeping bags?" "Sure!" Morrissey replied, "All I'd hear would be a chorus of 'bullshit' from the tents."

It was a long way down to Tukche. First we traversed on snow along a route that the porters had marked with large rock cairns and white gauze prayer flags; then we descended steeply down the yak pasture ridge in stiff, friendly winds and moist fog; then we met the trail and saw flat Tukche below us. First lichen, then clumps of moss, then stunted shrubs, then grass and

fifty-foot trees. We came to know green with the same precision that we had known drops of water on the hot glacier.

In Tukche we drank tea from glasses on the mud floor of a dimly lit house and ate pieces of goat from the hills above the town. Reichardt and Ngawang Samden were honored by the town with wreaths of yellow flowers. Ngawang Samden, Ang Dawa, and Pasang Tenzing went off to celebrate with friends in the Tibetan district. Sore from the long descent and generally diminished physically, the sahibs passively ate a magnificent dinner prepared by Ang Mingyur and drank *rakshi* until near dawn before stumbling off to sleep in the town square.

In the morning we organized ourselves slowly for the half-day walk to Lete. A few had the energy to bathe in the snow-fed Yamkin Khola, but most had very little strength to spare. Leaving town by twos and threes after noon, we made our way, gingerly stepping over drunken Sherpas here and there on the grey plain outside town. Ngawang Samden, Ang Dawa and Pasang Tenzing had celebrated Ngawang's summit success and their safe return so long that they could hardly stand. We were sympathetic, because though slightly more sober, we too were weak. Tibetans from Tukche were carrying the three Sherpas' packs and seemed to be taking care of them, so we smiled and went off.

We passed through town on the west side of the valley, spinning a row of Buddhist prayer wheels at the town gate, then passing a row of *mani* stones. The stones bear a *mantra,* or prayer, roughly transcribed as *om mani padme aum,* representing a specific theological meaning embodied in the sound of the human voice uttering the syllables. Merit accrues both to the one who places the stone, and to those who circumambulate it. The circumambulation is always clockwise, and the turn may be made by passing the stone on opposite sides going up and down the trail. Nearly three months before, we had passed with the stones to the right: returning, we completed the turn.

It was a very long half day. The rivers had begun to swell with monsoon rains, some seasonal bridges had already been washed away, and others were soon to go. Tricky footing in the thigh-deep tributaries of the Kali made us ford with our boots on. At Lete, we reclaimed our campsite from a small flock of sheep. Ang Dawa, glassy-eyed, arrived in time for dinner, but there was no sign of Ngawang Samden. In the morning, we found that spring had brought wild strawberries to the pine woods.

The following night in Tatopani, a kerosene lantern lighting a food shop on the main trail attracted our attention. The trail is wide there, paved with large, flat stones; a handful of shallow, open-fronted shops in the path are

Ang Tuta, spirit medium of Kumjung, the expedition's mailrunner.

open in the evening. The food shop had neat shelves of canned fruits and meats, "Panda" Chinese sweet condensed milk, packages of "Annapurna" biscuits and beer bottles sporting a wide variety of brand names. Labels in French, German, Polish, Spanish, and English on leftovers from a dozen expeditions gave the little shops a cosmopolitan air. We felt very civilized as we sat on wooden stools in the path, drinking Nepali Star beer and munching soggy pilot biscuits.

There was nothing noteworthy about the rest of the walk, only that we ate as much as we could, once stopping for a huge breakfast of potatoes and all the eggs in a house in Ghorepani, then crossing the trail to order thirty-two more, over easy. Bech started a *zuga* (Tibetan for leech) scare when he gravely rubbed his sneakers with salt before entering the rhododendron forest. As we walked along, the loathsome creatures rose up out of the bushes like trunks of tiny elephants in search of peanuts. We listened to tales of Rennie, two days ahead of the main party, a tall, gaunt figure clad in bright red parka and pants, dwarfing a tiny white Tibetan pony . . . solitary, mysterious, and silent as he ghosted through these towns. A sober Ngawang Samden rejoined us in Tirke where, with awkward contrition, he apologized for his absence while Morrissey tried to look stern, but the brief pantomime dissolved in laughter.

Nepal's economy relies on porter transportation, so there are well-placed stone load-rests along the trail. We stopped at every one. People who do not have to carry loads have inflated social status, so, on principle, we carried loads. Our packs were big, but often nearly empty. The high altitude Sherpas also carried, preferring to demonstrate their superiority by wearing expedition-issue long underwear and wool pants despite tropical temperatures. Ang Tuta, himself a porter, never sobered after the Tukche celebrations, so he had to subcontract with a local porter to carry his load.

Once in Pokhara, at our old camp by the lake, we nursed ourselves back to health on fresh fruit, cold beer, and mail: it was all we could do to paddle around the lake on air mattresses under the hot sun. On June 3, Al Read sent word from Kathmandu that Ambassador Laise wanted us at the Residence on the sixth for a reception. It was an honor, of course, but the tone of Read's footnote to the invitation made it a draft notice, too. We caught a plane and flew down that afternoon in time to dig out crumpled jackets and ties, and to arrange with Boris for a banquet at the Yak and Yeti after the reception.

In the cool of the ambassador's flower garden, the official Americans were present and with them were a collection of the denizens of Kathmandu, the explorers, adventurers, missionaries, and entrepreneurs who had settled in that dream-ridden town. Ngawang Samden wore a dark blue suit and was exceedingly humble, Ang Dawa wore climbing clothes and was drunk. We drank champagne, posed for pictures, and were as polite as our failing energies allowed. Drifting around the formal garden, drinks in hand, exhaustion, incipient amebiasis and a sense of abrupt transition conspired to build an atmosphere of fantasy. We went from there to the ornate mirrored ballroom of the Yak and Yeti, where good food, more drink, and the cool of evening completely destroyed the line between illusion and reality. Were we at an end, a beginning, or a pause in a cycle? The room became many rooms as mirrors reflected multiple images of our long table: were they images of the past, of other mountaineers who had feasted at Boris's after long expeditions, of our present, or of feasts yet uncooked?

A few days later, Sonam Girmi and the porters arrived in Kathmandu. We had been planning a party, an outdoor pig roast, as a celebration for them, but details piled up to push the idea aside. In the shuffle of payday and packing to go home, our energies went to peddling left-over supplies and buying inexpensive climbing gear in the bazaar. At first, we couldn't find a suitable place for a party. And then we couldn't find a suitable pig to roast. So the plan was nearly abandoned. Finally we made arrangements for another dinner at the Yak and Yeti.

The sahibs sat inside waiting for the Sherpas; the Sherpas sat outside, afraid to come in. An hour passed, until someone went outside to look, found the Sherpas and brought them in. Some had never even been to Kathmandu before, so the sight of the mirrored hall, polished floors and large chandeliers left them wide-eyed and speechless. They were on strict orders from Sonam Girmi to behave themselves, so they each politely took a single glass of beer and sat down stiffly and silently against the wall. We watched them uneasily as they watched us; the camaraderie of the mountain seemed lost in the palace. Jennifer Read rescued us all with a beer drinking game that pits two teams against each other in a race to get drunk. The first round was awkward; it nearly killed the sahibs who had to demonstrate the game over and over again. The porters nervously watched Sonam Girmi, who watched the memsahib orchestrating disorder. Sonam Girmi shrugged, binding the porters' behavior over to us. They relaxed at once, and laughter flooded the room.

The meal was a triumph of culinary art prepared to Sherpa taste for spicy foods, Boris's personal tribute to the Sherpas. Some of the porters had never used forks before, so most of us ate off the spotless china with our hands, as waiters poured wine into crystal goblets. The Sherpas faced this luxury with the same grace with which they had faced hardships on the mountain. We wallowed in it. We had been peasants together on the mountain, and we were royalty together that night. Morrissey and Sonam Girmi surveyed their court and were satisfied.

With the stiffness gone, the porters began to dance; first a small group, then a longer and longer line. The dance was a series of steps, and a chant, in which all the feet and all the voices act as one. That the sahibs were new to the steps did not matter.

The Dhaulagiri expedition danced together, and strong men wept with joy.

Note on Retinal Photography

BY DRUMMOND RENNIE

For two hundred years, doctors and scientists have realized that lack of oxygen has profound effects on the body and that a great many of the symptoms and signs they were seeing in patients were due to this lack. In the 1790's they first began to use the mountains for studying fit people taken up into a low-oxygen environment. Even now, despite a hundred years of experimentation with, and in, low-pressure chambers, the high mountains still provide the best, cheapest and most satisfactory "laboratory" in which to investigate oxygen deprivation and the consequent process of acclimatization.

In 1969 and 1970, a brilliant physiologist, Dr. Regina Frayzer, working with our group at the Arctic Institute camp on the summit plateau of Mount Logan in the Canadian Yukon, showed that fit people, suddenly transported by plane to an altitude of 17,600 feet, developed increased flow in the little blood vessels of the retina at the back of the eye, and that quite frequently hemorrhages from these blood vessels occurred—hemorrhages rather like those that occur in common diseases such as high blood pressure and anemia. (These changes have nothing to do with the condition of snow blindness which is a common mountaineering problem and can occur at any altitude.)

I saw that the Dhaulagiri expedition would be a perfect opportunity to look into the cause of this occurrence; guinea pigs (we climbers) would be going far higher and exercising far harder for very much longer periods than one could expect of any research volunteer. It was an opportunity I could not morally ignore. Moreover, photographing the back of the eye once at sea level before setting out, and once at Base Camp immediately after each climber had descended from his highest point, would involve me in only two days' work, and the others in only two brief photographing sessions. No one's climbing would be interrupted in any way (not even my own). There would be no tedious (and therefore impossible) collections of urine or blood to be made and therefore no complicated system for transporting the specimens back to the States. I felt embarrassed about the seeming simplicity of the experiment, and the small amount of work involved.

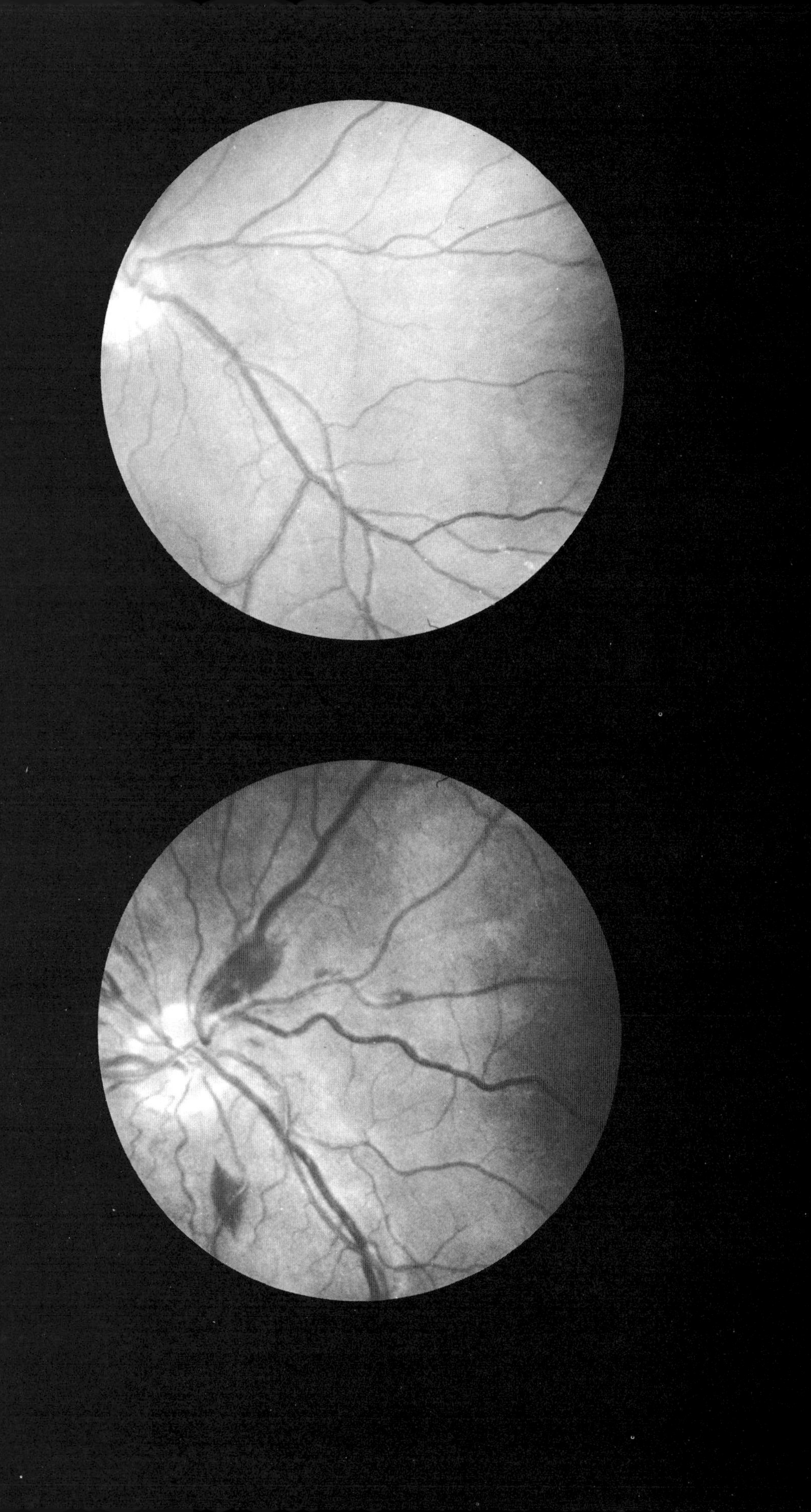

As with any ostensibly simple experiment, months of preparation and practice were necessary: retinal photography with a small, portable retinal camera was hard enough in my hospital. Taking such photographs kneeling down and bent double in a small tent with a camera, covered in condensation, wobbling on a pile of food boxes, its strobes and viewing lights working only intermittently as the tiny generator, also starved of oxygen, coughed and surged out in its box in the snow—and with the guinea-pig climber, just as cramped and breathless, trying to fix his eyes on an invisible light while keeping his head steady—all this turned out to be an exhausting business.

Back in Chicago, I studied the pictures; suddenly as I looked at the tracery of vessels and the red hemorrhages it all seemed worthwhile, and then, just as suddenly, I realized that I had merely clarified the problem, not solved it. I had not found the cause, just absolved the various factors I had considered as likely.

Retinal hemorrhages occurred in one third of the climbers: John Roskelley, Todd Thompson, Del Young, Andy Harvard, and Jim Morrissey. What distinguished this group of climbers from the others? Nothing: not loads carried, maximum height reached or cold endured; cough, fitness, or speed of acclimatization. They tended to be the younger members of the expedition—but Jim was the second oldest. Apart from that, they all had English-Irish names. Reichardt, Bech, Langbauer, Lev, and Duenwald were completely free of hemorrhages—so were the high altitude Sherpas. But then, so were Lyman, Rennie, Peterson, Fear, and Smith, none of whom have convincingly Sherpa-like names. In other words, in that the incidence was higher than on Mount Logan, I had shown only that altitude was a cause and that several other possible factors were irrelevant.

But that is research: more questions than answers, as usual—the candle taken out further into the darkness merely illumines a greater darkness.

Rennie prepares to dilate Harvard's eyes for retinal photography.

Rennie photographs the retina of Thompson's left eye.

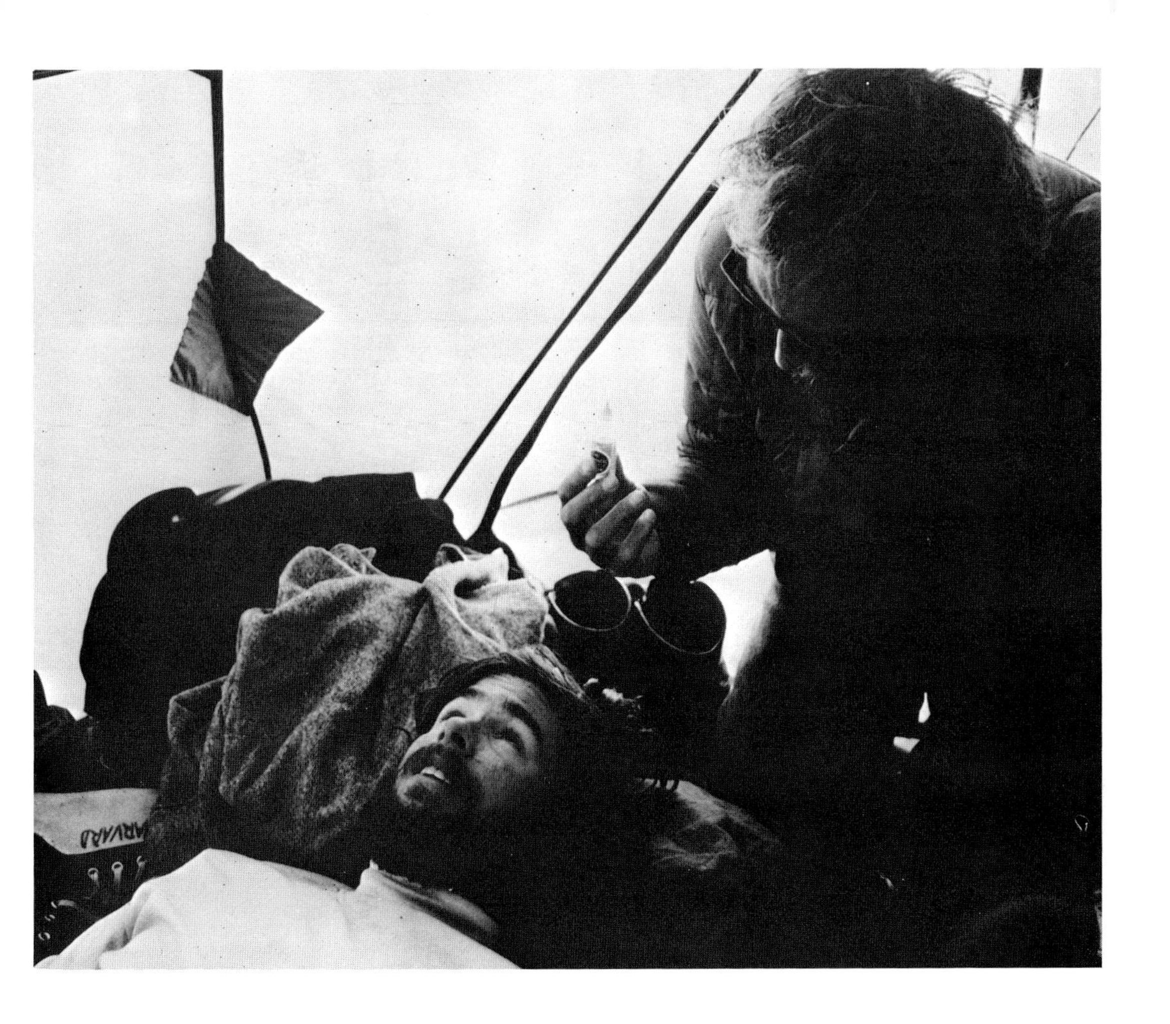

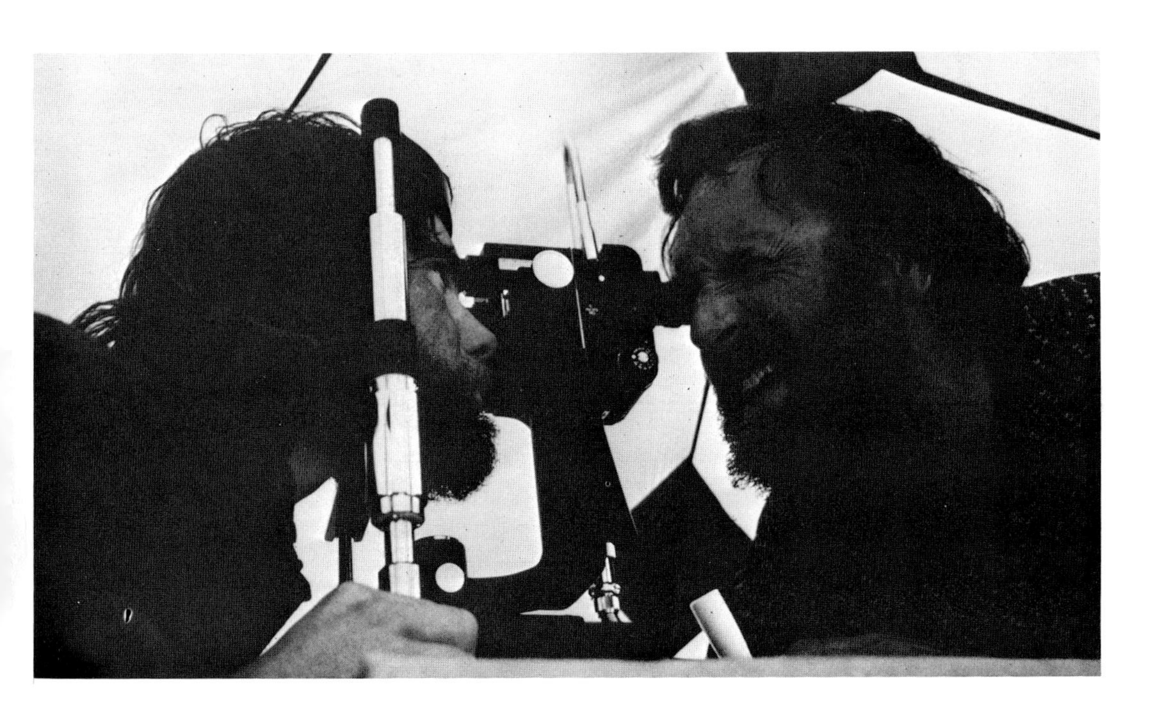

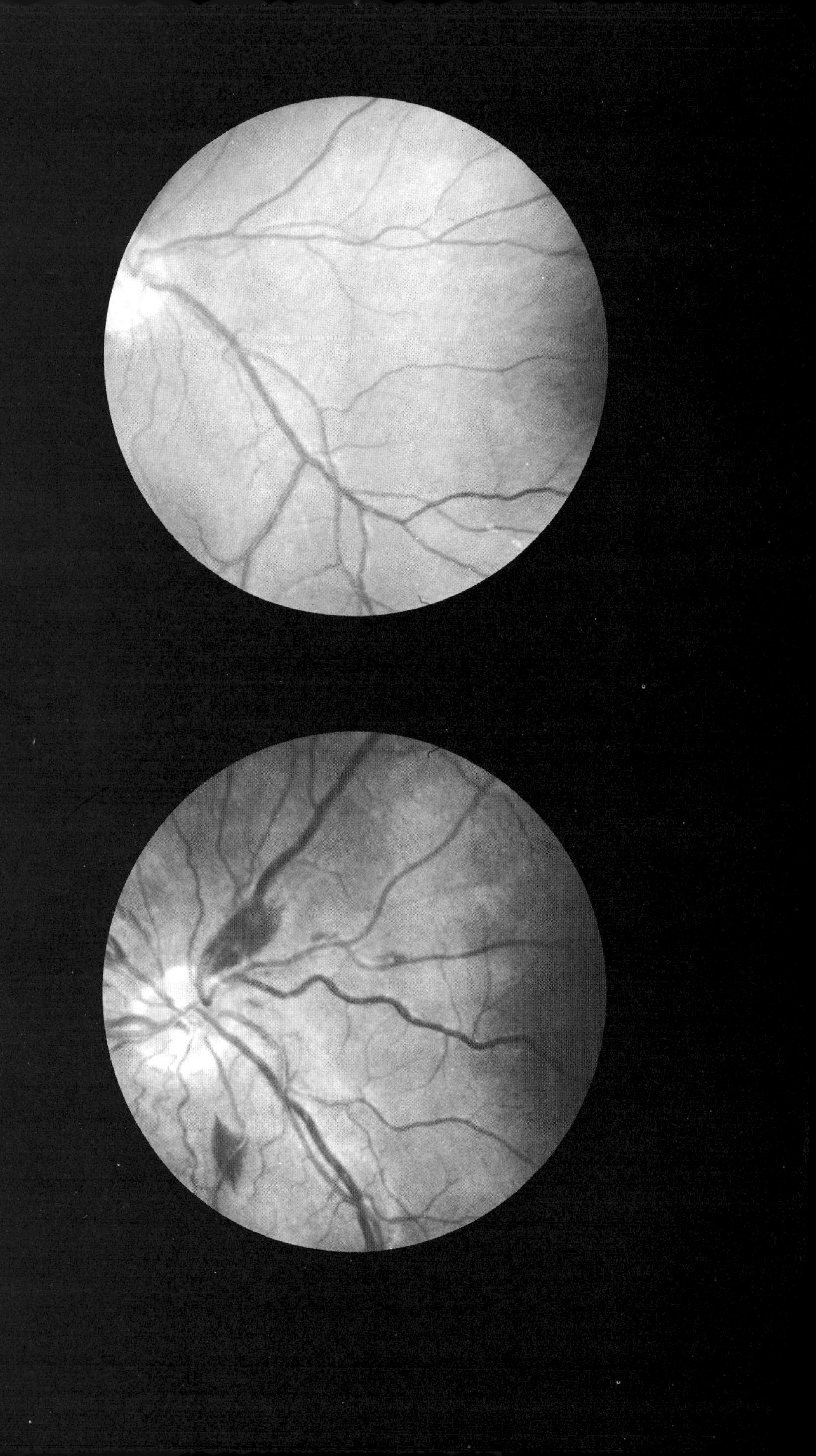

The back of Thompson's left eye, photographed before the start of the expedition at sea level in New York. The background is the retina or light sensitive membrane of the eye, and the small arteries and veins are radiating out over the retina from the disc which is the end of the optic nerve. This nerve carries all the information from the retina back to the brain. The veins are darker than the arteries because they have given up their oxygen to the totally oxygen-dependent nerve cells of the retina. The spot about one inch to the right is the macula and is the only part of the retina that is used for exact vision. The rest of the retina is concerned with peripheral vision.

The back of Thompson's right eye at Base Camp (19,300 feet) after his last descent from Camp II. The two or three dark smudges are hemorrhages or small leaks. The optic nerve is slightly swollen, suggesting that there was swelling in the brain which the nerve is connected directly to. There are no hemorrhages at the macula, which is why Thompson did not notice any trouble with his vision. A much smaller hemorrhage in the macula region would cause a dark spot in the middle of the field of vision. The blood vessels are wider than at sea level because they hold more blood and are more tortuous.

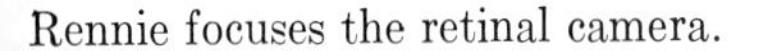

Rennie focuses the retinal camera.

Mountaineering History of Dhaulagiri I

1950 French reconnaissance of Dhaulagiri led by Maurice Herzog.

1953 Akademischer Alpen Klub Swiss expedition led by Bernard Lauterburg. Myagdi Khola approach; attempt on the Pear route reached 25,400 feet; reconnaissance of the northeast and south cols. Pfisterer determined that glacier landing on the northeast col is possible.

1954 Argentine Expedition attempt on the Pear reached 26,250 feet; Pasang Dawa Lama, sirdar; death by frostbite of leader Franciso Ibañez.

1955 Swiss-German Vegetarian Expedition led by Martin Meier of Munich; attempt on the Pear reached about twenty-five thousand feet; Pasang Dawa Lama, sirdar.

1956 Peron Argentine Expedition led by Colonel Huerta; attempt on the Pear reached about twenty-five thousand feet; death of Bal Bahadur, a porter.

1958 Swiss expedition led by Werner Stauble; attempt on the Pear reached 24,750; Pasang Dawa Lama, sirdar.

1959 Austrian Himalayan Association Expedition led by Fritz Moravec; first attempt of the northeast spur reached 25,250 feet; Pasang Dawa Lama, sirdar; crevasse death of Heini Roiss.

1960 International Swiss Expedition led by Max Eiselin; first ascent of Dhaulagiri by the northeast spur; Pilatus Porter aircraft flown by Ernst Saxer and Emil Wick used for transport of men and supplies to Dampus Pass and the northeast col.

1969 American Dhaulagiri Expedition led by Boyd N. Everett, Jr.; first attempt on the southeast ridge; approach from Lete by the southeast glacier; avalanche deaths of seven at 17,500 feet.

1970 Japanese expedition led by Tokufu Ota and Shoji Imanari; second ascent of Dhaulagiri via the northeast spur.

1971 Bech Reconnaissance to the northeast spur in preparation for the 1973 American Dhaulagiri Expedition.

1973 American Dhaulagiri Expedition led by James Morrissey; attempt on the southeast ridge reached 21,500 feet; third ascent of the mountain via the northeast spur; airdrops of supplies made by Emil Wick at French Pass (17,500 feet) and the northeast col (19,300 feet).

Chronology of the American Expeditions

1969

April 2	Everett and Read arrive in Kathmandu; team assembles during following weeks; purchase supplies, pack loads, hire Sherpas.
April 15	Team in Pokhara; advance party leaves for Lete.
April 16	Main body of expedition leaves Pokhara.
April 18	Advance party in Lete at foot of southeast glacier.
April 21	Base Camp established at fifteen thousand feet on southeast glacier.
April 22	Evacuation of Al Read begins.
April 26	Cache established at seventeen thousand feet on southeast glacier, reconnaissance to crevasse at 17,500 feet.
April 28	Avalanche at 17,500 feet kills seven.
April 29	Camp at 15,000 feet abandoned, survivors move to camp at 12,500 feet.
May 5	Team leaves Lete area.
May 12	Team in Kathmandu.

1973

February 18	Team arrives in Kathmandu; meets Sherpas.
February 25	Party to Calcutta to accompany supplies north.
March 3	Team in Pokhara for sorting of suppiles.
March 6	Expedition leaves Pokhara.
March 12	Expedition arrives in Tukche, leaves heavily traveled Kali Gandaki River valley.
March 13	Windy Corner camp occupied (12,000 feet).
March 17	Cornice camp occupied (14,500 feet).
March 22	Advance party occupies French Pass (17,500 feet).

March 23	Main party occupies Breast Camp (16,000 feet).
March 24	Airdrops begin at French Pass.
March 25	Main party moves to French Pass.
March 30	Advance party occupies northeast col (19,300 feet).
April 1 thru 5	Northeast col airdrops, Base Camp established at col, work on southeast ridge begins.
April 15	Southeast ridge attempt abandoned at 21,500 feet.
April 17	Camp I occupied on northeast spur (21,400 feet).
April 24	Camp II occupied on northeast spur (23,500 feet).
May 1	Camp III occupied on northeast spur (24,500 feet).
May 10	Camp IV occupied on northeast spur (25,700 feet).
May 12	Summit reached via northeast spur (26,795 feet).
May 15	Evacuation of Roskelley begins.
May 20	Last climbers off spur route in bad weather.
May 22	Expedition at R&R Camp below icefall (15,500 feet).
June 4	Expedition in Kathmandu.

Note on Terms

The vocabulary of mountain climbing can be confusing not so much because it contains obscure technical terms, but because, like any insiders' jargon, meanings rely as much on context, tone of voice, and prior usage as on specific definitions. We called one part of Dhaulagiri a "**ridge**" and another a "**spur**": different climbers might have switched the names around, or called them both ridges, or both spurs, or **corners,** or maybe even **buttresses.** No one would argue, but the distinctions might be hard to pin down.

One editor complained that we "mixed apples and pears" too often by using the term **expedition** to mean sometimes a group of people, sometimes a finite period of time, sometimes a specific goal, sometimes an event in mountaineering history and occasionally an abstract idea. **Climb,** with several meanings as a noun and others as a verb, causes more problems. Even simple words like **cache,** a place, a thing, and an action, and **anchor,** also two nouns and a verb, seem to have multiple meanings. We can only answer that this same editor insisted on an account which was "accurate in the context of word-meanings as actually expressed by climbers." Climbers claim to be able to use these terms without confusion; perhaps the reader can as well. Maybe the problem really lies in a climber's penchant to dream of apples and pears after weeks of living above the snowline.

But a few ambiguities do need special attention. **Sherpa** (from the Tibetan Shar-pa, meaning "easterners"): The Sherpa people are the members of a specific set of clans living in the Solu-Pharak-Khumbu region of Nepal, not far from Mount Everest. Sherpas are highlanders of Mongoloid extraction, they practice Tibetan Buddhism, and speak a language very closely related to Tibetan. Their land is mountainous, with settlements ranging from seven thousand to thirteen thousand feet. Namche Bazaar is the principal city in the area. Their economy is based on agriculture and cattle husbandry, with trade taking them north across the high passes into Tibet, and east to Darjeeling in Northern India.

Sherpas have been involved in expeditioneering since the turn of the century. In 1907, two Norwegians hired Sherpas in Darjeeling as porters for an expedition to climb a subsidiary peak of nearby Kanchenjunga (28,148 feet) and discovered the fitness for mountaineering of these tough, reliable hill people. When the British began their trips to Everest in 1921, they hired Sherpas as porters and began to train them in European climbing techniques. When Everest was climbed in 1953, the summit team was a Sherpa-United Kingdom partnership—Tenzing Norgay and Edmund Hillary, both now famous men. That partnership underscored the Sherpas' function on a climbing expedition. At home in the Himalaya, the Sherpas tend to acclimatize better and remain healthier than foreigners. The foreign Alpinists bring to the team technology, alpine climbing expertise and logistic organization; the Sherpas traditionally provide the depth of manpower.

A system of training and certification of climbing Sherpas was started in India in the twenties, developing into the highly structured system of today. The Sherpas favor rigid structuring because it helps maintain job standards, and fits comfortably with the Sherpas' own clan society.

A young Sherpa begins his career as a kitchen boy or a **low altitude porter,** working for a standard wage, and such equipment as is necessary for the terrain, usually below the base of the mountain, that he will work on. Porters can acquire mountain experience as **icefall porters,** carrying loads along established routes through the icefalls, high glaciers and lower slopes of the mountain. A big jump in status and pay comes with promotion to **high altitude porter:** this is the **"climbing Sherpa"** job, and the men who fill it are experienced expedition climbers. They are equipped as members of the expedition team, and are capable of working anywhere on the mountain. The leaders among the Sherpas are called **sirdars;** an expedition's chief sirdar has broad responsibilities for logistics and for supervision of the climbing Sherpas and porters.

Because of the Sherpa's close association with Himalayan mountaineering, the job description has become synonymous with the ethnic designation. Leaving both meanings as they are, one can remember: virtually all sherpas (job) are Sherpas (clansmen), but by no means are all Sherpas (clansmen) sherpas (job).

Ice and **snow** in the mountains, and in this book: like the Eskimos, climbers, seeing at close quarters a limitless variety of conditions of snow and ice, have developed a large vocabulary to describe every possible condition. The terms, drawing on several languages, cover variations in consistency, origin, geography, season, altitude, content, age, and time of day, and often the climber's mood and range of experience as well. It is a subjective system, but useful for comparative description when the terms can be linked to common experience. Most mountaineering accounts use a few technical terms like **"neve," "corn snow,"** or **"blue ice,"** for color and authenticity, then roughly divide everything that is not flowing water or solid rock into two broad classes: **snow** and **ice.** That should be simple enough—ice is anything that can be chipped off and put in a glass, snow can be molded and thrown. **Ice climbing** is a part of mountaineering which requires special skill, and is often more difficult than **snow climbing.** Techniques and equipment vary somewhat, with ice-climbing techniques generally representing a refinement of applied snow climbing and rock climbing techniques. Ice climbing is generally regarded as a higher state of the art, and it is a pursuit sometimes separated from mountaineering for weekend exercise on frozen waterfalls, gullies and roadcuts. Climbing steep ice can be beautiful to watch, it is usually intensely satisfying to do; it requires delicacy, control and imagination, and rewards a climber with a sense of freedom. Snow climbing, often laborious, rarely approaches any of those things. But confusion often occurs in mountain writing, where a great deal of snow turns to ice on the way from mountain to the manuscript. The technical terms really are specific, and translation problems can blur the distinction between hard-packed snow and soft ice. In treating two very different routes on Dhaulagiri, we have chosen to make the distinction quite clear. Ice in this text is ice: we were glad to find what ice we did, and happy to climb steep ice at high altitude, because most of the mountain, like most mountains, is covered with snow.

Acclimatization is the gradual process of becoming physically accustomed to living and working at high altitude. It is the cumulative effect of the numerous changes made by the body in response to low atmospheric oxygen pressure. The blood gradually becomes thicker to accommodate more oxygen; the circulation expands to contain a large increase in the actual amount of blood being pumped round; the way in which hemoglobin in the red cells of the blood picks up oxygen in the lungs and unloads it into the tissues is altered, and innumerable small changes in the brain, the muscles, the heart, the bones, and the kidneys occur to help increase oxygen delivery to the tissues.

The higher one climbs, the less oxygen there is to breathe, and the greater the effort expended, and hence oxygen required, in breathing. Most but not all people can readily acclimatize to heights of around twelve thousand to fourteen thousand feet provided they ascend slowly and do not exert themselves too hard for a few days.

The physiological changes required for acclimatization take hours, days, weeks, or even months to become complete. The higher one goes, the more radical the changes, until above a critical altitude of eighteen thousand to nineteen thousand feet (that is, below our Base Camp at 19,300 feet) they are never completed and it is impossible for anyone to live without a steady deterioration in health and performance.

On going up to higher altitudes, the physiological processes begin at once, and since they stop when they have brought oxygen delivery back up to normal, they do not progress very far if one does not go very high. At any altitude, the oxygen demands of the body are enormously increased by exercising, so extra acclimatization is needed at each new step before one can climb or carry higher. Every time one moves up to a higher camp, the processes are stimulated all over again.

For the first few days at an increased altitude, the acclimatization processes will not have had time to occur, so activity should be strictly limited. During that time, a climber runs a high risk of **acute mountain sickness.** Typically lasting forty-eight hours or so before disappearing spontaneously, mountain sickness is usually no more than breathlessness, headache, nausea, loss of appetite, dizziness, and problems with balance and sleeping, often accompanied by lassitude, depression, and irritability. Its extreme manifestations, which include fluid accumulation in the cranial cavity and fluid in the lungs (**cerebral and pulmonary edema**), may be fatal. Successful treatment relies on rapid descent to lower altitude.

Acute mountain sickness is a disease of civilization: airplanes, helicopters, ski lifts, and ever tighter schedules rush tourists and climbers up quicker and higher, sometimes to a rapid death. It never occurs after the first few days at high altitudes, even though acclimatization may not yet be complete.

GLOSSARY

anchor 1) the point in a rope system where the fixed ropes are secured, normally by a rock or ice piton, or a snow picket.

2) the hardware used to secure a rope.

approach The problem, often consuming more time and energy than the climb itself, of reaching the base of a mountain.

belay The protection one climber can afford another using a rope system. Climbing in pairs where falling is a potential danger, the lead climber is protected by the second who is secured to an anchor. The second belays the leader by paying out rope to him as he climbs. The leader then anchors himself, and belays as the second climbs. Most climbing on fixed ropes is done without belay. Crossing snowfields and glaciers where crevasses are a danger, or climbing on easy terrain at high altitude, climbers are roped together for safety, but move continuously without belay.

bivouac A planned or unplanned night out on a mountain with minimal equipment.

bergschrund A large crevasse separating the upper slopes of a glacier from the steeper slopes of ice or rock above. Considered to be the point at which the glacier ends and the mountain begins.

col A high, snowy pass between two peaks.

cornice Overhanging lip of snow on a ridge, sculpted by the wind, generally in the shape of a wave.

couloir A gully, usually a steep ice or snow gully.

crampons Steel spikes fitted to climbing boots for climbing on ice and snow.

Dhaulagiri (Sanskrit) White Mountain. In the text, Dhaulagiri, unless otherwise specified, refers to Dhaulagiri I (26,795 feet), the principal mountain in the Dhaulagiri massif.

fixed rope Rope anchored in place on a climbing route. Leaving fixed ropes during a climb facilitates repeated carries up and down a route.

gendarme A tower of rock.

glacier A river of ice. A **hanging glacier** is one that flows to a precipice and ends in a steep wall of ice that breaks off periodically. An **icefall** is that part of a glacier that falls down steep underlying terrain forming a mass of broken ice blocks. A **crevasse** is a crack in the surface of a glacier caused by a change in the slope underneath.

glissade A controlled or uncontrolled slide down a snow slope in either standing or sitting position.

hardware The collective term for the technical equipment a climber uses on a mountain: ice and rock **pitons, nuts,** chockstones, snow **pickets** and **dead-man anchors** are all used to secure anchors and protection points. **Carabiners** are small oval snaplinks used in rope systems. **Piton hammers,** and **alpine hammers,** carried in holsters, are the tools of technical climbing; **ice axes** are the tools of general mountaineering. Nylon **slings** are used as links in the rope system. A **seat harness** or **swami belt** links the climber to the ropes.

jumar (n) a spring-loaded handle for climbing first ropes. Clipped to a rope, the jumar slides up, but holds under tension. Other devices perform the same function, all of them replacing a knot, the prussik, which slides up a rope but holds under tension.

(v) to climb a fixed rope using jumar handles.

massif 1) a group of mountains, geologically related, and geographically distinct from the surrounding mountains.

2) the main mass of a large mountain, usually a mountain with several summits.

monsoon A front of warm, wet weather which moves north across India to bring heavy rains to Nepal at the end of May. The monsoon brings the end of the main climbing season with heavy snows which make the mountains dangerous, and rains which flood the valleys, making transportation difficult. There is a short post-monsoon climbing season in the fall before the winter storms and cold weather set in.

objective danger Hazards over which a climber has no control, such as bad weather, rockfall, or avalanche. Climbers can estimate the degree of objective danger in light of prevailing conditions, and take precautions, choosing optimum routes and times of travel, but never eliminate entirely the element of chance.

pitch The section of climbing between two belay anchors: normally about the length of a single climbing rope, 150 feet.

pooh Dhaulagiri's regular afternoon fog.

rakshi A spiritous liquor distilled from **chang,** rice beer.

rappel Descent along a rope. Friction slows the climber and gives him control. A brake system is made of carabiners attached to the climber's harness for steep or overhanging rappels. On a gentle slope, a **hothand rappel** without brake is used, the rope simply providing directional control.

ridge The intersection of two faces of a mountain. A **spur** is a ridge or subsidiary rise extending laterally from a mountain or range. In the text, we use **spur** to indicate the sloping northeast ridge, and **ridge** for the long, sharp southeast ridge.

sahib (pron: sa'h'b) Term of address used by the Sherpas for the foreigners who employ them. The great gulf in status and privilege which the term once implied has closed considerably. Sherpas can call any climber "sahib," thus avoiding the problem of confusing and unfamiliar surnames which all sound alike. The relationship between sahibs and Sherpas could be compared to an army, the sahibs being officers and the Sherpas N.C.O.'s. As in an army, some of the wise old sergeants have more experience than the young lieutenants and more common sense than the blustering generals. A **memsahib** is a female sahib; the **bara-sahib** is the leader of the sahibs.

scree The accumulation, sometimes extensive, of loose stones on a mountainside.

serac A wall or tower of ice.

thakali Clan living in the Dhaulagiri region of Nepal.

tumpline Strap looped around a load and hung from the forehead back across the shoulders.

wand A bamboo stake used to mark a route in the snow on a glacier or a low slope. Wands are placed one to two hundred feet apart for easy visibility in storm conditions.

whiteout The condition in which blown snow or clouds on a snowfield make it impossible to distinguish between the sky and the ground.

yeti The legendary abominable snowman of the Himalaya; the name of the 1960 Swiss expedition's aircraft.

Note on Loadcarrying

Loadcarrying, building the logistic pyramid, is the daily fare of a large expeditionary assault on a big mountain. One can, if one chooses, tell the entire story of an expedition in the record of carries alone. We did not do so, because the resulting picture, though accurate as far as it goes, is as incomplete as it is colorless. The same criticism would apply to a statistical picture of days leading, days in support, or days above or below a given altitude. The excitement of leading or breaking trail, the joy of changing surroundings, the satisfaction of visible progress; silences, sounds, weather . . . all of the things which make up a carry are lost to dry numbers, the least important aspect of a day spent carrying a pack. But a diary of statistics does help to explain how an expedition works. The following record is the daily log kept by Louis Reichardt. We have chosen to use his because it includes the summit and the highest camps on the spur; a similar log could be constructed for each of the other sahibs and climbing sherpas. The weights represent Reichardt's estimate, against the standard sixty pounds, the "load" unit as ordained by tradition and measured by the sirdar. High on the mountain, we had no scale, but one can, if really interested, become a very astute estimator of weights, with consistent accuracy to plus or minus five pounds, the direction of the error reflecting the carrier's mood of the time. Elevations, in feet, indicate the daily carry made up or down, and the camp elevations for the nights indicate the gradual uphill, then rapid downhill progress of the climber.

While different climbers carried diflerent amounts, moved up or down at different rates, and took different rest days, the pattern of this log reflects the general pattern of expedition activity.

DAILY LOG MARCH 14–MAY 24

March 14—50 lb. 8,500 to 12,100 (Windy Corner)	night at 12,100
March 15—60 lb. 12,100 to 13,000	night at 12,100
March 16—rest (sick)	night at 12,100
March 17—rest (sick)	night at 12,100
March 18—rest (sick)	night at 12,100
March 19—30 lb. 12,100 to 13,000	night at 12,100
March 20—50 lb. 12,100 to 14,500 (Cornice Camp)	night at 14,500
March 21—75 lb. 14,500 to 16,000	night at 14,500
March 22—20 lb. 14,500 to 16,000 (trail breaking)	night at 14,500
March 23—50 lb. 14,500 to 16,000 (Breast Camp)	night at 16,000
March 24—60 lb. 16,000 to 17,000 (Dampus Pass)	night at 16,000
March 25—50 lb. 16,000 to 17,500 (French Pass)	night at 17,500
March 26—80 lb. 17,500 to 15,500 (R&R Camp)	night at 17,500
March 27—50 lb. carried + 60 lb. dragged 17,500 to 15,500	night at 15,500
March 28—55 lb. 15,500 to 17,000 (to Glacier)	
45 lb. 17,500 to 15,500 (French Pass to R&R)	night at 15,500
March 29—80 lb. 15,500 to 17,000; 70 lb. 17,000 to 17,800	night at 15,500
March 30—rest	night at 15,500
March 31—60 lb. 15,500 to 17,000; 70 lb. 17,800 to 17,000	night at 17,000
April 1—50 lb. 15,500 to 17,000 (Glacier)	night at 17,000
April 2—50 lb. 17,000 to 19,300 (Base)	night at 19,300
April 3—50 lb. 19,300 to 19,400 (Foot of S.E.R.)	night at 19,300
April 4—50 lb. 19,300 to 20,000	night at 19,300
April 5—60 lb. 17,000 to 19,300	night at 19,300
April 6—rest (storm)	night at 19,300
April 7—rest day	night at 19,300
April 8—rest (storm)	night at 19,300
April 9—50 lb. 19,400	night at 19,300
April 10—rest (wind)	night at 19,300
April 11—60 lb. 17,600 to 19,300 (Glacier to Base)	night at 19,300
April 12—40 lb. 19,300 to 21,000 (on southeast ridge)	night at 19,300
April 13—rest	night at 19,300
April 14—45 lb. 19,300 to 21,400 (on NE spur)	night at 19,300
April 15—60 lb. 19,300 to 21,400	night at 19,300
April 16—60 lb. 19,400 to 19,300	night at 19,300
April 17—rest	night at 19,300
April 18—70 lb. to 21,400	night at 19,300

April 19—45 lb. to 21,400 (Camp I)	night at 21,400
April 20—30 lb. to 22,700	night at 21,400
April 21—50 lb. to 23,500	night at 21,400
April 22—50 lb. to 23,500	night at 21,400
April 23—50 lb. to 23,500	night at 21,400
April 24—50 lb. to 23,500 (Camp II)	night at 23,500
April 25—rest	night at 23,500
April 26—50 lb. 23,500 to 24,200	
40 lb. 24,200 to 24,600	night at 23,500
April 27—45 lb. 23,500 to 24,600	night at 23,500
April 28—rest (wind)	night at 23,500
April 29—55 lb. 23,500 to 24,600	
50 lb. 24,300 to 24,600	night at 23,500
April 30—rest	night at 23,500
May 1—50 lb. 23,500 to 24,500 (Camp III)	night at 24,500
May 2—exploring route (bad weather)	night at 24,500
May 3—rest (bad weather)	night at 24,500
May 4—rest (high winds)	night at 24,500
May 5—rest (high winds)	night at 24,500
May 6—55 lb. 23,500 to 24,500 (high winds)	night at 24,500
May 7—rest (high winds)	night at 24,500
May 8—rest (high winds)	night at 24,500
May 9—rest (winds)	night at 24,500
May 10—50 lb. 24,500 to 25,700 (Camp IV)	night at 25,700
May 11—rest (winds and storm)	night at 25,700
May 12—20 lb. 25,700 to 26,800 and return (summit)	night at 25,700
May 13—40 lb. 25,700 to 23,500 (IV to II)	night at 23,500
May 14—55 lb. 23,500 to 19,300 (II to Base)	night at 19,300
May 15—rest at Base	night at 19,300
May 16—55 lb. 19,300 to 15,500	night at 15,500
May 17—rest	night at 15,500
May 18—rest	night at 15,500
May 19—80 lb. 16,800 to 15,500	night at 15,500
May 20—80 lb. 16,800 to 15,500	night at 15,500
May 21—80 lb. 16,800 to 15,500	night at 15,500
May 22—60 lb. 17,700 to 15,500	night at 15,500
May 23—rest	night at 15,500
May 24—leave 15,500 for Dampus Pass	

Note on the Teams

AMERICAN DHAULAGIRI EXPEDITION 1969

Boyd N. Everett, Jr., leader	Bill Ross
Al Read, deputy leader	David Seidman
Terry Bech	Phu Dorje II, sirdar
Jeffrey Duenwald	Pangboche Tenzing
Paul Gerhard	Pemba Phutar
Vin Hoeman	Mingma Norbu
James Janney	Phu Tharkay
James Morrissey	Pemba Norbu
Louis Reichardt	Ang Pasang

AMERICAN DHAULAGIRI EXPEDITION 1973

James Morrissey, M.D.	*36, Stockton, California; married, three children; cardiothoracic surgeon; expedition leader.*
Craig Anderson	*26, Bremerton, Washington; married; science teacher.*
Terry Bech	*33, Kathmandu, Nepal; married, one child; ethno-musicologist; director, U.S. Educational Foundation in Nepal; expedition transportation officer.*
Jeffrey Duenwald, D.V.M.	*30, Pullman, Washington; married, two children; veterinarian, clinical virologist; expedition deputy leader.*
Ron Fear	*29, Tacoma, Washington; single; promotional representative for Raichle-Molitor, USA, mountain guide.*
Andrew Harvard	*23, Woodford, Vermont; single; forester, mountain guide; expedition photographic coordinator and business agent.*

Del Langbauer, Ph.D.	*29, Tacoma, Washington; married; professor of philosophy, expedition equipment coordinator.*
Peter Lev	*33, Alta, Utah; separated; mountain guide, USFS snow ranger; expedition avalanche pundit.*
Thomas Lyman	*30, Littleton, New Hampshire; married; science teacher, mountain guide.*
David Peterson, M.D.	*31, Olympia, Washington; married; physician.*
Louis Reichardt, Ph.D.	*30, La Canada, California; married; biologist.*
Drummond Rennie, M.D.	*37, Lake Forest, Illinois; married, two children; nephrologist, high altitude physiologist; expedition scientific coordinator.*
John Roskelley	*24, Spokane, Washington; married, one child; mountaineering equipment retailer.*
Lowell Smith	*36, Los Altos, California; married, two children; physicist.*
Todd Thompson	*24, Friday Harbor, Washington; single; earthquake researcher, mountain guide; expedition secretary.*
Del Young	*25, Wenatchee, Washington; single; mountain guide, graduate student in psychology.*
Sonam Girmi	*1972 German Lhotse Expedition, 1971 International Himalayan Expedition (Everest), 1970 British Army Annapurna Expedition, 1969 Swiss Tukche Expedition, sirdar for Mountain Travel; expedition sirdar.**
Ngawang Samden	*1971 French Makalu Expedition, 1970 Japanese Everest Expedition; expedition deputy sirdar.*
Ang Dawa	*1960 International Swiss Expedition (to Dhaulagiri I) German Cho Oyu Expedition; expedition high altitude porter.*
Ang Namgyal	*1972 German Everest Expedition, 1971 French Makalu Expedition; expedition cook.*
Gyaltsen	*1971 International Himalayan Expedition (Everest); expedition high altitude porter.*
Nang Tenzing	*1971 International Himalayan Expedition (Everest); expedition high altitude porter.*
Pasang Tenzing	*1972 German Everest Expedition, German Cho Oyu Expedition, Japanese Manaslu Expedition,*

* These lists are representative of the Sherpas' experience; they are by no means complete.

	1959 Argentine Dhaulagiri I Expedition; expedition high altitude porter.
Sonam Tsering	*High altitude porter*
Ang Mingyur	*Kitchen*
Phuntso (Pinzo)	*Kitchen*

Low Altitude Porters

Pemba I
Pemba II
Pemba Tsering
Sangay
Ang Pasang I
Ang Dorje
Ang Putarang
A. Puah
Ba Dorje
Mingma Chortar
Min Temba
Tenzing Mingma
Ang Pasang II
O. Pasang
Nyima Norbu
P. Tenzing
Pasang Sonam
Lhakpa Tenzing
Pemba Chotar
Lhakpa Chotar
Shitah Tsering
Ang R.
Ang C.
Ang Tuta
Ang Shitah
Sanggye
Nyima Norbu
Lhakpa Dorje
Gyaltsen

Sub-inspector of Police Samrajya Bahadur Pande—Liaison officer
Henry S. Hall, Jr.—Patron
Elizabeth Hawley—Expedition communications agent
Nola Morrissey—Treasurer
John Skow—Expedition agent in Pokhara; airdrop kicker for RNAC
Emil Wick—Pilot, RNAC

List of Sponsors and Suppliers

The members of the expedition wish to express their gratitude and appreciation to the individuals and institutions assisting the expedition. The following lists are incomplete; there were literally hundreds of people who made contributions of time, expertise, goods, services, money, and good will as the net of the expedition drew in sixteen climbers from across the country and grew over a period of years. Particular thanks to those who are not mentioned here.

Lew Allyn (Welch-Allyn Company)
Barbara Annan
Suzanne Clarke Falk
Norman J. Fisher
Carlton P. Fuller
Marilyn Gerhard (memorial to Paul A. Gerhard)
Henry S. Hall, Jr.
Elizabeth Knowlton
Mr. and Mrs. William Krueger
Lester L. Lev
Samuel F. Thomas, M.D.

American Alpine Club, Boyd N. Everett, Jr. Memorial Fund
Air India
Arthur Kahn Company, Inc.
Eddie Bauer Expedition Outfitters
Garcia Corporation, Thomas T. Lenk Foundation
Harvard Travellers' Club
Research Foundation, State University of New York
Sierra Club Foundation
U.S. Forest Service Avalanche Control Center (for avalanche research)
YKK Zipper Company

We would like to thank the following suppliers of equipment and food for their generous support, and their assistance in procuring the items listed:

A. B. Optimus, Inc.	*Optimus Stoves and Lanterns*
AGA Corporation	*altimeters*
Allen-A Corporation	*fish net, light weight and heavy weight long underwear, turtleneck shirts*
Applications des Gaz	*Bluet stoves and fuel cartridges*
Aris Glove	*Mylar glove liners*
Arvid's of Norway	*cross country skis, poles, boots and running wax*
Bausch and Lomb Corporation	*goggles and sunglasses*
Beck Outdoor Enterprises	*neoprene crampon straps*
Bonne Bell, Inc.	*sun cream, high altitude cream*
Bushnell	*400 mm. lens*
Cello Corporation	*plastic bags*
Coast to Coast Hardware	*tools*
Day Pant Company	*shorts, custom made climbing pants, pants for porters*
Dillon-Beck, Inc.	*plastic jugs*
Donner Mountain Corporation	*Edelweiss climbing ropes, candle lanterns, candles*
Eastern Mountain Sports	*pressure cookers, foam pads, overboots*
Eiger Mountain Sports	*Salewa crampons*
Ethyl Corporation	*use of an industrial wind tunnel for testing*
ESB, Inc.	*Ray-O-Vac batteries for radios, tape recorders, flashlights*
Farwest Garments, Inc.	*custom wind suits, stuff sacks*
Fuji Photo Film USA, Inc.	*Fujica 701 and 801 35 mm. SLR cameras, 8 mm. P-300 and P-800 movie cameras and Fujichrome 35 mm. and 8 mm. color film*
Garcia Corporation	*corporate liaison with Applications des Gaz*
Gott Manufacturing Company	*plastic jugs*
Howe and Brainbridge, Inc.	*ripstop nylon tape*
The Hanover Press	*printing*
HMW Industries, Inc.	*Pulsar Time Computers*
Imports International	*Labiosan lip salve*
J. C. Penney and Company	*Palco cookware, J. C. Penney binoculars*
J. B. Rivory-Joanny	*9 mm., 7 mm., and 5.5 mm. perlon climbing rope*
Arthur Kahn Corporation	*Dhaulagiri cloth for windsuits*
Kelwood Corporation	*base camp tents of eight-, four- and two-man size*
Laerdal Medical Corporation	*drugs*
Leon Greenman, Inc.	*Dachstein mitts*
Eli Lilly	*drugs*

L. L. Bean	*Norwegian sweaters, duffle bags, wind shirts*
Longview Fiber Company	*fiberboard boxes*
Lord Charles Cosmetics	*bio-wash soap, sun lotions*
Mallory Battery Company	*flashlights*
Metal Textile Company	*pot cleaners*
Michael's of Oregon	*compasses*
Miller-Morton Company	*Chap-Stick, Chap-ans Lotion*
Mobil Chemical Company	*Hefty plastic bags*
Nalge Company, Division of Sybron Corporation	*water bottles, assorted plastic containers*
Mountain Paraphernalia	*nylon webbing, agents for Galibier boots*
Northwest Staple Company	*use of an industrial stapler, staples*
Northwest Snowshoe Company	*snowshoes*
Panasonic Corporation	*walkie-talkie radios, tape recorders*
Primary Source, Inc.	*liaison with J. B. Rivory-Joanny, Simond ice axes*
The Press on Washington Street	*printing*
Raichle-Molitor USA	*high altitude boots, hiking boots*
Recreational Equipment, Inc.	*McKinley and Cascade tents, rain parkas, ponchos, agents for imported climbing equipment*
Rescue Products, Inc.	*rescue sled, medical emergency kit*
Reynes Products, Inc.	*Frostguard, Sunguard creams*
Robert Shaw Corporation	*oxygen regulator*
Roche Pharmaceuticals	*drugs*
Ronson Lighter Company, Inc.	*Varaflame lighters, butane fuel*
Scott USA	*Smith goggles*
Seattle Manufacturing Corporation	*pitons, carabiners*
Smith, Kline and French	*drugs*
Squires Manufacturing Co.	*stuff sacks*
Stebco Industries, Inc.	*air mattresses*
Survival Systems, Inc.	*signal flares and smoke bombs*
Sunvan and Storage Co., Inc.	*freight forwarding*
Texas Pharmaceutical Company	*A-fil, Maxafil, sun stick*
Total Pole	*adjustable ski poles*
Tupperware International	*plastic boxes*
Union Manufacturing Company	*stainless steel vacuum bottles*
United Textile and Supply Co.	*Cordura nylon for packs*
Universal Field Equipment Co.	*frame packs, custom expedition rucksacks, seat harnesses, stuff sacks*
Wigwam Mills, Inc.	*rag socks, stretch socks, knee socks, wool hats*
William Krueger Associates, Inc.	*aluminum snow anchors*
Wilshire Foam Products	*closed cell foam mats*
Woolrich Woollen Mills	*wool shirts and knickers*
YKK Zipper Company	*zippers for down clothing and sleeping bags*

American Kitchen Products Company	*bouillon*
Amstar Corporation	*sugar*
Astro Foods	*use of a vacuum packing machine*
Azar Nut Company	*fresh, salted and dry roasted nuts*
Best Foods	*Skippy Peanut Butter*
Bumble Bee Seafoods	*canned fish*
California Vegetable Concentrates	*dried vegetables*
Continental Mills, Inc.	*Krusteaz pancake mix*
Crescent Foods	*black pepper*
David and Sons, Inc.	*sunflower seeds*
Devonsheer Melba Corporation	*assorted crackers*
Diamond Walnut Corporation	*walnuts, walnugget food bars*
The Dickinson Family	*jams and preserves*
El Molino Mills	*carob-drink mix, Cara-Coa brownie mix*
Facelle Company, Division of International Paper	*paper towels and toilet tissue*
Farmers Rice Cooperative	*brown rice*
Foremost McKesson	*Milkman powdered milk*
Freeze-Dried Foods, Ltd.	*freezedried meats, vegetables and fruits*
General Converting Corp.	*plastic bags for vacuum packing*
Gerber Cheese Company, Inc.	*Swiss Knight knives*
Graves-Chambers, Inc.	*agents for Swiss Miss cocoa*
The Grist Mill	*granola*
H. J. Heinz Company, West Coast Division	*mustard, catsup*
Hershey Foods	*tropical chocolate bars*
Hickory Farms of Ohio, Inc.	*cheese, Yankee Trader soup, seasoned rice, canned cakes, banana chips*
Hills of Westchester	*canned fruitcakes*
International Multifoods Corporation	*Kretschmer wheat germ*
Jack Daniel's Distillery	*Black Label sour mash whiskey*
Jeno's, Inc.	*canned fruit pie fillings*
Joyva Corporation	*sesame bars*
Ken's Foods	*freezedried foods*
Kikkoman Internations, Inc.	*soy sauce*
L. B. Yount Company	*agents for Wyler's lemonade mix*
Lindsay International	*canned ripe olives*
McCormick and Company, Inc.	*packaged sauce mixes*
Morton Salt Company	*salt*
Mountain Pass Canning Company	*canned peppers*
Nabob Foods	*orange marmalade*
National Confectioners' Association: Andes Candies, California Peanut Company, Chocolate House, Inc., E. J. Brach & Sons, F. and F. Laboratories, Luden's Inc.	*candy bars, hard candy*

National Confectioners' Association (Cont.)	*candy bars, hard candy*
Miss Saylor's Chocolates	
Peter Paul	
Reed Candy Company	
Societe Candy Company	
Sunline	
Tom's Foods	
Tootsie Roll	
Natural Sales Company	*canned fruitcake, sunflower seeds*
Nugget Distributors, Inc.	*canned fruit*
Ocean Spray Cranberries, Inc.	*cranberry sauce*
Oregon Freeze Dried Foods, Inc.	*freezedried dinners*
Pet, Inc. Grocery Products Division	*evaporated milk, cheese dips*
Peter Paul	*canned cookies, candy bars*
The Prairie Market #329	*various grocery services*
R-A Formula	*Formula A dietary supplement capsules*
R. C. Bigelow	*Constant Comment tea and coffee*
Ralston Purina Company	*instant Ralston cereal*
Richter Brothers, Inc.	*Familia cereal*
Roman Meal Company	*Roman Meal cereal*
S. Gumpert Company	*powdered eggs, fruit drink mixes*
Sanna, Inc.	*Swiss Miss Cocoa*
Sioux Honey Association	*honey*
Smokecraft	*beef jerky, pemmican*
Spice Islands, Inc.	*spices*
Starbuck's	*tea*
Starkist Foods, Inc.	*canned fish*
Wasa Ry-King, Inc.	*rye crackers*
William Underwood Company	*canned meat spreads*
Wilson Certified Foods, Inc.	*bacon bars, meat bars, freezedried meats*

Sample Menus

Sample unit-portions for four men for one day:

13 oz. Pet evaporated milk
6 oz. brown sugar
4 ind. packs lemon flavored white sugar
4 packs cocoa
2 tea bags
12 oz. canned cake
5 qts. cold drink mix
24 oz. candy bars
10 oz. hard candy
4 oz. raisins
4 cubes bouillon
7 oz. brown rice
7 oz. rye crackers
4 oz. Smokecraft pemmican
1 lb. canned bacon
1 oz. freeze-dried ham
1 small package Morton's salt
8 oz. Granola
5 oz. honey
3 pkgs. Hickory Farms Yankee Trader soup mix
8 oz. jam
8 oz. Hickory Farms pasteurized cheese
1 pkg. jello
16 oz. nuts
1 pkg. freeze-dried pears
1 pkg. sauce mix
1 pkg. freeze-dried corn

Lightweight four-man-day unit: for high altitude use:

10 oz. spiced rice
2 tea bags
4 qts. Wyler's lemonade mix
24 oz. candy bars
10 oz. hard candy
16 oz. nuts (Azar)
4 pkgs. Swiss Miss Cocoa
8 oz. Peter Paul canned cookies
1 raspberry cobbler dessert
2 pkg. Yankee Trader soup mix
2 oz. Milkman powdered whole milk
salt
7 oz. crackers
4 freeze-dried beef steaks
4 bouillon cubes
8 oz. dehydrated potatoes
1 pkg. freeze-dried green beans
1 pkg. dehydrated eggs

Main dishes, starches, protein foods and sweets varied widely in fifteen basic menus. These menus were adequate. Insofar as they were based on the collective experience of the members of the team, they reflected a common miscalculation: On Dhaulagiri, because of our lengthy approach, we were better acclimatized than any of us had ever been before. As a result, we wanted more solid foods and fewer snacks and sweets than we were accustomed to want at high altitude; we were eating better at above twenty-four thousand feet than we ever had at nineteen or twenty thousand feet. Beyond that, the only real flaw was an inexplicable, and unforgiveable, error in the amount of tea in the high altitude packs; fluids are essential, and tea is the least offensive to dry, sore throats.

These rations were liberally supplemented with rice, sugar, potatoes, flour, and cabbage carried by the Sherpas as high as Base Camp, and by beer, butter and beef airdropped to the sahibs at 19,300. The low altitude porters chose their own rations, supplementing a basic menu of rice, tea, cabbage, and flour with treats from the airdrop cache at French Pass. The high altitude Sherpas, who regarded the sahibs' eating habits as barbaric, lived on packaged foods only at the highest camps, where the sahibs tried to keep the food bland for their chapped lips and raw throats, while the Sherpas added Old El Paso hot chili peppers to everything but the jello. Below Camp I, a workable compromise was reached to satisfy both the Sherpas' preference for bulk starches and the sahibs' preference for protein foods and sweets. There was complete agreement on soup, fats and sherpa-style "tea" which is any heated solution or colloidal mixture of something dark (tea, coffee, cocoa, broth or a combination thereof) and something light (sugar and powdered or condensed milk) in apparently equal parts.

Because we started with liberal estimates, then added an error-, emergency-, and loss-factor, then planned to stock camps on two routes for as many as twenty-four climbers, and then had unprecedented success in recovering airdropped supplies, we had an overall surplus of food throughout the expedition. As for the original man-day estimates, the rations were probably on the short side, a development we attribute to the general good health, hence hearty appetites of the team, and to the abundance of food almost everywhere on the mountain.